D0387608

Peculiar People: The Story of My Life

Peculiar People:
The Story of My Life

AUGUSTUS HARE

Edited by Anita Miller and James Papp

ILLUSTRATIONS BY AUGUSTUS HARE
AND JULIA ANDERSON-MILLER

ACADEMY CHICAGO PUBLISHERS
– 1995 –

Published in 1995 by
Academy Chicago Publishers
363 West Erie Street
Chicago, Illinois 60610

© Anita Miller 1995
Introduction © James Papp 1995

Printed and bound in the U.S.A.

Library of Congress Cataloging-in-Publication Data

Hare, Augustus J. C. (Augustus John Cuthbert), 1834-1903.
         Peculiar people : the story of my life / Augustus Hare ; edited by
    Anita Miller and James Papp ; illustrations by Augustus Hare and
    Julia Anderson-Miller.
              p.   cm.
         Includes index.
         ISBN 0-89733-388-8 $26.95
         1. Hare, Augustus J. C. (Augustus John Cuthbert), 1834–1903.
    2. Great Britain—History—Victoria, 1837-1901—Biography.
    3. Eccentrics and eccentricities—Great Britain. 4. Travel writers—
    Great Britain—Biography. I. Miller, Anita, 1926-   . II. Papp,
    James. III. Title.

         DA565.H2A3 1994   94-33759
         941.081'092—dc20   CIP
         [B]

Contents

Introduction by James Papp

Who was Augustus John Cuthbert Hare? Nancy Mitford's grandfather called him a "tedious toady"; Sacheverell Sitwell considered him as "a person of formidable learning and acuity, a huge inexhaustible store of historical knowledge, and an extraordinary repository ... of spine-chilling anecdote and story"—more, perhaps, a large box filled with interesting things, than a human being.

Augustus Hare was born in 1834 at the Villa Strozzi in Rome, into an aristocratic and decidedly eccentric English family. With a certain careless abandon, his parents gave him as an infant to a widowed aunt, Maria Hare, who took him to live in Hurstmonceaux, Sussex, near his uncle Julius, who was the local rector and Archdeacon of Lewes. When Uncle Julius married Esther Maurice, the most alarming member of an influential family of religious fanatics, little Augustus's life became darkly Dickensian. The story of his childhood and adolescence has to be read to be believed.

His escape to Oxford in the spring of 1853 was a welcome one. After he left Oxford in 1857, he travelled with Maria Hare —"The Mother"—and spent a year in Rome, where he established a sort of relationship with his real mother—his father was long dead—whom he called "Italima" and his sister Anne Frances Maria Louisa, called "Esmeralda." They had both converted to Catholicism, to the intense disgust of the Hare family, and they introduced Augustus into upper class Roman society. At this point Augustus embarked upon a career as a travel writer, producing two handbooks on English counties for the publisher John Murray. He received little money for this work but he found it most congenial. He was able to visit old buildings, and cultivate social connections. Like most Englishmen belonging to great families, Augustus had access to a network of carefully nurtured relationships and alliances throughout the island. He collected cousins as others collect stamps, knew everyone's history and everyone's worth. In those days, one could descend, respectably dressed, from a gig at the door of a country house and, if the owner's great-grandfather was one's aunt's cousin several times removed, one could count on a good lunch at the least.

So was established the rhythm of the rest of Augustus Hare's life: escaping the English winter to Rome or the south of France, driving cross country with sketchbook and watercolors, collecting historical detail and lively anecdotes, cultivating the society of the *upper* upper classes and, of course, writing the travel books which established his reputation—almost two dozen altogether, among them *A Winter at Mentone* (1862), *Walks in Rome* (1871), *Wanderings in Spain* (1873) and *Studies in Russia* (1885). He became a literary celebrity in his day. He began his travels in the days of the horse-drawn coach when there was enough danger and discomfort to make travelling an adventure in itself; his Guides were published as railway lines were becoming ubiquitous and the middle classes, encouraged by Thomas Cook, were trooping across Europe armed with Baedakers. They were armed also, as Hare observed with satisfaction, with "the familiar little red and black volumes" of *Walks in Rome*, his most popular guide, which had gone into fifteen editions by the end of the nineteenth century, and twenty-two by 1925, fifty years after its first publication. He had great success, too, with his books of biography and letters. His first, a life of Maria Hare called *Memorials of a Quiet Life*, written over the strong objection of his family, sold out within three days, and twelve years later was in its nineteenth printing. The book reduced Carlyle to tears and convinced the Queen of Sweden-Norway to entrust the rather dull Crown Prince to Augustus for some English polish. In all, Augustus Hare produced thirty books, ten of which ran to multiple volumes.

These books were written for people with a good deal of leisure time. The travel guides begin with a chapter titled "Dull-Useful Information"—lists of hotels, shops and restaurants which are the stuff of travel guides today. There were fewer hotels, shops and restaurants in Hare's day (at least those suitable for English patronage), but there was possibly more appetite for information about art and history. The 678 pages of *Walks in Rome* brim with anecdotes, but even the more discursive volumes are studded with useful information. In *Studies in Russia*, Hare's party encounters a religious procession outside Novgorod and follows it "slowly, with bare heads like our drivers, through the red walls of the Kremlin enclosure, and across the broad Volkoff to the good and reasonable Hotel Solovieff."

But it is the six volumes of *The Story of My Life* for which Augustus Hare is remembered today; it intrigued many and infuriated as many others since the first three volumes appeared in 1896 and the second three in 1900. Because of this hiatus Hare was able, in the second half, to discuss the critical reception of the first half. "It is funny," he writes, "how each reviewer wants a different part left out—one the childhood, one the youth, one the experiences of a later life; there would be nothing left but the little anecdotes about already well-known people, which they all wish to keep."

Strange stories were the hallmark of the Hares and their connections. These stories were Augustus's only inheritance. At Harrow he amused his classmates with them. On the country house circuit, children clamored for them, and not children alone. Lady Waterford said she preferred Hare's stories to novels, and Lady Salisbury assembled her guests to hear him; on one occasion Gladstone loitered nearby to listen. European princesses sent their ladies-in-waiting to listen, with instructions not to return without at least one tale from Mr Hare. And people told him their own stories too.

Mrs Winthrop Chanler described Augustus's story-telling: "He told them slowly, in a curious rather nasal voice which had an extraordinary variety of tone and pitch. As he neared the climax, he would tremble and break and rise almost to a shriek, while he writhed in his chair, twisting and wringing his hands, tortured as it were by the intolerable horror of what he was telling." The Crown Princess of Sweden commented to Augustus that "every hair of her head had curled up."

This could signify something deeper than one man attempting to be amusing. It could reflect the obsession of a society with the tale, the myth.

We now commonly make a distinction between written Western literature, in which authors and readers act as individuals, and the oral tribal culture of much of the world, a shared process in which people gather to talk and to listen. This oral culture seems to have existed in the drawing rooms of the country houses and refurbished castles of the Victorian landed gentry.

One can, surprisingly, find similarities between the Plains Indians and this English gentry, who were to some extent nomadic, moving with the seasons from one watering place to another—and sharing both a tradition of hospitality and a code based on bravery in battle and sport.

The gentry were of course less egalitarian than the Sioux, being drawn together by social stratum rather than geography, although they felt a duty toward the less fortunate in their families and on their estates. They were close-knit; they had strict codes of behavior and frowned on individualism. They did not however object to what we today would consider outrageous eccentricity. Evelyn Waugh wrote to Nancy Mitford that English society seemed to him to be "a complex of tribes, each with its chiefs and elders and witch-doctors and braves, each with its own dialect and deity, each strongly xenophobic."

Stories and a story-teller are necessary to such tribes. Hare's stories—of customs, families, sickness and death, of wild eccentricities—constructed a society for his listeners as they reconstruct that society for us today. They demand a set of beliefs and at the same time a suspension of disbelief.

Augustus Hare had survived one of the most extravagantly cruel Victorian childhoods in one of the maddest of Victorian families, to create a society for us in which he was placed psychologically and socially to become both master story teller and historian. He did not originate these stories; he collected them meticulously. His tribe had the means, the character and the tradition to exceed the ordinary. He told Somerset Maugham, "The only people worth writing about are the lower classes and the upper. No one wants to read about the middle classes."

A Note on the Text
Anita Miller

It was James Papp who brought Augustus Hare to the attention of Academy Chicago; he had prepared a collection of Hare's stories and anecdotes culled from the pages of *The Story of My Life* and arranged by subject matter: Ghost Stories, Royalty, Sickness and Death, and so forth. Inevitably much of this material was fascinating, but Dr Papp's introductory essay on Hare's tormented childhood and adolescence aroused in me—as I know Dr Papp intended it should in any reader—a strong desire to read the six-volume autobiography. I was fortunate to find the volumes at Northwestern University Library where I was allowed to take them home, although they were not in the best condition. It seemed to me after reading them, that Hare's extraordinary story should be available to modern readers in a one-volume edition and that the tales and anecdotes should remain embedded in the text where Hare had originally put them.

Consequently I spent several months condensing this work. As Hare himself pointed out, the original English edition had very large print and unusually wide leading, so that six volumes were excessive to begin with. At first I indicated the cuts by using ellipses, but this seemed to give the pages both a tentative aspect and a speckled look, so for the most part I decided not to use ellipses, except for Augustus's own. Hare had already studded the narrative with extracts from letters and journal entries; its flow, it seemed to me, should not be further interrupted by artificial devices.

I eliminated most of the description of landscapes, churches and other points of interest encountered by Hare during his travels. Malcolm Barnes had included much of this material in his two-volume abridgement of *The Story of My Life* which appeared in the 1950s; I chose to concentrate instead on the more central events of Hare's life, and on the stories and anecdotes which have so enchanted Dr Papp and many others since the appearance of the second volume of the autobiography in 1900. These remain in the text, as I have said, in the setting—country house or London dinner party—where Hare first heard them and remain attributed to those acquaintances from whom he heard them.

I have chosen to use footnotes to translate most French phrases, and here and there to elucidate references to events eliminated in the condensation.

Finally it should be noted that among the most charming elements of the original edition are Augustus's own drawings; he was a talented artist. We have reprinted as many here as we could. To heighten the effect of some of the extraordinary events recounted by Augustus, Julia Anderson-Miller has added her inimitable illustrations.

I believe that what we have here is both a portrait of a genuine Victorian eccentric and a priceless treasury of English social history.

I. THE HARES

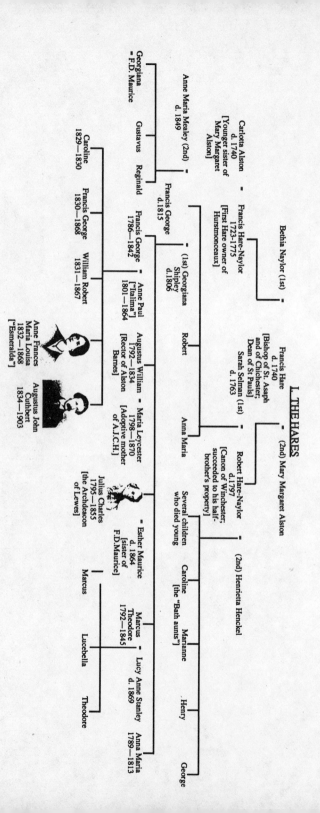

Francis Hare-Naylor
1723–1775
[First Hare owner of
Hurstmonceaux]
=
Carlotta Alston
d. 1740
[Younger sister of
Mary Margaret
Alston]

Bethia Naylor (1st)   =   Francis Hare
d. 1740
[Bishop of St. Asaph
and of Chichester,
Dean of St Pauls]
Sarah Selman (1st)
d. 1763
=   =   (2nd) Mary Margaret Alston

Robert Hare-Naylor
d. 1797
[Canon of Winchester;
succeeded to his half-
brother's property]
=   (2nd) Henrietta Henckel

Anne Maria Mealey (2nd)
d. 1849
=   Francis George
d. 1815
=   (1st) Georgiana
Shipley
d. 1806

Robert   Anna Maria   Several children
who died young

Caroline
[the "Bath aunts"]   Marianne   Henry   George

Georgiana
= F.D. Maurice

Gustavus   Reginald

Francis George
1786–1842
=   Anne Paul
["Italima"]
1801–1864

Caroline
1829–1830   Francis George
1830–1868   William Robert
1831–1867

Augustus William
1792–1834
[Rector of Alston
Barnes]
=   Maria Leycester
1798–1870
[Adoptive mother
of A.J.C.H.]

Anne Frances
Maria Louisa
1832–1868
["Esmeralda"]   Augustus John
Cuthbert
1834–1903

Julius Charles
1795–1855
[the Archdeacon
of Lewes]
=   Esther Maurice
d. 1864
[sister of
F.D. Maurice]

Marcus   Lucebella   Theodore

Marcus
Theodore
1792–1845
=   Lucy Anne Stanley
d. 1869   Anna Maria
1789–1813

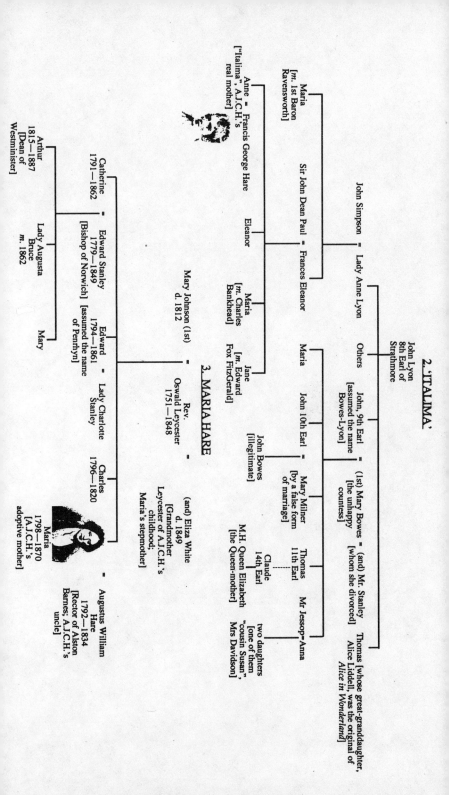

2. 'ITALIMA'

3. MARIA HARE

John Simpson = Lady Anne Lyon

John Lyon 8th Earl of Strathmore

Maria [m. 1st Baron Ravensworth]

Anne = Francis George Hare ["Italima", A.J.C.H.'s real mother]

Sir John Dean Paul = Frances Eleanor

Eleanor

Maria [m. Charles Bankhead]

Jane [m. Edward Fox FitzGerald]

Others

John, 9th Earl [assumed the name Bowes-Lyon]

Maria

John 10th Earl = Mary Milner [by a false form of marriage]

John Bowes [illegitimate]

(1st) Mary Bowes [the unhappy countess] = (and) Mr. Stanley [whom she divorced]

Thomas [whose great-granddaughter, Alice Liddell, was the original of Alice in Wonderland]

Thomas 11th Earl = Mr Jessop-Anna

Claude 14th Earl - - - M.H. Queen Elizabeth [the Queen-mother]

two daughters [one of them "cousin Susan", Mrs Davidson]

Mary Johnson (1st) d. 1812

Rev. Oswald Leycester 1751—1848 = (and) Eliza White d. 1849 [Grandmother Leycester of A.J.C.H.'s childhood; Maria's stepmother]

Catherine 1791—1862 = Edward Stanley 1779—1849 [Bishop of Norwich]

Arthur 1815—1887 [Dean of Westminister]

Lady Augusta Bruce m. 1862

Mary

Edward 1794—1861 [assumed the name of Penrhyn] = Lady Charlotte Stanley

Charles 1796—1820 = Maria 1798—1870 [A.J.C.H.'s adoptive mother]

Augustus William Hare 1792—1834 [Rector of Alston Barnes; A.J.C.H.'s uncle]

Peculiar People: The Story of My Life

I. ANTECEDENTS

GEORGIANA HARE NAYLOR

In 1727, the year of George the First's death, Miss Grace Naylor of Hurstmonceaux, though she was beloved, charming and beautiful, died very mysteriously in her twenty-first year, in the immense and weird old castle of which she had been the heiress. She was affirmed to have been starved by her former governess, who lived alone with her, but the fact was never proved. Her property passed to her first cousin Francis Hare, who forthwith assumed the name of Naylor. He died after a life of wildest dissipation, without leaving any children. So the property of Hurstmonceaux went to his half-brother Robert, Canon of Winchester—whose first wife Sarah Hare, in the zenith of her youth and loveliness, died very suddenly from eating ices when overheated at a ball. She left two children, Francis and Robert.

Soon afterwards Robert married a second wife—the rich Henrietta Henckle, who pulled down Hurstmonceaux Castle. She did this because she was jealous of the sons of her predecessor, and wished to build a large new house, which she persuaded her husband to settle upon her own children, who were numerous, although only two daughters lived to any great age. The second Frances Hare-Naylor and his brother Robert had a most unhappy home in their boyhood. Their stepmother ruled their weak-minded father with a rod of iron. She ostentatiously burnt the portrait of their beautiful mother. Every year she sold a farm from his paternal inheritance and spent the money in extravagance. But she was justly punished, for when Robert Hare died, it was discovered that the great house, now known as Hurstmonceaux Place, was erected upon entailed land, so that the house, stripped of furniture, and the property, shorn of its most valuable farms, passed to Francis Hare-Naylor, son of Sarah Hare.

Mrs Henckle Hare lived on to a great age, and when "the burden of her years came on her" she repented of her avarice and injustice and coming back to Hurstmonceaux in childish senility, would wander round and round the castle ruins in the early morning and late evening, wringing her hands and saying, "Who could have done such a wicked thing—Oh, who could have done such a wicked thing, as to pull down this beautiful old place?"

Then her daughters, Caroline and Marianne, walking beside her, would say, "Oh dear mamma, it was you who did it, it was you yourself who did it, you know."

And she would despairingly resume, "Oh no, that is impossible; it could not have been me. I could not have done such a wicked thing; it could not have been me that did it."

My cousin Marcus Hare had at Abbots Kerwell a picture of Mrs Henckle Hare, which was always surrounded with crape bows.

Hurstmonceaux Place was then and is still a large but ugly house. It forms a massy square, with projecting circular bows at the corners, the appearance of which produces a frightful effect outside, but is exceedingly comfortable within. The staircase, the floors and the handsome doors, were brought from the castle. The west side of the house, decorated with some Ionic columns, is part of an older manor house, which existed before the castle was dismantled. In this part of the building is a small old panelled hall, hung round with stags' horns from the ancient deer park. The house is surrounded by spacious pleasure grounds.

For several years our grandparents carried on a most laborious contest of dignity with poverty on their ruined estate of Hurstmonceaux. Finding no congenial associates in the neighbourhood, my grandmother, Georgiana Hare-Naylor, consoled herself with keeping up an animated correspondence with all the learned men of Europe, while her husband wrote dull plays and duller histories, which have all been published but which few people read then and nobody reads now. It is still remembered at Hurstmonceaux how our grandmother rode on an ass to drink at the mineral springs which abound in the park, how she always wore white, and how a beautiful white doe always accompanied her in her walks, and even to church, standing, during the service, at her pew door.

While my father Francis was being tutored at Aberdeen, my grandmother formed the design of leaving to her children a perfect series of large finished watercolour drawings, representing all the different parts of Hurstmonceaux Castle, interior as well as exterior, before its destruction. She never relaxed her labour and care till the whole were finished, but the minute application for so long a period, seriously affected her health and produced disease of the optic nerve, which ended in total blindness.

She removed to Weimar, where the friendship of the Grand

Duchess and the society of Goethe, Schiller and the other learned men who formed the brilliantly intellectual circle of the little court did all that was possible to mitigate the affliction. But her health continued to fail and her favorite son Francis was summoned to her side, arriving in time to accompany her to Lausanne, where she expired, full of faith, hope and resignation, on Easter Sunday, 1806.

After his wife's death Mr Hare-Naylor could never bear to return to Hurstmonceaux, and sold the remnant of his ancestral estate for £60,000, to the great sorrow of his children. They were almost more distressed, however, by his second marriage to a Mrs Mealey, the Mrs Hare-Naylor of my own childhood, who was less and less liked by her stepsons as years went on. In 1815, Mr Hare-Naylor died at Tours and was buried at Hurstmonceaux.

My father Francis was during the years 1819 to 1826 chiefly at Florence, where he spent much time with the family of Lady Paul, who had brought her four daughters to spend several years in Italy. One of her objects in coming abroad had been the hope of breaking through an attachment which her daughter Maria had formed for Charles Bankhead, an exceedingly handsome and fascinating, but penniless young attaché with whom she had fallen in love at first sight, declaring that nothing should ever induce her to marry anyone else.

Unfortunately, the first place to which Lady Paul took her daughters was Geneva, and Mr Bankhead, finding out where they were, came hither (from Frankfort, where he was attaché) dressed in a long cloak and with false hair and beard. In this disguise, he climbed up and looked into a room where Maria Paul was writing, with her face toward the window. She recognized him at once, but thought it was his double, and fainted away. On her recovery, finding her family still inexorable, she one day, when her mother and sisters were out, tried to make away with herself.

Her room faced the stairs, and as Prince Lardoria, an old friend of the family, was coming up, she threw open the door and exclaimed, *"Je meurs, Prince, je meurs, je me suis empoisonné."*[*]

"Oh Miladi, Miladi," screamed the Prince, but Miladi was not there, so he rushed into the kitchen, and seizing a large bottle of oil, dashed upstairs with it and throwing Maria Paul upon the ground, poured the contents down her throat.

After this, Lady Paul looked upon the marriage as inevitable, and sent Maria to England to her aunt Lady Ravenswood, from whose house she was married to Charles Bankhead, neither her mother nor sisters being present. Shortly afterwards Mr Bankhead was appointed minister in Mexico and, his wife accompanying him thither, remained there for many years, and had many extraordinary adventures, especially during a great earthquake, in which she was saved by her presence of mind in swinging upon a door while "the cathedral rocked like a wave on the sea" and the town was laid in ruins.

In 1828 Francis made a formal proposal of marriage to Anne Paul. On receiving her answer, he sent his banker's book to Sir John Paul, begging him to examine and see if, after all his extravagancies, he still possessed at least "fifteen hundred a year, clear of every possible deduction and charge, to spend withal, that is, four pounds a day," and to consider, if the examination proved satisfactory, that he begged to propose for the hand of his eldest daughter!

In the autumn of 1833 my father rented the beautiful Villa Strozzi at Rome, then standing in large gardens of its own facing

[*] I am dying, Prince, I am dying, I have taken poison.

– 5 –

the grounds of the noble old Villa Negroni. Here on the 13th of March, 1834, I was born—the youngest child of the family, and a most unwelcome addition to the population of this troublesome world, as both my father and Mrs Hare were greatly annoyed at the birth of another child, and beyond measure disgusted that it was another son.

II. My Childhood
1834—1843

IN JUNE, 1829, MY UNCLE Augustus Hare was married to Maria Leycester, then in her thirty-first year. In their every thought and feeling they were united and all early associations had combined to fit them more entirely for each other's companionship. Four years of perfect happiness were permitted them—years spent almost entirely in the quiet of their little rectory in the singularly small parish of Alton Barnes amid the Wiltshire downs, where the inhabitants, less than two hundred in number, living close to each other's doors, around two or three small pastures, grew to regard Augustus Hare and his wife with the affection of children for their parents. So close was the tie which united them that when the rich family living at Hurstmonceaux fell vacant on the death of our great-uncle Robert, Augustus Hare could not bear to leave his little Alton and implored my father to persuade his brother Julius to give up his fellowship at Trinity and to take it instead. But Augustus Hare caught a chill when he was in Cheshire for his brother's marriage; it was the first cause of his fatal illness. It was soon after considered necessary that he should spend the winter abroad with his wife. At Genoa the illness of Augustus became alarming, but he reached Rome, and there he expired on the 14th of February, 1834, full of faith and hope, and comforting those who surrounded him to the last.

When Augustus was laid to rest at the foot of the pyramid of Caius Cestius, my father's most earnest wish was to comfort his widowed sister-in-law, and in the hope of arousing an interest which might still give some semblance of an earthly tie to one who seemed then upon the very borderland of heaven, he entreated, when I was born in the following month, that she would become my godmother, promising that she should be permitted to influence my future in any way she pleased and wishing that I should be called Augustus after him she had lost.

I was baptized on the first of April in the Villa Strozzi by Mr Burgess. The widow of Augustus held me in her arms, and I received the names of "Augustus John Cuthbert," the two last from my godfathers (the old Sir John Paul and Mr Cuthbert Ellison), who never did anything for me, the first from my godmother, to whom I owe everything in the world.

Soon afterward my godmother returned to England with her faithful maid Mary Lea, accompanied by the Marcus Hares. She had already decided to fix her future home in the parish of Julius, who, more than any other, was a fellow mourner with her. As regarded me, nothing more than the tie of a godmother had to that time been thought of; but in the quiet hours of her long return journey to England, while sadly looking forward to the solitary future before her, it occurred to Augustus Hare's widow as just possible that my parents might be induced to give me up altogether to live with her as her own child.

In July she wrote her petition, and was almost surprised at the glad acceptance it met with. Mrs Hare's answer was very brief—

"My dear Maria, how very kind of you! Yes, certainly, the baby shall be sent as soon as it is weaned; and if anyone else would like one, would you kindly recollect that we have others."

After another winter at Rome, the family went to Lausanne and thence my father, with my beautiful Albanese nurse, Lucia Cecinelli, took me to meet Mrs Gayford, the English nurse sent out to fetch me by my adopted mother. There the formal exchange took place which gave me a happy and loving home. I saw my father afterwards, but he seldom noticed me. Many years afterward I knew Mrs Hare well and had much to do with her; but I have never at any time spoken to her or of her as a "mother," and I have never in any way regarded her as such. She gave me up wholly and entirely. She renounced every claim upon me, either of affection or interest. I was sent over to England with a little green carpet bag containing two little white night-shirts and a red coral necklace —my whole trousseau and patrimony. At the same time it was indicated that if the Marcus Hares should also wish to adopt a child, my parents had another to dispose of: my second brother William had never at any time any share in their affections.

It was in October, 1835, that my mother moved from the

Rectory to Lime—our own dear home for the next five-and-twenty years. Those who visit Hurstmonceaux now can hardly imagine Lime as it then was, all is so changed. The old white gabled house, with clustered chimneys and roofs rich in color, rose in a brilliant flower-garden sheltered on every side by trees. On the side towards the Rectory, a drive between close walls of laurel led to the old-fashioned porch which opened into a small double hall. The double drawing room and the dining room, admirably proportioned, though small, looked across the lawn, and one of the great glistening pools which belonged to an old monastery (once on the site of the house), and which lay at the foot of a very steep bank carpeted with primroses in spring. Beyond the pool was our high field, over which the stumpy spire of the church could be seen, at about a mile and a half distant, cutting the silver line of the sea. The castle was in a hollow farther still and not visible.

No description can give an idea of the complete seclusion of life at Lime, of the silence which was only broken by the cackling of the poultry or the distant threshing in the barn. No sound from the "world," in its usually accepted sense, would ever have penetrated, if it had not been for the variety of literary guests who frequented the Rectory, and one or other of whom constantly accompanied my uncle Julius when he came down, as he did every day of his life, to his sister-in-law's quiet six o'clock dinner, returning about eight.

In 1838 I was four years old, and I have a vivid recollection of all that happened from this time—often a clearer remembrance than of things which occurred last year. From this time I never had any playthings, they were all banished to the loft, and, as I had no companions, I never recollect a game of any kind or ever having played at anything. There was a little boy of my own age called Philip Hunnisett, son of a respectable poor woman who lived close to our gate and whom my mother often visited. I remember always longing to play with him, and once trying to do so in a hay-field, to Lea's supreme indignation, and my being punished for it, and never trying again.

From the earliest age I heartily detested Hurstmonceaux Rectory, because it took me away from Lime, to which I was devoted, and brought me into the presence of Uncle Julius, who frightened me out of my wits; but to all rational and unprejudiced people the Rectory was at this time a very delightful place. It is situated on a hill in a lonely situation two miles from the church and castle, and more than a mile from any of the five villages which were then included in the parish of Hurstmonceaux; but it was surrounded by large gardens with fine trees, had a wide distant view over levels and sea, and was in all respects externally more like the house of a squire than a clergyman. Inside it was lined with books from top to bottom; not only the living rooms, but the passages and every available space in the bedrooms were walled with bookcases from floor to ceiling, containing more than 14,000 works.

Most unpleasant figures who held a preeminent place in those childish years were my step grandmother, Mrs Hare Naylor—and her daughter Georgiana. Mrs H. Naylor had been beautiful in her youth and still, with snow-white hair, was an extremely pretty petite old lady. She was suspicious, exacting, and jealous to a degree. If she once took an impression of anyone, it was impossible to eradicate, however utterly false it might be. She was very deaf and only heard through a long trumpet. She would make the most frightful tirades against people, especially my mother and other members of the family, bring the most unpleasant accusations against them, and the instant they attempted to defend themselves, she took down her trumpet.

I have been told that her daughter Georgiana was once a pretty lively girl. I only remember her as a sickly discontented petulant woman. When she was young, she was very fond of dancing, and once, at Bonn, she undertook to dance the clock round. She performed her feat but it ruined her health, and she had to lie on her back for a year. From this time, she defied the Italian proverb, "Let well alone," and dosed herself incessantly. She had acquired "*l'habitude d' être malade*"; she liked the sympathy she excited and henceforth *preferred* being ill. Once or twice every year she was dying, the family were summoned, everyone was in tears, they knelt around her bed; it was the most delicious excitement.

Mrs Hare Naylor had a house at St Leonards, on Maize Hill, where there were only three houses then. We went annually to visit her for a day, and she and "Aunt Georgiana" generally spent several months every year at Hurstmonceaux Rectory —employing themselves in general abuse of all the family. I offended Aunt Georgiana (who wore her hair down her back in two long plaits) mortally, at a very early age, by saying, "Chelu (the Rectory dog) has only one tail, but Aunt Georgie has two."

In the autumn of 1838 my father came alone to Hurstmonceaux Rectory. I remember him then—tall and thin, lying upon a sofa. My father never once noticed my existence during his long stay at the Rectory. On the last day before he left, my mother said laughingly, "Really, Francis, I don't think you have ever found out that such a little being as Augustus is in existence here." He was amused, and said, "Oh no, really!" and he called me to him and patted my head, saying, "Good little Wolf; good little Wolf!" It was the only notice he ever took of me.*

We spent part of the winter of 1838-39 with the Marcus Hares at Torquay. Their home was a most beautiful one— Rockend, at the point of the bay, with very large grounds and endless delightful walks winding amongst rocks and flowers, or terraces overhanging the natural cliffs . . . . Nevertheless I recollect this time as one of the utmost misery. My Aunt Lucy, having heard someone say that I was more intelligent than little Marcus, had conceived the most violent jealousy of me, and I was cowed and snubbed by her in every possible way. Little Marcus himself was encouraged not only to carry off my little properties—shells, fossils, &c.— but to slap, bite, and otherwise ill-treat me as much as he liked, and when, the first day, I ventured, boylike, to retaliate, and cuff him again, I was shut up for two days on bread and water—"to break my spirit"—and most utterly miserable I became, especially as my dear mother treated it as wholesome discipline, and wondered that I was not devoted to little Marcus, whereas, on looking back, I wonder how —even in a modified way—I ever endured him.

* Augustus's father died in 1842.

FROM MY MOTHER'S JOURNAL.

Torquay, Jan. 7 [1839].—It has been a trial to him on coming here to find himself quite a secondary object of attention. At first he was so cowed by it that he seemed to have lost all his gaiety, instead of being pleased to play with little Marcus. In taking his playthings, little Marcus excited a great desire to defend his own property, and though he gives up to him in most things, he shows a feeling of trying to keep his own things to himself, rather than any willingness to share them. By degrees they have learnt to play together more freely . . . . But I see strongly brought out the self-seeking of my dear child, the desire of being first, together with a want of true hearty love for his little companion . . . .

Stoke, Feb. 26—All the time of our stay at Rockend, Augustus was under an unnatural constraint, and though he played for the most part good-humourdly with little Marcus, it was evident he had no great pleasure in him, and instead of being willing to give him anything, he seemed to *shut up* all his generous feelings, and to begin to think only of how he might secure his own property from invasion: in short, all the self-ishness of his nature seemed thus to be drawn out. For the most part he was good and obedient, but the influence of reward and dread of punishment seemed to cause it. He has gained much greater self-command, and will stop his screams on being threatened with the loss of any pleasure immediately, and I fear the greater part of his kindness to little Marcus arose from fear of his Aunt Lucy if he failed to show it. Only once did he return a blow, and knock little Marcus down. He was two days kept upstairs for it, and afterward bore patiently all the scratches he received; but it worked inwardly and gave a dislike to his feeling towards his cousin . . . . He seemed relieved when we left Torquay.

March 13 [1839].—My little Augustus is now five years old. Strong personal identity, reference of everything to himself, greediness of pleasure and possessions, are I fear prominent features in his disposition. May I be taught how best to correct these his sinful propensities with judgment, and to draw him out of self to live for others.

On leaving Torquay, we went to Exeter and from thence to Bath, to the house of "the Bath Aunts": Caroline and Marianne Hare, daughters of that Henrietta Henckel who pulled down Hurstmonceaux Castle. Old Mrs Hare was of a very sharp disposition. Her niece, Lady Taylor, has told me how she went to visit her at Eastbourne as a child, and one day left her work upon the table when she went out. When she came in, she missed it, and Mrs Hare quietly observed, "You left your work about, my dear, so I've thrown it all out of the window." And sure enough, on the beach her thimble, scissors, &c. were all still lying, no one having picked them up!

The Bath Aunts had two brothers (our great-uncles) who lived to grow up. The eldest of these was Henry (born 1778). He was sent abroad, and was said to be drowned, but the fact was never well established. Lady Taylor remembered that, in their later life, a beggar once came to the door of the Aunts at Bath, and declared he was their brother Henry. The Aunts came down and looked at him, but not recognizing any likeness to their brother, they sent him away with a few shillings.

At the time we were at Bath, Aunt Caroline was no longer living there. Having been positively in love with my Uncle Marcus—she always wrote of him as her "treasure"—she had become so furiously jealous of Mrs Marcus Hare, that she had to be kept under restraint, and though not actually mad, she lived alone with an attendant in a cottage at Burnet near Corsham. There she died some years after, very unhappy, poor thing, to the last. Her companion was a Mrs Barbara, with whom Aunt Caroline was most furious at times. She had a large pension after her death. It used to be said that the reason why Mrs Barbara had only one arm and part of another was that Aunt Caroline had eaten the rest.

It was when we were staying with Aunt Marianne in 1839 that I first saw my real mother. I watched her arrival and, through the banisters of the stairwell, saw her cross the hall, and was on the tiptoe of expectation; but she displayed no interest about seeing me, and did not ask for me at all until late in the evening when all enthusiasm had died away.

How many happy recollections I have of hot summer days in the unbroken tranquillity of Lime. Often, awake in the night now, I recall, out of the multiplicity of pretty, even valuable things, with which my house of Holmhurst is filled, how few of them belonged to our dear simple home in these early days. The small double hall had nothing in it, I think, except a few chairs, and some cloaks hanging on pegs against the wall, and the simple furniture of the double drawing room consisted chiefly of the gifts made to my mother by her family when she went to Alton. One wall—the longest—was, however, occupied by a great bookcase, filled with handsomely bound books, chiefly divinity, many of them German. On the other wall hung a very few valuable engravings, mostly from Raphael . . . . The only point of colour in the room, not given by flowers, came from a large panel picture presented by Landor—a Madonna and Child by Raffaellino da Colle, in a fine old Italian frame. The few china ornaments on the chimney-piece beneath were many of them broken, but they were infinitely precious to us. In the dining room were only a few prints . . . . Simpler still were the bedrooms, where the curtains of the windows and beds were of white dimity. In my mother's room, however, were some beautiful sketches of the older family by Flaxman. The "pantry," which was Lea's special sitting room, where the walls were covered with pictures and the mantelpiece laden with china, had more the look of rooms of the present time.

My mother and I breakfasted every morning at eight (as far as I can remember, I never had any meal in the so-called nursery) in the dining room, which, as well as the drawing room, had wide glass doors always open to the little terrace of the garden, from which the smell of new-mown grass or dewy pinks and syringa was wafted into the room. If it was very hot too, our breakfast took place *on* the terrace, in the deep shadow of the house, outside the little drawing-room window.

After breakfast I began my lessons which, though my mother and uncle always considered me a dunce, I now think to have been rather advanced for a child of five years old, as beside English reading, writing and spelling, history, arithmetic and geography, I had to do German reading and *writing*, and a little Latin. Botany and drawing I was also taught, but they were an intense delight. Through plans, maps, and raised models, I was made perfectly familiar with the topography of Jerusalem and the architecture of the Temple, though utterly ignorant of the topography of Rome or London and of the architecture of St Peter's or St Paul's. But in-

DRAWING ROOM, LIME.

deed I never recollect the moment of (indoor) childhood in which I was not undergoing education of some kind, and generally of an unwelcome kind. There was often a good deal of screaming and crying over the writing and arithmetic and I never got on satisfactorily with the former till my Aunt Kitty or my grandmother took it in hand, sitting over me with a ruler and by a succession of hearty bangs on the knuckles, forced my fingers to go the right way.

At twelve o'clock I went out with my mother, sometimes to Lime Cross (village) and to the fields behind it, where I used to make nosegays. At one we had dinner—almost always roast mutton and rice pudding—and then I read aloud —Josephus at a *very* early age, and then Froissart's Chronicles. At three we went out in the carriage to distant cottages, often ending at the Rectory. At five I was allowed to "amuse myself," which generally meant nursing the cat for half an hour and "hearing its lessons." All the day I had been with my mother, and now generally went to my dear nurse Lea, for half an hour, when I had tea in the cool "servants' hall" (where, however, the servants never sat—preferring the kitchen), after which I returned to find Uncle Julius arrived, who stayed till my bedtime.

As Uncle Julius was never captivating to children, it is a great pity that he was turned into an additional bugbear, by being always sent for to whip me when I was naughty! These executions generally took place with a riding-whip, and looking back dispassionately through the distance of years, I am conscious that, for a delicate child, they were a great deal too severe. I always screamed dreadfully in the anticipation of them, but bore them without a sound or a tear. I remember one very hot summer's day, when I had been very naughty over my lessons, Froissart's Chronicles having been particularly uninteresting . . . that Uncle Julius was summoned.

He arrived, and I was sent upstairs to "prepare." Then, as I knew I was going to be whipped anyway, I thought I might as well do something horrible to be whipped *for*, and as soon as I reached the head of the stairs, gave three of the most awful, appalling and eldritch shrieks that ever were heard in Hurstmonceaux. Then I fled for my life. Through the nursery was a small bedroom, where Lea slept, and where I knew that a large black traveling "imperial" was kept under the bed. Under the bed I crawled, and wedged myself into the narrow space behind the imperial, between it and the wall. I was only just in time. In an instant all the household —mother, uncle, servants—were in motion, and a search was on foot all over the house. I turn cold still when I remember the agony of fright with which I heard Uncle Julius enter the nursery, and then, with which, through a chink, I could see his large feet moving about the very room in which I was. He *looked under the bed*, but he saw only a large black box. I held my breath, motionless, and he turned away. Others looked under the bed too; but my concealment was effectual.

I lay under the bed for an hour—stifling—agonised. Then all sounds died away, and I knew that the search in the house was over, and that they were searching the garden. At last my curiosity would no longer allow me to be still, and I crept from under the bed and crawled to the window of my mother's bedroom, whence I could overlook the garden without being seen. Every dark shrub, every odd corner was being ransacked. The whole household and the gardeners were engaged in the pursuit. At last I could see by their actions—for I could not hear words—that a dreadful idea had presented itself. In my paroxysms I had rushed down the steep bank, and tumbled or thrown myself into the pond! I saw my mother look very wretched and Uncle Julius try to calm her. At last they sent for people to drag the pond. Then I could bear my dear mother's expression no longer, and, from my high window, I gave a little hoot. Instantly all was changed; Lea rushed upstairs to embrace me; there was great talking and excitement, and everyone forgot that I had not been whipped! That, however, was the only time I ever escaped.

In the most literal sense, and in every other, I was "brought up at the point of the rod." My dearest mother was so afraid of over-indulgence that she always went into the opposite extreme: and her constant habits of self-examination made her detect the slightest act of especial kindness into which she had been betrayed, and instantly determine not to repeat it. Nevertheless, I loved her most passionately, and many tearful fits, for which I was severely punished as fits of naughtiness, were really caused by anguish at the thought that I had displeased her or been a trouble to her. From never daring to express my wishes in words, which she would have thought it a duty to meet by an immediate refusal, I early became a coward as to concealing what I really desired. I remember once, in my longing for childish companionship, so intensely desiring that the little Coshams—a family of children who lived in the parish—might come to play with me, that I entreated that they might come to have tea in the summerhouse on my Hurstmonceaux birthday (the day of my adoption), and that the mere request was not only refused, but so punished that I never dared to express a wish to play with any child again. At the same time I was *expected* to play with little Marcus, then an indulged disagreeable child whom I could not endure, and because I was not fond of *him*, was thought intensely selfish and self-seeking.

As an example of the severe discipline which was maintained with regard to me, I remember that one day when we went to visit the curate, a lady (Miss Garden) very innocently gave me a lollypop, which I ate. This crime was discovered when we came home by the smell of peppermint, and a large dose of rhubarb and soda was at once administered with a forcing-spoon, though I was in robust health at the time, to teach me to avoid such carnal indulgences as lollypops for the future. For two years, also, I was obliged to swallow a dose of rhubarb every morning and every evening because— according to old-fashioned ideas—it was supposed to "strengthen the stomach"! I am sure it did me a great deal of harm, and had much to do with accounting for my after-sickliness. Sometimes I believe the medicine itself induced fits of fretfulness; but if I cried more than usual, it was supposed to be from want of additional medicine, and the next morning senna tea was added to the rhubarb. I remember the misery of sitting on the back stairs in the morning and having it in a teacup, with milk and sugar.

At a very early age I was made to go to church—once, which very soon grew into twice, on a Sunday. Uncle Julius's endless sermons were my detestation. I remember someone speaking of him to an old man in the parish, and being surprised by the statement that he was "not a good winter parson," which was explained to mean that he kept the people so long with his sermons, that they could not get home before dark.

With the utmost real kindness of heart, Uncle Julius had often the sharpest and most insulting manner I have ever known in speaking to those who disagreed with him. I remember an instance of this when Mr Simpkinson had lately come to Hurstmonceax as my uncle's curate. His sister, then a very handsome young lady, had come down from London to visit him, and my mother took her to church in the carriage. That Sunday happened to be Michaelmas Day. As we were driving slowly away from church through the crowd of those who had formed the congregation, Uncle Julius holding the reins, something was said about the day. Without a suspicion of giving offense, Miss Simpkinson, who was sitting behind me, said in a careless way, "As for me, my chief association with Michaelmas Day is a roast goose." Then Uncle Julius turned round, and, in a voice of *thunder*, audible to everyone on the road, exclaimed, "Ignorant and presumptuous young woman!" He had never seen her till that day. As she said to me years after, when she was a wife and mother, "That the Archdeacon should call me ignorant and presumptuous was trying; still, I could bear that very well; but that he should dare to call me a *young woman* was not to be endured." However her only alternative was to bear the affront and be driven two miles home, or to insist on getting out of the carriage and walking home through the mud, and she chose the former course, and afterwards my uncle, when he knew her good qualities, both admired and liked her.

I was not six years old before my mother—under the influence of the Maurices—began to follow out a code of penance with regard to me which was worthy of the ascetics of the desert. Hitherto I had never been allowed anything but roast mutton and rice pudding for dinner. Now all was changed.

The most delicious puddings were talked of—dilated on—until I became, not greedy, but exceedingly curious about them. At length "*le grand moment*" arrived. They were put on the table before me, and then, just as I was going to eat some of them, they were snatched away, and I was told to get up and carry them off to some poor person in the village.

FROM MY MOTHER'S JOURNAL.
Lime, June 18 [1839].—In all the books of education I do not find what I believe is the useful view taken of the actual labor of learning to read—that of forcing the child's attention to a thing irksome to it and without interest . . . . Now it seems to me to be an excellent discipline whereby daily some self-denial and command may be acquired in overcoming the repugnance to doing from duty what has in itself no attraction. In the first struggle to fix the attention and learn that which is without interest, but which *must be done*, a habit is gained of great importance . . . .

I find in giving any order to a child, it is always better not to *look* to see if he obeys, but to take for granted it will be done. If one appears to doubt the obedience, there is occasion given for the child to hesitate, "Shall I do it or no?" If you seem not to question the possibility of non-compliance, he feels a trust committed to him to keep and fulfill it. It is best never to repeat a command, never to answer the oft-asked question "Why?"

Augustus would, I believe, always do a thing if *reasoned* with about it, but the necessity of obedience without reasoning is especially necessary to such a disposition as his. The will is the thing that needs being brought into subjection.

The withholding a pleasure is a safe punishment for naughtiness, more safe, I think, than giving a reward for goodness. "If you are naughty I must punish you," is often a necessary threat: but it is not good to hold out a bribe for goodness—"If you are good I will give you such a thing."

The happiest days of my childish years were all condensed in the five months which we annually spent at Stoke (away from Uncle Julius, Aunt Georgiana and the Maurices). Grandpapa did not take much notice of my existence, but when he did, it was always in kindness, though I believe he had rather resented my adoption. Grannie (who was only my mother's stepmother but married to Grandpapa when she was quite a child) was tremendously severe, but also very good to me: she never "kept me at a distance," so, though she often punished me, I was never afraid of her . . . I had my breakfast in the little room of Mrs Cowbourne, my Grannie's dear old maid, which was through the kitchen, and deliciously warm and comfortable. Sometimes I went in to see the men and maids have their breakfast at the long table in the servants' hall: the maids had only great bowls of bread and milk; tea and bread and butter were never thought of below the housekeeper's room.

I did my lessons in my mother's room upstairs. Spelling and geography were always trials, the latter because the geography book was so dreadfully uninteresting; it told us how many inhabitants there were in the States of Lucca and Modena. I never had any playthings at Stoke: my amusement was to draw on all the bits of paper I could get hold of; but I only drew two subjects over and over again—the Day of Judgment, and Adam and Eve being turned out of Paradise: these were of inexhaustible interest.

The curates always came to luncheon at the Rectory on Sundays. They were always compelled to come in ignominiously at the back door, lest they should dirty the entrance; only Mr Egerton was allowed to come in at the front door, because he was a "gentleman born." How Grannie used to bully the curates! They were expected not to talk at luncheon; if they did they were soon put down. As soon as the curates had swallowed a proper amount of cold veal, they were called upon to "give an account to Mrs Leycester" of all that they had done in the week in the four quarters of the parish . . . and soundly were they rated if their actions did not correspond with her intentions.

After the curates came the schoolgirls to practice their singing, and my mother was set down to strum the piano by the hour together as an accompaniment, while Grannie occupied herself in seeing that they opened their mouths wide enough, dragging their mouths open by force, and if they would not sing properly, putting her fingers so far down their throats that she made them sick. One day, when she was doing this, Margaret Beeston bit her violently. Mr Egerton was desired to talk to her afterwards about the wickedness of her conduct. "How could you be such a naughty girl, Margaret, as to bite Mrs Leycester?"

"What'n her put her fingers down my throat for? Oi'll bite she harder next time," replied the impenitent Margaret.

Grannie used to talk of chaney (china), laylocks (lilacs), and gould (gold): of the Prooshians and the Rooshians: of things being "plaguey dear" or "plaguey bad." In my childhood, however, half my elders used such expressions, which now seem to be almost extinct. "Obleege me by passing the cowcumber," Uncle Julius always used to say.

Grannie was very severe to all her dependants, but to no one more than to three young lady *protegées* who lived with her in turn—whom she fed on skim milk and dry bread, and treated so harshly that the youngest and most adventurous of them, Charlotte Atkinson, ran away altogether, joined a party of strolling players, and eventually married an actor. I remember Grannie going down into the kitchen one day and scolding the cook till she could bear it no longer, when she seized the dinner bell from the shelf and rang it in her ears till she ran out of the kitchen.

When there was a "wash" at Stoke, which was about every third week, it was a rule with Grannie that, summer or winter, it must always begin at one a.m. At that hour old Hannah Berry used to arrive from the village, the coppers were heated and the maids at work. The ladies-maids, who were expected to do all the fine muslins, &c., themselves, had always to be at the wash-tubs at three a.m.—by candlelight. If anyone was late, the housekeeper reported to Mrs Leycester, who was soon down on them pretty sharply. Generally, however, her real practical kindness and generosity prevented anyone minding Mrs Leycester's severity; it was looked upon as only "her way;" for people were not so tender in those days as they are now, and certainly no servant would have thought of giving up a place which was essentially a good one because they were a little roughly handled by their mistress.

In those days servants were as liable to personal chastise-

STOKE RECTORY, THE GARDEN SIDE

ment as the children of the house, and would as little have thought of resenting it. "You don't suppose I'm going to hurt *my* fingers in boxing *your* ears," said Grannie, when about to chastise the schoolchildren she was teaching, and she would take up a book from the table and use it soundly, and then say, "Now we mustn't let the other ear be jealous," and turn the child round and lay on again at the other side. Grannie constantly boxed her housemaid's ears, and alas! when he grew very old, she used to box dear Grandpapa's though she loved him dearly, the great source of offence being that he would sometimes slyly give the servant's elbow a tip when his daily tablespoonful of brandy was being poured out.

As I have said, Grannie was quite devoted to Grandpapa, yet as she was twenty years younger, his great age could not but accustom her to the thought of his death, and she constantly talked before him, to his great amusement, of what she should do as a widow. One day the party sitting in the drawing room were astonished to see the family carriage drive up to the door with Spragg the butler on the box. "I was only seeing how Spragg would look as coachman when your grandpapa is dead," said Grannie, and Grandpapa looked on at the arrangements and enjoyed them heartily.

In the autumn [of 1842] Mrs Hare came with her children to spend some time at Hurstmonceaux Rectory. It was then arranged that I should call her "Italima" (being a corruption of "Italian Mama"), and by that name I will henceforth speak of her in these memoirs, but this must not be taken to imply any greater intimacy, as she never treated me familiarly or with affection. I remember the party arriving in their black dress*—Italima, Francis, William, Esmeralda .... My sister, as a little child, was always called "the Tigress," but as she grew older, her cousin Lord Normanby remonstrated at this. "Then give her another name," said Italima. "Esmeralda,"— and Esmeralda she was now always called.

Italima must have found it intensely dull at the Rectory. She used to walk daily to Gardner Street, where the sight of "*somebody*" and the village shops was a consolation to her.

---

* They were in mourning for their husband and father, Francis Hare, Augustus's father, who had died that year.

She used to make my sister practice on the pianoforte for hours, and if she did not play well she shut her up for the rest of the day in a dressing room, and I used to go and push fairy stories to her under the door. Though she was so severe to my sister, she resented exceedingly any scoldings which Uncle Julius gave to Francis, who richly deserved them, and was terribly spoilt. Altogether my own brothers and sister being as children infinitely more attractive than the Marcus Hares', I was much happier with them, which was terribly resented in the family, and any sign I gave of real enjoyment was always followed by some privation, for fear I should be over excited by it.

Among other visitors of 1843, I must mention our cousin Penelope, Mrs Warren, who spent some days at the Rectory with her daughters, because under her protection I had my only sight of the upper part of Hurstmonceaux Castle. One of the staircases remained then, and the timbers of many of the upper rooms were left, though the floors were gone. One day we were with my mother and uncle in the ruins, and they were saying how no one would ever see the upper floor again, when, to their horror, Mrs Warren seized me in her arms and darted up the staircase. "Look, child, look!" she said, "for no one will ever see this again," and she leapt with me from beam to beam. I recollect the old chimney-pieces, the falling look of everything. It was wonderful that we came down safe; the staircase was removed immediately after, that no one might follow in our footsteps.

I remember Carlyle coming to stay at the Rectory, where they did not like him much. He came in a high hat—every one wore high hats then. The day he arrived, the wind blew his hat off into a ditch as he was getting over a stile: and he went off at once into one of his unbounded furies against "the most absurd outrageous head covering in the world, which the vanity of the Prince Regent had caused people to adopt."

Aunt Lucy and the Maurices had long urged my mother to send me to school, and perhaps in many ways my terrible fits of naughtiness made it desirable, although they chiefly rose from nervousness, caused by the incessant "nagging" I received at home from everyone except my mother and Lea. But the choice of the school to which I was sent at nine years old was very unfortunate.

The greater portion of Mr Kilvert's scholars—his "little flock of lambs in Christ's fold"—were a set of little monsters. All infantine immoralities were highly popular, and—in such close quarters—it would have been difficult for the most pure and high-minded boy to escape from them. The first evening I was there, at nine years old, I was compelled to eat Eve's apple quite up—indeed, the Tree of the Knowledge of Good and Evil was stripped absolutely bare; there was no fruit left to gather.

It was leaving my mother that I minded, not the going to school, to which my misery was put down: though, as I had never had any companions, the idea of being left suddenly amongst a horde of young savages was anything but comforting. But my nervous temperament was tortured with the idea that my mother would die before I saw her again (I had read a story of this kind), that our life was over, that my aunts would persuade her to cease to care for me—indeed, the anguish was so great and so little understood, that though it is more than fifty years ago, as I write this, I can scarcely bear to think of it.

III. MY BOYHOOD
1843-1848

AUGUSTUS J. C. HARE

IN THE SUMMER [OF 1844] I was delivered from Hurstmonceaux, going first with my mother to our dear Stoke home and thence to the English lakes, where the delight was not unalloyed, for, though Uncle Julius accompanied us, my mother took Esther Maurice with her, wishing to give her a holiday after her hard work in schoolteaching at Reading, and never foreseeing, what everyone else foresaw, that Uncle Julius, who had always a passion for governesses, would certainly propose to her. Bitter were the tears which my mother shed when this result — to her alone unexpected — actually took place. It was the most dismal of betrothals; Esther sobbed and cried, my mother sobbed and cried, Uncle Julius sobbed and cried daily. I used to see them sitting holding each other's hands and crying on the banks of the Rotha.

These scenes for the most part took place at Foxhow, where we paid a long visit to Mrs Arnold, whose children were delightful companions to me. Afterward we rented a small damp house near Ambleside —Rotha Cottage — for some weeks, but I was very ill from its unhealthiness . . . . Matthew Arnold, then a very handsome young man, was always excessively kind to me, and I often had great fun with him and his brothers, but he was not considered then to give any promise of the intellectual powers he showed afterwards.

From Foxhow and Rotha Cottage we constantly visited Wordsworth and his dear old wife at Rydal Mount, and we walked with him to the Rydal Falls. He always talked a good deal about himself and his own poems, and I have a sense of his being not vain, but conceited. I have been told since, in confirmation of this, that when Milton's watch—preserved somewhere — was shown to him, he instantly and involuntarily drew out his own watch, and compared not the watches, but the poets.

The winter of 1844–45 was the first of many which were made unutterably wretched by Aunt Esther. Aunt Lucy was a very refined person, and a very charming and delightful companion to those she loved, and, had she loved me, I should have been devoted to her. Aunt Esther was, from her own personal characteristics, a person I never could have loved. Yet my uncle was now entirely ruled by her, and my gentle mother considered her interference in everything as a cross which was "sent to her" to be meekly endured. The society at the Rectory was now entirely changed: all the relations of the Hare family, except the Marcus Hares, were given to understand that their visits were unwelcome, and the house was entirely filled with the relations of Aunt Esther—old Mr and Mrs Maurice; their married daughter Lucilla Powell, with her husband and children; their unmarried daughters—Mary, Priscilla and Harriet—Priscilla, who now never left her bed, and who was violently sick after everything she ate (yet with the most enormous appetite), often for many months together.

With the inmates of the house, the whole "tone" of the Rectory society was changed. It was impossible entirely to silence Uncle Julius, yet at times even he was subdued by his new surroundings, the circle around him being incessantly occupied with the trivialities of domestic or parochial detail, varied by the gossip of such a tenth-rate provincial town as Reading, or reminiscences of the boarding school which had been their occupation and pride for so many years. Frequently also the spare rooms were filled by former pupils—"young ladies" of a kind who would announce their engagement by: "The infinite grace of God has put it into the heart of his servant Edmund to propose to me," or "I have been led by the mysterious workings of God's providence to accept the hand of Edgar"—expressions which Aunt Esther, who wrote good and simple English herself, would describe as touching evidences of a Christian spirit in her younger friends.

But what was far more trying to me was that in order to prove that her marriage had made no difference in the sisterly and brotherly relations which existed between my mother and Uncle Julius, Aunt Esther insisted that my mother should dine at the Rectory *every* night, and as in winter, the late return in an open carriage was impossible, this involved our sleeping at the Rectory and returning home every morning in the bitter cold before breakfast. The hours after five o'clock in every day of the much-longed-for, eagerly counted holidays, were now absolute purgatory.

Once landed at the Rectory, I was generally left in a dark room till dinner at seven o'clock, for candles were never allowed in winter in the room where I was left alone. After dinner, I was never permitted to amuse myself, or to do *anything* except oc-

casionally to net. If I spoke, Aunt Esther would say, with a satir-
ical smile, "As if you ever *could* say anything worth hearing, as
if it was ever *possible* that anyone could want to hear what you
have to say." If I took up a book, I was told instantly to put it
down again, it was "disrespect to my uncle." If I murmured, Aunt
Esther, whose temper was absolutely unexcitable, quelled it by
her icy rigidity. Thus gradually I got into the habit of absolute
silence at the Rectory—a habit which it took me years to break
through; and I often still suffer from the want of self-confidence
engendered by reproaches and taunts which never ceased: for a
day—for a week—for a year they would have been nothing: but
for *always,* with no escape but my own death or that of my tor-
mentor! Water dripping forever on a stone wears through the
stone at last.

The cruelty which I received from my new aunt was repeated
in various forms by her sisters, one or the other of whom was
always at the Rectory. Only Priscilla occasionally sent a kindly
message or spoke a kindly word to me from her sickbed, which I
repaid by constant offerings of flowers. Most of all, however,
did I feel the conduct of Mary Maurice, who, by pretended sympathy and affection, wormed from me all my little secrets — how
miserable my uncle's marriage had made my home-life, how I
never was alone with my mother now, &c.— and repeated the
whole to Aunt Esther.

From this time Aunt Esther resolutely set herself to subdue me
thoroughly—to make me feel that any remission of misery at
home, any comparative comfort, was a gift from her. But to make
me feel this thoroughly, it was necessary that all pleasure and
comfort in my home should first be annihilated. I was a very
delicate child, and suffered absolute agonies from chilblains,

which were often large open wounds on my feet. Therefore I was put to sleep in "the Barracks"—two dismal, unfurnished, uncarpeted north rooms, without fireplaces, looking into a damp courtyard, with a well and a howling dog. My only bed was a rough deal trestle, my only bedding a straw palliasse, with a single coarse blanket. The only other furniture in the room was a deal chair, and a washing-basin on a tripod. No one was allowed to bring me any hot water; and as the water in my room always froze with an intense cold, I had to break the ice with a brass candlestick, or, if that were taken away, with my wounded hands. If when I came down in the morning, as was often the case, I was almost speechless from sickness and misery, it was always declared to be "temper." I was given "saur-kraut" to eat because the very smell of it made me sick.

When Aunt Esther discovered the comfort I found in getting away to my dear old Lea, she persuaded my mother that Lea's influence over me was a very bad one, and obliged her to keep me away from her.

A favorite torment was reviling all my relations before me—my sister, &c.—and there was no end to the insulting things Aunt Esther said of them.

People may wonder, and oh! how often have I wondered, that my mother did not put an end to it all. But, inexplicable as it may seem, it was her extraordinary religious opinions which prevented her from doing so. She literally believed and taught that when a person struck you on the right cheek you were to invite them to strike you on the left also, and therefore if Aunt Esther injured or insulted me in one way, it was right that I should give her the opportunity of injuring or insulting me in another! I do not think that my misery cost her nothing, she felt it acutely;

but because she felt it thus, she welcomed it, as a fiery trial to be endured. Lea, however, was less patient, and openly expressed her abhorrence of her own trial in having to come up to the Rectory daily to dress my mother for dinner, and walk back to Lime through the dark night, coming again, shine or shower, in the early morning, before my mother was up.

I would not have any one suppose that I can see no merits in my Aunt Esther Hare. The austerities which she enforced upon my mother with regard to me she fully carried out as regarded herself. She was the Inquisition in person. She probed and analyzed herself and the motive of her every action quite as bitterly and mercilessly as she probed and analyzed others. She fasted and denied herself in everything. To such of the poor as accepted her absolute authority, Aunt Esther was unboundably kind, generous and considerate. To her own sisters and other members of her family her heart and home were ever open, with unvarying affection. To her husband, to whom her severe creed taught her to show the same inflexible obedience she exacted from others, she was utterly devoted. His requirement that she should receive his old friend Mrs Alexander as a permanent inmate, almost on an equality with herself in the family home, and surround her with loving attentions, she bowed to without a murmur. But to a little boy who was, to a certain degree, independent of her, and who had from the first somewhat resented her interference, she knew how to be—oh! she was—most cruel.

Open war was declared at length between Aunt Esther and myself. I had a favourite cat called Selma, which I adored, and which followed me about at Lime wherever I went. Aunt Esther saw this, and at once insisted that the cat must be given up to her. I wept over it in agonies of grief; but Aunt Esther insisted.

My mother was relentless in saying that I must be taught to give up my own way and pleasure to others; and would be forced to give it up if I would not do so willingly, and with many tears I took Selma to the Rectory. For some days it almost comforted me for going to the Rectory, because then I possibly saw my idolized Selma. But soon there came a day when Selma was missing: Aunt Esther had ordered her to be . . . hung!

From this time I never attempted to conceal that I loathed Aunt Esther. I constantly gave her the presents which my mother made me save up all my money to buy—for her birthday, Christmas, New Year, &c.—but I never spoke to her unnecessarily. On these occasions I always received a present from her in return—"The Rudiments of Architecture," price ninepence, in a red cover. It was always the same, which not only saved expense, but also the trouble of thinking. I have a number of copies of "The Rudiments of Architecture" now, of which I thus became the possessor.

Only from Saturday to Monday we had a reprieve. The nearness of Lime to the school which my mother undertook to teach on Sundays was the excuse, but, as I see from her journal, only the excuse, which she made to give me one happy day in the week. How well I remember the ecstasy of these Saturday evenings, when I was once more alone with the mother of my childhood, who was all the world to me, and she was almost as happy as I was playing with my kittens or my little black spaniel . . . and dear Lea was able to come in and out undisturbed in the old familiar way.

Even the pleasures of this home-Sunday, however, were marred in the summer, when my mother gave in to the suggestion of Aunt Esther that I should be locked into the vestry of the church between services. Miserable indeed were the three hours which

—provided with a sandwich for dinner—I had weekly to spend there; and though I did not expect to see ghosts, the utter isolation of Hurstmonceaux church, far away from all haunts of men, gave my imprisonment an unusual eerieness. Sometimes I used to clamber over the tomb of the Lords Dacre, which rises like a screen against one side of the vestry, and be stricken with vague terrors by the two grim white figures lying upon it in the silent desolation, in which the scamper of a rat across the floor seemed to make a noise like a whirlwind. At that time two grinning skulls (of the founder and foundress of the church, it was believed) lay on the ledge of the tomb; but soon after this Uncle Julius and Aunt Esther made a weird excursion to the churchyard with a spade, and buried them in the dusk with their own hands. In the winter holidays, the intense cold of the unwarmed church made me so ill that it led to my miserable penance being remitted.

It was a sort of comfort to me, in the real church-time, to repeat vigorously all the worst curses in the Psalms, those in which David showed his most appalling degree of malice (Psalm XXXV. 7-16, Psalm LIX, Psalm LXIX. 22-29, Psalm CXL. 9, 10 for instance) and apply them to Aunt Esther & Co. As all the psalms were extolled as beatific, and the Church of England used them constantly for edification, their sentiments were all right, I supposed.

In the summer of 1845 I went with my mother to her old home of Alton for the first time. On leaving Alton, we went to join the Marcus Hares in the express train at Swindon. Uncle Marcus, Aunt Lucy, her maid Griffiths, and my mother were in one compartment of the carriage; my little cousin Lucebella, Lea, an elderly peer and I were in the other, for carriages on the Great

Western were then divided by a door. As we neared Windsor, my little cousin begged to be held up that she might see if the

THE VESTRY, HURSTMONCEAUX.

flag were flying on the castle. At that moment there was a frightful crash, and the carriage dashed violently from side to side. In an instant the dust was so intense that all became pitch darkness. "For God's sake put up your feet and press backwards; I've been in this before," cried Lord S., and we did so. In the other compartment all the inmates were thrown violently on the floor, and jerked upwards with every lurch of the train. If the darkness cleared for an instant, I saw Lea's set teeth and livid face opposite. I learned then for the first time that to put hand bags in the net along the top of the carriage is most alarming in case of accident. They are dashed hither and thither like so many cannon balls. A dressing case must be fatal.

After what seemed to be an endless time, the train suddenly stopped with a crash. We had really, I believe, been three minutes off the line. Instantly a number of men surrounded the carriage. "There is not an instant to lose, another train is upon you, they may not be able stop it"— and we were all dragged out and up the steep bank of the railway cutting. Most strange, I remember, was the appearance of our ruined train beneath, lying quite across the line. The wheels of the luggage van at the end had come off, and the rest of the train had been dragged off the line gradually, the last carriages first. Soon two trains were waiting (stopped) on the blocked line behind. We had to wait on the top of the bank till a new train came to fetch us from Slough, and when we arrived there, we found the platform full of anxious inquirers, and much sympathy we excited, quite black and blue with bruises, though none of us seriously hurt.

Soon after we reached Hurstmonceaux, my Uncle Marcus became seriously ill at the Rectory. As we came back in the hot evening, we were met by a messenger desiring us not to drive up to the house, as Uncle Marcus must not be disturbed by the sound of wheels. Then his children were sent to Lime, and my mother was almost constantly at the Rectory. At last one morning I was summoned to go up to the Rectory with all three children. I remember the scene as a picture, and Aunt Lucy sitting stonily at the bed's head in a violet silk dress. In the night my mother and Uncle Julius said the "Te Deum" aloud, and, as they reached the last verse, he died.

Aunt Lucy never saw him again. She insisted upon being brought away immediately to Lime, and shut herself up there. She was very peculiar at this time, and for a year afterward, one of her odd fancies being that her maid Griffiths was always to breakfast and have luncheon with the family and be waited on as a lady. We children all went to the funeral, driving in the family chariot. I had no real affection for Uncle Marcus, but felt unusually solemnized by the tears around me. When, however, a peacock butterfly, for which I had always longed, actually perched upon my prayer-book as I was standing by the open grave in the most solemn moment, I could not resist closing the book on it, and my prayer-book still has the marks of the butterfly's death. I returned to school in August [1845] under the care of Mr Hull, a very old friend of the family, who had come to the funeral . . . .

How vividly, how acutely, I recollect that—in my passionate devotion to my mother—I used, as the holidays approached, to conjure up the most vivid mental pictures of my return to her, and appease my longing with the thought of how she would rush out to meet me, of her ecstatic delight, &c.; and then how terrible was the bathos of the reality, when I drove up to the silent door of Lime, and nobody but Lea took any notice of my coming; and of the awful chill of going into the drawing room and seeing my longed-for and pined-for mother sit still in her chair by the fire till I went up and kissed her. To her, who had been taught to curtsey not only to her father, but even to her father's chair, it was only natural; but I often sobbed myself to sleep in a little-understood agony of anguish — an anguish that she could not really care for me.

In the winter of 1845–46, Aunt Lucy let Rockend to Lord Beverley, and came to live at Lime for six months with her three children, a governess, and two, sometimes three, servants. As she fancied herself poor, and this plan was economical, it was frequently repeated afterwards. On the whole, the arrangement was satisfactory to me, although Aunt Lucy was excessively unkind to me, and often did not speak a single word to me for several weeks together, and though the children were most tormenting, Aunt Esther—a far greater enemy—was at least kept at bay, for Aunt Lucy detested her influence and going to the Rectory quite as cordially as I did.

How often I remember my ever-impatient rebellion against the doctrine I was always taught as fundamental—that my uncles and aunts must always be right, and that to question the absolute wisdom and justice of their every act—to me so utterly selfish—was typical of the meanest and vilest nature. How odd it is that parents, and still more uncles and aunts, never will understand, that whilst they are criticizing and scrutinizing their children or nephews, the latter are also scrutinizing and criticizing them. Yet so it is: investigation and judgment of character is usually mutual. During this winter, however, I imagine that the aunts were especially amiable, as in the child's play which I wrote, and which we all acted —"The Hope of the Katzekoffs"—they, with my mother represented the three fairies —"Brigida, Rigida, and Frigida"—Aunt Lucy, I need hardly say, being Frigida, and Aunt Esther Rigida.

Being very ill with the measles kept me at home till the middle of February. Aunt Lucy's three children also had the measles and were very ill; and it is well remembered as characteristic of Aunt Esther that she said when they were at the worst—"I am *very glad* they are so ill; it is a well-deserved punishment because their mother would not let them go to church for fear they should catch it there." Church and love of church was the standard by which Aunt Esther measured everything. In all things she had the inflexible cruelty of a Dominican. She would willingly and proudly undergo martyrdom herself for her own principles, but she would torture without remorse those who differed from her.

When we were recovering, Aunt Lucy read "Guy Mannering" aloud to us. It was enchanting. But usually, as Aunt Lucy and my mother sat together, their conversation was almost entirely about the spiritual things in which their hearts, their mental powers, their whole being were absorbed. They would talk of heaven in detail just as worldly people would talk of the place where they were going for a change of air. At this time, I remember, they both wished—no, I suppose they only thought they wished—to die; they talked of longing, pining for "the coming of the kingdom," but when they grew really old, when the time which they had wished for before was in all probability really near, and when they were, I believe, far more really prepared for it, they ceased to wish for it. "By-and-by" would do. I imagine it is always thus.

In March the news that my dear (Mary) Lea was going to marry our manservant John Gidman was an awful shock to me. My mother might easily have prevented this (most unequal) marriage which, as far as Mrs Leycester was concerned, was an elopement. It was productive of great trouble to us afterwards, and obliged me to endure John Gidman, to wear him like a hair-shirt, for forty years. Certainly no ascetic torments can be so severe as those which Providence occasionally ordains for us. As for our dear Lea herself, her marriage brought her misery enough, but her troubles always stayed in her heart and never filtered through. As I once read in an American novel, "There ain't so much difference in the troubles on this earth, as there is in the folks who have to bear them."

The great age of my dear Grandfather Leycester, ninety-five, had always made his life seem to us to hang upon a thread, and very soon after I returned home for my summer holidays [1846], we were summoned to Stoke by the news of his death. This was a great grief to me, not only because I was truly attached to the kind old man, but because it involved the parting with the happiest scenes of my childhood, the only home in which I had ever been really happy. Grannie drove in her own carriage all the way to her house in New Street, Spring Gardens, the posting journey, so often talked of, actually taking place at last.

I thought the house in New Street charming—the cool, old-fashioned, bow-windowed rooms, which we should now think very scantily furnished, and like those of many a country inn; the dining room opening upon wide leads, which Grannie soon turned into a garden; the drawing room, which had a view through the trees of the Admiralty garden to the Tilting Yard, with the Horse Guards and towers of Westminster Abbey.

The grief of leaving Stoke made me miserably unwell, and a doctor was sent for as soon as I arrived at the Stanley's house, 38 Lower Brook Street, who came to me straight from a patient ill with the scarlatina, and gave me the disorder. For three weeks I was very seriously ill in hot summer weather, in stifling rooms, looking on the little black garden and chimney pots at the back of the house. Mary and Kate Stanley were sent away from the infection, and no one came near me except my faithful friend Miss Clinton, who brought me eau-de-cologne and flowers. It was long foolishly concealed from me that I had the scarlatina, and therefore, as I felt day after day of the precious holidays ebbing away, while I was pining for coolness and fresh country air, my mental fever added much to my bodily ailments, whereas, when once told that I was seriously ill, I was quite contented to lie still.

Before I quite recovered, my dear nurse Lea became worn-out with attending to me, and we had scarcely reached Lime before she became most dangerously ill with a brain-fever. For many days and nights she lay on the brink of the grave, and great was my agony while this precious life was in danger. Aunt Esther, who on *great* occasions generally behaved kindly, was very good at this time, ceased to persecute me, and took a very active part in the nursing.

At length our dear Lea was better, and, as I was still very fragile, I went with my mother and Anne Brooke, our cook, to Eastbourne—then a single row of little old-fashioned houses by the sea—where we inhabited, I should think, the very smallest and humblest lodging that was ever seen.... The Misses Thomas of Wratton came to see us there, and could hardly suppress their astonishment at finding us in such a place—and when the three tall smart ladies had once got into our room, no one was able to move, and all had to go out in the order in which they were nearest the door.

When I returned to Harnish I was still wretchedly ill, and the constant sickness under which I suffered, with the extreme and often unjust severity of Mr Kilvert, made the next half-year a miserable one. In the three years and a half which I had spent at Harnish, I had been taught next to nothing—all our time having been frittered in learning Psalms by heart, and the Articles of the Church of England (I could say the whole thirty-nine straight off when eleven years old), &c. Our history was what Arrowsmith's Atlas used to describe Central Africa to be —"a barren country only productive of dates." I could scarcely construe even the easiest passages of Caesar. Still less had I learned to play at any ordinary boys' games; for, as we had no play-ground, we had naturally never had a chance of any. I was glad of any change. It was delightful to leave Harnish for good at Christmas, 1846, and the prospect of Harrow was that of a voyage of adventure.

In January, 1847, my mother took me to Harrow. It was a wonderfully new life upon which I entered; but though a public school was a very much rougher thing then than it is now, and though the fagging for little boys was almost ceaseless, it would not have been an unpleasant life if I had not been so dreadfully weak and sickly, which sometimes unfitted me for enduring the roughness to which I was subjected. It was a great amusement to write to my mother all that occurred. In reading it, people might imagine my narration was intended for complaint, but it was nothing of the kind; indeed, had I wished to complain, I should have known my mother far too well to complain to *her*.

To my mother. *Harrow, Jan. 19 [1847].*—In the evening two big boys rushed up and seizing Buller (another new boy) and me, dragged us into a room where a number of boys were assembled. I was led into the midst. Bob Smith whispered to me to do as I was bid and I should not be hurt. On the other side of the room were cold chicken, cake, fruit, &c., and in a corner were a number of boys holding open little Dirom's mouth and pouring something horrible stirred up with a tallow candle down his throat. A great boy came up to me and told me to sing or drink some of this dreadful mixture. I did sing—at least I made a noise—and the boys were pleased because I made no fuss, and loaded me with oranges and cakes.

Jan. 21—What do you think happened last night? Before prayers I was desired to go into the fifth form room, as they were having some game there. A boy met me at the door, ushered me in, and told me to make my salaam to the Emperor of Morocco, who was seated cross-legged in the middle of a large counterpane, surrounded by twenty or more boys as his servingmen. I was directed to sit down by the Emperor, and in the same way. He made me sing, and then jumped off the counterpane, as he said, to get me some cake. Instantly all the boys seized the counterpane and tossed away. Up to the ceiling I went and down again, but they had no mercy, and it was up and down, head over heels, topsy-turvy, till some one called out "Satus"— and I was let out, very sick and giddy at first, but soon all right again . . . . I am not much bullied except by Davenport, who sleeps in my room.

Jan. 22—Today it has snowed so hard that there has been nothing but snow-balling, and as I was coming out of school, hit by a shower of snowballs, I tumbled the whole way down the two flights of stairs headlong from the top to the bottom.

Jan. 23—Yesterday I was in my room, delighted to be alone for once, and very much interested in the book I was reading, when D. came in and found the fire out, so I got a good licking. He makes me his fag to do errands, and do all he bids me, and if I don't do it, he beats me, but I don't mind much. However, I have got some friends, for when I refused to do my weekday lessons on a Sunday, and was being very much laughed at for it, some-one came in and said, "No, Hare, you're quite right; never mind being laughed at." However I am rather lonely still with no one to speak to or care about me. Sometimes I take refuge in Bur-roughs' study, but I cannot do that often, or he would soon get tired of me. I think I shall like Waldegrave, a new boy who has come, but all the others hate him. Bloomfield is a nice boy, but his room is very far away. Indeed, our room is so secluded, that it would be a delightful place if D. did not live in it. In playtime I go here, there, everywhere, but with no one and doing nothing. Yet I like Harrow very much, though I am much teased even in my form by one big boy, who takes me for a drum, and hammers on my two sides all lesson-time with doubled fists . . . .

Jan. 30—There are certain fellows here who read my last letter to you, and gave me a great lecture for mentioning boys' names; but you must never repeat what I say: it could only get me into trouble. The other night I did a desperate thing. I appealed to the other boys in the house against D. Stapleton was moved by my story, and Hankey and the other boys listened. Then a boy called Sturt was very much enraged at D., and threatened him greatly, and finally D., after heaping all the abuse he could think of upon me, got so frightened that he begged me to be friends with him. I cannot tell you how I have suffered and do suffer from my chilblains, which have become so dreadfully bad from going out so early and in all weathers.

June [1847].—On Sunday in the middle of the Commandments it was so hot in chapel that Kindersley fell down in a fit. He was seized head and foot and carried out, struggling terribly, by Smith and Vernon and others; and the boys say that in his fit he seized hold of Mr. Middlemist's (the Mathematical Master's) nose and gave it a very hard tweak; but how far this is true I cannot tell. However, the whole chapel rose up in consternation, some thinking one thing and some another, and some not knowing what to think, while others thought as I did, that the roof was coming down. Dr Vaughn went on reading the prayers, and Kindersley shrieking, but at last all was quiet. Soon, however, there was another row, for Miles fainted, and he was carried out, and then several others followed his example. The night was so hot that many of the boys slept on the bare floor, and had no bedclothes on but the next day it rained and got quite cold, and last night we were glad of our counterpanes and blankets again.

The winter of 1847–48 was one of those which were rendered quite miserable to me by the way in which I was driven to the Rectory, where Aunt Esther made me more wretched than ever, and by being scarcely ever permitted to remain in my own dear home. I fear that in later days I should have acted a part, and pretended to *like* going to the Rectory, when it would instantly have been considered unnecessary, the one thought in the mind of all the family being that it was a duty to force me to do what I disliked; but at that time I was too ingenuous to indulge in even the most innocent kinds of deception. My own brothers, Francis and William, who were now at Eton, came to the Rectory for part of their holidays, but their upbringing and their characters had so little in common with my own, that we were never very intimate, though I rather liked them than otherwise. They hated the Rectory, and got away from it whenever they could.

Of all the miserable days in the year, Christmas was the worst. I regarded it with loathing unutterable. The presents of the quintessence of rubbish which I had to receive from my aunts with outward grace and gratitude. The finding all my usual avocations and interests cleared away. The having to sit for hours and hours pretending to be deeply interested in the six huge volumes of Foxe's "Book of Martyrs," one of which was always doled out for my mental sustenance. The being compelled — usually with agonizing chilblains — to walk twice to church, eight miles through the snow or piercing winds, and sit for hours in mute anguish of congelation, with one of Uncle Julius's interminable sermons in the afternoon, about which at that time I heartily agreed with a poor woman, Philadelphia Isted, who declared that they were "the biggest of nonsense." Then, far the worst of all, the Rectory and its sneerings and snubbings in the evening.

My mother took little or no notice of all this—her thoughts, her heart, were far away. To her Christmas was simply "the festival of the birth of Christ." Her whole spiritual being was absorbed by it: earth did not signify: she did not and could not understand why it was not always the same with her little boy.

I was not allowed to have any holidays this year, and was obliged to do lessons all morning with Mr Venables, the curate. At this I wonder now, as every day my health was growing worse. I was constantly sick, and grew so thin that I was almost a skeleton, which I really believe now to have been entirely caused by the way in which the miseries of my home life preyed upon my excessive sensitive nervous disposition. And instead of my mind being braced, I was continually talked to about death and hell, and urged to meditate upon them. Towards the close of the holidays I was so ill that at last my mother was alarmed, and took me to a Mr Bigg, who declared that I had distinct curvature of the spine, and put my poor little back into a terrible iron frame, into which my shoulders were fastened as into a vice. Of course, *with* this, I ought never to have been sent back to Harrow, but this was not understood. Then, as hundreds of times afterwards, when

I saw that my mother was really unhappy about me, I bore any amount of suffering without a word rather than add to her distress, and I see now that my letters are full of allusions to the ease with which I was bearing "my armour" at school, while my own recollection is one of intolerable anguish, stooping being almost impossible.

That I got on tolerably well at Harrow, even with my "armour" on, is a proof that I never was ill-treated there. I have often, however, with Lord Eustace Cecil (who was at Harrow with me), recalled since how terrible the bullying was in our time — of the constant cruelty at "Harris's," where the little boys were always made to come down and box in the evening for the delectation of the fifth form:—of how little boys were constantly sent in the evening to Famish's—halfway to the cricket ground, to bring back porter under their greatcoats, certain to be flogged by the headmaster if they were caught, and to be "wapped" by the sixth form boys if they did not go, and infinitely preferring the former: —of how, if the boys did not "keep up" at football, they were made to cut large thorn sticks out of the hedges, and flogged with them till the blood poured down outside their jerseys. Indeed, what with fagging and bullying, servility was as much inculcated at Harrow in those days as if it was likely to be a desirable acquirement in afterlife.

I may truly say that I never learnt anything useful at Harrow, and had little chance of learning anything. Hours and hours were wasted daily on useless Latin verses with sickening monotony. A boy's school education at this time, except in the highest forms, was hopelessly inane.

In some ways, however, this "quarter" at Harrow was much pleasanter than preceding ones. I had a more established place in the school, and was on more friendly terms with all the boys in my own house; also, with my "armour," the hated racket-fagging was an impossibility. I had many scrambles about the country with Buller in search of eggs and flowers, which we painted afterwards most carefully and preservingly; and assisted by Buller, I got up a sort of private theatricals on a very primitive scale, turning Grimms' fairy stories into little plays, which were exceedingly popular with the house, but strictly forbidden by the tutor, Mr Simpkinson or "Simmy." Thus I was constantly in hot water about them. One day when we had got up a magnificent scene, in which I, as "Snowdrop," lay locked in a magic sleep in an imaginary cave, watched by dwarfs and fairies, Simmy came in and stood quietly amongst the spectators, and I was suddenly awakened from my trance by the *sauve qui peut*[*] which followed the discovery. Great punishments were the result. Yet, not long after, we could not resist a play on a grander scale — something about the "Fairy Tilburina" out of the "Man in the Moon," for which we learnt our parts and had regular dresses made. It was to take place in the fifth-form room on the ground-floor between the two divisions of the house, and just as Tilburina (Buller) was descending one staircase in full bridal attire, followed by her bridesmaids, of whom I was one, Simmy himself suddenly appeared on the opposite staircase and caught us.

At Easter, 1848, I left Harrow for the holidays, little imagining that I should never return there. I should have been very sorry had I known it. On the whole, the pleasurable "adventures" of a public-school life had always outweighed its disagreeables; though I was never in strong enough health for any real benefit or enjoyment.

[*] "Save (oneself) who can", thus, flight from an overwhelming defeat.

IV. LYNCOMBE

MARIA LEYCESTER HARE

OF ALL THE UNHAPPY SUMMERS of my boyhood, that of 1848 was the most miserable. When I left Harrow at Easter, I was really very ill. The iron frame which had been made for my back had seriously injured the spine which it was intended to cure, and a bad fall down the school steps at Harrow had increased the malady. When Sir Benjamin Brodie saw me, he said that I must lie down for at least the greater part of many months, and that a return to Harrow was quite out of the question. This, however, was concealed from me at first, and when I knew it, I was too ill to have any regrets.

I was so ill when we returned home, almost everything I ate producing violent sickness, that it is astonishing my health should not have been considered a primary object. A few weeks of healthy life on moors or by the seaside, with freedom from the gnawing mental misery and depression under which I suffered, would probably have restored me; a visit to German baths might have cured me, and saved years of ill-health. Had the family only had any practical common sense! But, on religious grounds, it was thought wrong to contend against "the wonderful leadings of God's Providence"—pain was "sent" to be endured, sickness as a tractor to draw its victims to heaven; and all simple and rational means of restoration to a healthy and healthful life were disregarded. Sago with brandy in it was provided instead of meat for my physical, and an inexhaustible supply of tracts, hymns, and little sermons for my mental digestion. Patient endurance of suffering, the following of the most unpleasant path which duty could be thought to point out, and that without hope of either reward or release, were the virtues which even my mother most inculcated at this time.

Then a private tutor was sent for—not by knowledge, not by inquiry at the Universities, not by careful investigation of attainments for teaching, but by an advertisement. The inquiry as to all the letters which answered it was whether they appeared to be "those of truly pious men"—*i.e.*, whether they were written in the peculiar phraseology then supposed to denote such a character. At last one was accepted, and a tutor arrived, who was—well, I will not describe him further than as certainly the most unprepossessing of human beings: nature had been so terribly hard upon him.

With this truly unfortunate man I was shut up every morning in the hope that he would teach me something, a task he was wholly unequal to; and then I had to walk out with him. Naturally there were scenes and recriminations on both sides, in which I was by no means blameless. But daily my health grew worse, and scarcely a morning passed without my having an agonizing fit of suffocation, from contraction of the muscles of the throat, gasping for breath in misery unutterable. The aunts said it was all nervous. I have no doubt it was: I have had plenty of experience of hysteria since, and it is the most dreadful disorder that exists.

At last my sufferings were such, from the relaxing air of Hurstmonceaux, that I was taken to Eastbourne, but an attempt was still made to chain me down for six or eight hours a day in a stuffy lodging at lessons with my tutor, who had not an idea of teaching and knew nothing to teach. Poor man! He was at least quite as wretched as I was, and I know that he thirsted quite as much for the fresh air of the downs. Aunt Esther came over, and used cruelly to talk, in my presence, of the fatigue and trouble my ill-health caused my mother, and of the burden which she had thus brought upon herself by adopting me. It is only by God's mercy that I did not commit suicide. I was often on the point of throwing myself over the cliffs, when all would have been over in an instant, and was *only* restrained by my intense love for my mother, and the feeling that her apparently dormant affection would be awakened by such a catastrophe, and that she would always be miserable in such an event. Twenty-two years afterwards when we were as closely united as it was possible for any mother and son to be, my darling mother reverted of her own accord to this terrible time: she could never die happy, she said, unless she knew that her after-love had quite effaced the recollection of it.

When I went in 1877, to visit Alfred Tennyson the poet, he asked me to give him a subject for "A Domestic Village Tragedy." The story which I told him occurred at Hurstmonceaux this summer [1848]. Mrs Coleman, who kept the "dame's school" at Flowers Green had a niece, Caroline Crowhurst, a very pretty girl, the belle of the parish, and as amiable and good as she was pretty, so that everyone was friends with her. She became engaged, rather against the will of her family, to a commercial traveler from a distance. He wrote to her, and she wrote to him, maidenly letters, but full of deep affection. One day they had a little quarrel, and the man, the fiend, took the most intimate, the most caressing of these letters and nailed it up against the Brewery in the center of Gardener Street, where all the village might read it and scoff at it. As the people knew Caroline, no one scoffed and all pitied her. But Caroline herself came to the village shop that afternoon; she saw her letter hanging there, and it broke her heart. She said nothing about it to anyone, and she did not shed a tear, but she went home and kissed her aunt and her mother more tenderly then usual; she gathered the prettiest flowers in her little garden and put them in her bosom, and then she opened the lid of the draw-well close to her home and let herself in. The lid closed upon her.

I remember the news coming to Lime one evening that Caroline Crowhurst was missing, and the dreadful shock the next morning when we heard that the poor girl had been found in the well.

At the end of July my real mother, "Italima," with my sister, came to stay at the Rectory. The visit was arranged to last a month, but, unhappily, on the second day of her stay, Italima went out with Aunt Esther. They came home walking on different sides of the road, and as soon as she entered the house Italima sent for post-horses to her carriage and drove away. I never heard what happened, but Italima never came to the Rectory again. Soon afterwards she fixed her residence at Rome in the Palazzo Parisiani . . . .

In August [1848] it was decided to send me away to a private tutor's and my mother and Uncle Julius went with me to Lyncombe, near Bath. My tutor was the Rev. H.S.R., son of a well-known evangelical writer, but by no means of the same spiritual grace: indeed I never could discover that he had any grace whatever; neither had he any mental acquirements, or the slightest power of teaching. He was "*un homme absolument nul,*" and though paid a very large salary, he grossly and systematically neglected all his duties as a tutor. Uncle Julius must have been perfectly aware how inefficient the education at Lyncombe would be, but he was probably not to blame for sending me there. Because I did not "get on" (really because I was never taught), he regarded me as the slave of indolence. He considered me, however, to be harmless, though fit for nothing and therefore one to be sent where I should probably get no harm, though certainly no good either. It was the system he went upon with my brothers also, and in their case he had all the responsibility, being their guardian.

I went to Lyncombe with the utmost curiosity. The house was a large villa, oddly built upon arches in the bellow of a wooded valley about a mile from Bath, behind the well-known Breechen Cliff. We all had rooms to ourselves at Lyncombe, scantily furnished, and with barely a strip of carpet, but we could decorate them with pictures, &c. if we liked. We did our lessons, when we were supposed to do them, at regular hours, in the dining room, where we had our meals, and after work was finished in the evening, and eight-o'clock tea, we were expected to sit with Mrs R. in the drawing-room.

But we had an immense deal of time to ourselves —the whole afternoon we were free to go where we liked; we were not expected to give any account of what we did, and might get into as much mischief as we chose. Also, we too frequently had whole holidays, which Mr R.'s idle habits made him only too glad to bestow, but which I often did not in the least know what to do with.

On the whole, at first I was not unhappy at Lyncombe. I liked the almost unlimited time for roaming over the country, and the fresh air did much to strengthen me. But gradually, when I had seen all the places within reach this freedom palled, and I felt with disgust that, terribly ignorant as I was, I was learning nothing, and that I had no chance of learning anything except what I could teach myself. I made, in desperation, great efforts to instruct myself, which, with no books and with every possible hindrance from without, was difficult enough. After a fashion, however, I succeeded in teaching myself French, stumbling through an interesting storybook with Grammar and Dictionary, till I had learnt to read with ease; of the pronunciation I naturally knew nothing.

Two miserable years and a half of life were utterly wasted at Lyncombe, before Arthur Stanley came to visit me there, and rescued me by his representation of the utter neglect and stagnation in which I was living. It had been so hammered into my head by my aunts that I was a burden to my mother, and that she was worn out with the trouble I had given her in finding my first private tutor, that I should never of myself have ventured to try to persuade her to look out for a second.

Once a week at least I used to go into Bath itself to dine with my father's old friend Walter Savage Landor, who had been driven away from his Florentine home by his wife's violent temper. Mr Landor's rooms (in Catherine Place, and afterwards at 2 Rivers Street) were covered entirely with pictures, the frames fitting close to one another, leaving not the smallest space of wall visible. One or two of these pictures were real works of art, but as a rule he bought them at Bath, quite willing to imagine that the little shops of the Bath dealers could be storehouses of Titians, Giorgiones, and Vandycks. The Bath picture dealers never had such a time; for some years almost all their wares made their way to Mr Landor's walls. Mr Landor lived alone with his beautiful white Spitz dog Pomero, which he allowed to do whatever it liked, and frequently to sit in the oddest way on the bald top of his head. He would talk to Pomero by the hour together, poetry, philosophy, whatever he was thinking of, all of it imbued with his own powerful personality, and would often roar with laughter till the whole house seemed to shake. In the evenings he would sit in impassioned contemplation; in the mornings he wrote incessantly, to fling off sheet after sheet for the *Examiner*, seldom looking them over afterwards.

He scarcely ever read, for he only possessed one shelf of books. If anyone gave him a volume, he mastered it and gave it away, and this he did because he believed that if he knew he was to keep the book and be able to refer to it, he should not be able to absorb its contents so as to retain them. When he left Florence, he had made over all he possessed to his wife, retaining only £200 a year—afterwards increased to £400—for himself, and this sufficed for his simple needs. He never bought any new clothes, and a chimneysweep would have been ashamed to wear his coat, which was always the same as long as I knew him, though it in no way detracted from his majestic and lion-like appearance. But he was very particular about his little dinners, and it was about these that his violent explosions of passion usually took place. I have seen him take a pheasant up by the legs when it was brought to table and throw it into the back of the fire over the head of the servant in attendance. This was always a failing, and, in later days, I have heard Mr Browning describe how in his fury at being kept waiting for dinner at Siena, he shouted: "I will not eat it now, I will not eat it if it comes," and, when it came, threw it all out of the window.

At the same time nothing could be more nobly courteous than his manner to his guests, and this was as marked towards an ignorant schoolboy as towards his most distinguished visitor; and his conversation, whilst calculated to put all his visitors at their ease and draw out their best points, was always wise, chivalrous, pure, and witty.

At one time Mr Landor's son Walter came to stay with him, but he was an ignorant rough youth, and never got on well with his father. I believe Mr Landor preferred me at this time to any of his own children, and liked better to have me with him; yet he must often have been grievously disappointed that I could so little reciprocate about the Latin verses of which he so constantly talked to me, and

WALTER SAVAGE LANDOR

that indeed I could seldom understand them, though he was so generous and highbred that he never would allow me to feel mortified.

My dear grandmother, Mrs Leycester, had been failing all the autumn, and my mother was much with her at her house in New Street. Towards the end of October she seemed better, and my mother returned to Lime, but on the 3rd of November she was suddenly recalled. As so often happens in serious cases, for the only time in her life she missed the train, and when she arrived, after many hours' delay, she found that dear Grannie had died, an hour before, wishing and longing for her to the last.

Grannie was buried in the vaults of St Martin's Church, Trafalgar Square, her coffin being laid upon that of Uncle Hugh. The vaults were a very awful place—coffins piled upon one another up to the ceiling, and often in a very bad state of preservation—and the funeral was a very ghastly one, all of the ladies being enveloped in huge black hooded mantles, which covered them from head to foot like pillars of crape. Grannie is one of the few persons whose memory is always evergreen to me, and for whom I have a most lasting affection.

During the autumn at Lyncombe I was almost constantly ill, and very often ill in the winter at home, which the Marcus Hares all spent at Lime. It was a miserable trial to me that, in her anxiety lest I should miss an hour of a school where I was taught nothing, my mother sent me back a week too early—and I was for that time alone in the prison of my abomination, in unutterable dreariness, with nothing in the world to do. This term, a most disagreeable vulgar boy called W—— was added to the establishment at Lyncombe, who was my detested companion for the next two years; and from this time in every way life at Lyncombe became indescribably wretched—chiefly from the utter waste of time— and, as I constantly wrote to my mother, I was always wishing that I were dead. My only consolation, and that a most dismal and solitary one, was in the long excursions which I made; but I look back upon these as times of acute suffering from poverty and hunger, as I never had any allowance, and was always sent back to my tutor's with only five shillings in my pocket. Thus, though I walked sometimes twenty-four miles in a day, and was out for eight or ten hours, I never had a penny with which to buy even a bit of bread, and many a time sank down by the wayside from the faintness of sheer starvation, often most gratefully accepting some of their food from the common working people I met. If I went out with my companions, the utmost mortification was added to the actual suffering of hunger, because, when they went into the village inns to have a good well-earned luncheon, I was always left starving outside, as I never had the means of paying for any food. I believe my companions were very sorry for me, but they never allowed their pity to be any expense to them. After a time, too, the food at Lyncombe itself became extremely stinted and of the very worst quality—a suet dumpling filled with coarse odds and ends of meat being our dinner on at least five days out of seven, which of course was very bad for an extremely delicate rapidly growing youth—and, if I was ill from want of food, which was frequently the case, I was given nothing but rice.

What indescribably miserable years those were! I still feel, in passing Bath by railway, sick at heart from the recollection, and I long in this volume to hurry over a portion of life so filled with wretched recollections, and which had scarcely a redeeming feature, except Mr Landor's constant kindness and friendship. It was also a terrible disappointment that my mother never would consent to my going for a few days to see "Italima" and my brothers, who were then living at Torquay, and who vainly begged for it. My endless letters to my mother (for I wrote several sheets daily) are so crushed and disconsolate that I find little to select.

In my summer holidays of 1849 my mother took me for the second time to Alton. It was very hot weather, and we lived entirely amongst the affectionate primitive cottagers, going afterwards to stay with Lady Gore at Wilcot House — an old haunted house, with a tower where a tailor (I forget how he got there) committed suicide. With Mrs Pile we drove through the open Wiltshire country to her farmhouse home of Tufton, where we spent several days very pleasantly. On the day of our leaving Tufton we visited Winchester, and as we were going thence to Portsmouth by rail, we had an adventure which might have ended seriously.

The train was already in motion, and my mother and I were alone in the carriage, when three men came running along the platform and attempted to enter it. Only one succeeded, for before the others could follow him, the train had left the platform. In a minute we saw that the man who was alone in the carriage with us was a maniac, and that those left behind were his keepers. He uttered a shrill hoot and glared at us. Fortunately, as the door banged to, the tassel of the window was thrown up, and this attracted him, and he yelled with laughter. We sat motionless at the other side of the carriage opposite each other. He seized the tassel and kept throwing it up and down, hooting and roaring with laughter. Once or twice we fancied he was about to pounce upon us, but then the tassel attracted him again. After about eight minutes the train stopped. His keepers had succeeded in getting upon the guard's box as the train left the station, and hearing his shouts, stopped the train, and he was removed by force.

Up to this time, as afterward, no preparation for social life had ever been thought of as far as I was concerned. I was never encouraged to talk at home; indeed if I ever spoke, I was instantly suppressed. I knew nothing of any game; I was never taught to ride or swim, and dancing was absolutely prohibited as an invention of the evil one. The boys must have thought me a terrible ass, but it was not really quite my own fault. Oh! how heartily I agree with Archbishop Whately who said that "the God of the Calvinists is the devil with 'God' written on his forehead."

In the summer [1850] my maternal grandfather, Sir John Paul, came to stay at a hotel at Bath and I saw him frequently, but never found anything in common with him, though he was an exceedingly clever artist. In my daily letters to my mother, I see that I described his first reception of me with "How do you do, sir"—just like any distant acquaintance. He was at this time married to his third wife, who presented a very youthful appearance. Her step children, who never liked her, declared that on the day after her marriage one of her eyebrows fell off into her soup. But to me she was always very kind and I was fond of her, in spite of her many ancient frivolities.

It was in April 1850 that a happy missing of his train at Bath produced a visit at Lyncombe of Arthur Stanley, who was horrified at my ignorance, and at the absence, which he discovered, of all pains in teaching me. His representations to my mother at last induced her to promise to remove me, for which I shall ever be eternally grateful to him in recollection. Nevertheless I was unaccountably left at Lyncombe till Christmas; nine wretched and utterly useless months; for when he knew I was going to leave, after my return in the summer, Mr R. dropped even the pretense of attempting to teach me, so that I often remained in total neglect, without any work whatever, for several weeks. In their anger at the distant prospect of my escaping them, the R.'s now never spoke to me, and my life was passed in total and miserable silence, even at mealtimes. If it had not been for the neighbourhood of Bath, I should often have been many weeks together without speaking a single word. My mother in vain remonstrated over my sickeningly doleful letters, and told me to "catch all the sunbeams within reach"; I could only reply there were no sunbeams to catch—that "you would think at meals that you were in the Inquisition from the cold, morose, joyless, motionless faces around the table." Then Aunt Esther would make my mother urge me to accept all these small trials, these "guidings," in a more Christian spirit, which made me furious: I could not express religious sentiments when such sentiments were quite unborn. I also wrote to my mother—

"We are in the last extremities as regards food. I will give you a perfectly correct account of the last few days. Saturday, dinner, boiled beef. Sunday, breakfast, ditto cold with bread and butter. Luncheon, a very small portion of ditto with dry bread and part of the rind of a decayed cheese. Dinner, a little of ditto with a doughy plum-tart. Monday, breakfast, ditto with two very small square pieces of bread. Luncheon, ditto with bread and butter! Dinner, ditto and a rice-pudding. Tuesday, breakfast, ditto; luncheon, a very small fragment of ditto and one potato apiece doled around. Dinner, ditto. Wednesday, breakfast, scraps of ditto; luncheon, fat and parings ditto. We all have to sit and do our work by the light of a single bedcandle. Oh! I am more thankful every day that you will at last let me leave this place. Any change must be for the better, and I should not mind if it was to the centre of the desert, if only I could feel I should learn something, for I am learning nothing here, and never have learnt anything. . . . Would you very much mind giving me an umbrella, for I have got wet through almost every day: on Sundays it is especially inconvenient. Mr R. asked me the other day how I like the thoughts of going away!—but I was very good, and only said "I should not mind it very much!"

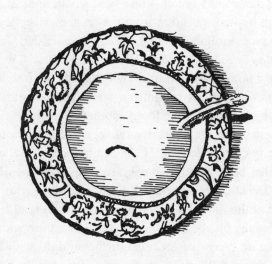

V. SOUTHGATE

FRANCIS GEORGE HARE

MY NEW TUTOR, THE REV. Charles Bradley, was selected by
Arthur Stanley. The life at Southgate for the next two years was
certainly the reverse of luxurious, and I did not get on well with
my tutor owing to his extraordinary peculiarities, and probably to
my many faults also; but I feel that mentally I owe everything to
Mr Bradley.

My mother determined at the end of the quarter to make a short
tour in Normandy—a plan with which I was intensely delighted.
To go abroad was positively enchanting. But *anything* would have
been better than staying at Hurstmonceaux, so overrun was it
with Maurices. We crossed to Boulogne, saw Amiens and had a
glimpse of Paris. We spent delightful days at Rouen . . . . From
Havre we went by sea to Caen from whence we made excursions
to Bayeux and Falaise. From Falaise we went to Lisieux, which
was then one of the most beautiful old towns in France, almost
entirely of black and white timber houses. My mother and cousin
returned to England from thence, but I was left for some weeks at
Caen to study French at the home of M. Melun, a Protestant pas-
teur in a quiet side-street close to the great Abbaye des Dames,

where Matilda of Flanders is buried.

Want of money was still always the great trouble of my boy-hood, as my dear mother could never be persuaded to see the necessity of my having any, and after she had made a minute calculation of the necessary pennies that came into her head, always gave me just that sum and no more, never allowing anything for the ever-recurring incidents and exigencies of daily life. When I was sixteen she was persuaded to allow me £10 a year, but out of this I was expected to buy all the smaller articles of dress, boots, hats, gloves, &c., so, as may be imagined, my annual allowance was almost nil; and my excursions at South-gate had been only possible by starvation, and because the third-class ticket to London cost only fourpence. When I was left at Caen, just the absolutely needful sum for my return journey was given me, and no allowance made for any personal expenses of my stay—for washerwoman, fees to servants, or payments for the many purchases which my mother wrote to desire me to make for her. Thus, when the time came for setting out home-wards, with the nine packages which were to be taken to my mother, I was in the greatest embarrassment and many were my adventures; yet my dread of a sea voyage still made me refuse altogether to go by Havre and Southhampton, and my longing to see a historical spot which I had long read and heard of made me determine if possible—if I half died for it on the way—to visit St. Denis, a place I had always had a special longing after. The journey entailed a singular chapter of accidents.

During the whole of the first long day—twelve hours' diligence journey—I had nothing whatever to eat but a brioche and some plums; but at seventeen starvation is not one of the worst things in life, and when I arrived at Evreux, the fair of St. Taurinus, the patron saint of the place, was going on and I was in ecstasies the next morning over the costumes which it brought into the town, as well as over the old Bishop's Palace and the beautiful cathedral with its lace-work architecture.

From Evreux the diligence had to be taken again to Bonnières, where I joined the railway to Paris, and in the evening reached St. Denis. I had no money to go to a hotel, but spent the night in a wretched café which was open for carters under the walls of the cathedral, where I got some sour bread and eggs, having had no food all day. At five in the morning the doors of the Abbey were opened, and in my raptures over the monuments of Dagobert, Francis I, &c., I forgot all my miseries—especially in the crypt, full then of royal tombs and statues. At half-past twelve, when I was ready to leave, I found that no more trains for Boulogne would stop at St. Denis that day, and that I must return to Paris. I went in the omnibus, but owing to my ignorance of French, was carried far beyond my point, and had to be dropped, with all my packages, in a strange street, whence with some difficulty I got a porter to drag my things to the station, but arrived when the train was just gone, and no other till half-past seven, and it was then two. Hungry and forlorn, I made my way, losing it often, on foot, to the Tuileries gardens, where I felt that the beauty of the flowers repaid me for the immense walk, though I was disconcerted when I found that sitting down on a chair cost the two sous I had saved to buy bread with. In my return walk, ignorance and mistakes brought me to the railway for Rouen (Gare S. Lazare), instead of that for Boulogne (Gare du Nord). However, in time I reached the right place.

As we were halfway to the coast in the express, a strong smell of burning was borne on the wind, and the carriage soon filled with smoke. Looking out, we saw a line of screaming faces, and the roof of one of the front carriages in flames. Pieces of burning stuff rushed flaming past. A young lady in our carriage—"Gabrielle"—fell on her knees and said her prayers to the Virgin. Suddenly we stopped, and heard the rush of water above us. The engine driver, to save the train, had, with terrible risk to the passengers, pushed on at a frightful speed to the *pompe d'incendie** of Pontoise.

At half-past one in the morning we reached Boulogne. I was told that the steamer for Folkestone would not start for an hour. An official in blue with silver lace said that he would call for me then. At the time, but rather late, he came. A cab was ready, and we were only just in time to catch the steamer. The official, as I was going on board, desired that I would pay my fare. I supposed it was all right, and gave up almost all my few remaining shillings. I was assured the packet was the one for Folkestone, and though surprised at having no ticket, supposed it was because most of the passengers had through tickets from Paris to London, and because my going on was an afterthought.

The steamer started, but, before leaving the harbour, concussed with another vessel, which broke one of the paddle-boxes and delayed us an hour. Meantime it began to pour in torrents, the deck swam with water, and before we got out to sea the wind had risen and the sea was very rough. The vessel was fearfully crowded with three hundred and fifty people going to the Hyde Park Exhibition, and more than half of them were seasick.

At last day broke, and with it the English coast came in sight. But it was very odd; it was not a coast I knew, and Dover Castle seemed to be on the wrong side. Then a man came for the tickets, and said I must have had one if I had paid: as I had not one, I

* Fire engine.

could not have paid. It was in vain that I protested I had paid already. "When I get to Folkestone," I said, "I should see someone who could prove my identity," &c. The man grinned. "It will be a long time before *you* get to Folkestone," he said, and he went away.

Then I saw Dover Castle fade away, and we still coasted on, and I saw a little town which looked strangely like the pictures of Deal. At last a man next to me, recovering from a paroxysm of seasickness, said, "You think you're in the boat for Folkestone, but you are in the boat for London!" I had been swindled at Boulogne by a notorious rogue. Some weeks afterwards I saw in the papers that he had been arrested, after a similar case.

I was in despair, not so much because of the long voyage, as because to *pay* for it was impossible. We were not to reach London till four in the afternoon. I implored the captain to set me down, we were so near the coast. "No," he said, "go to London you must."

At last, as we passed Margate, he said I might perhaps get out, but it was rather too much to sacrifice the comfort of three hundred and fifty passengers to one. However, the three hundred and fifty seemed very glad of a break in the monotony of their voyage, and as there was another passenger anxious to land, a boat was hailed and reached the vessel. All my packages were thrown overboard and I after them with injunctions to sit perfectly still and hold fast, as it was so frightfully rough. The injunctions were unnecessary, since, exhausted as I was, I very soon became unconscious, as I have so often done since in rough sea.

It was too rough to land at the pier, so we were landed on a ridge of rocks at some distance from the shore. Seeing all my packages, the coastguardsmen naturally took us for smugglers, and were soon on the spot to seize our goods and carry them to the custom-house. Here I had to pay away all that remained to me except sixpence.

With that sixpence I reached Ramsgate.

There were four hours to wait for a train, and I spent it in observing the directions on the luggage of all arriving passengers, to see if there was any one I could beg of. But no help came; so eventually I told my story to the stationmaster, who kindly gave me a railway pass. At Ashford I had four hours more to wait, and I lay almost unconscious (from want of food) upon the floor of the waiting room. Lying thus, I looked up, and saw the astonished face of my cousin Mary Stanley gazing in through the window at me. She was leaving in two minutes for France, but had time to give me a sovereign; with that sovereign, late in the night, I reached home in a gig from Hastings.

I think it must have been on leaving Southgate for the summer that I paid a visit of one day to "Italima" and my sister in a house which had been lent them in Grosvenor Square. It was then that my sister said, "Mamma, Augustus is only with us for one day. We ought to take the opportunity of telling him what may be of great importance to him: we ought to tell him the story of the 'Family Spy.'" What I heard then was as follows—

For many years my sister had observed that she and her mother were followed and watched by a particular person. Wherever they went or whatever they did, she was aware of the same tall thin man dressed in grey, who seemed to take a silent interest in all that happened to them. At last this surveillance became quite disagreeable and they tried to escape it. One spring they pretended that they were going to leave Rome on a particular day, announced it to their friends, and made secret preparations for quitting Rome a week earlier. They arrived in safety within a few miles of Florence, when looking up at a tall tower by the side of the road, my sister saw the face of the Family Spy watching them from its battlements. Another time they heard that the Spy was ill and confined to his bed, and they took the opportunity of moving at once. As their vetturino carriage turned out of the piazza into the Via S. Claudio in order to attain the Corso, which must be passed before reaching the gate of the city, the narrow street was almost blocked up by another carriage, in which my sister saw the emaciated form of the Family Spy propped on pillows and lying on a mattress, and which immediately followed them. Constant inquires had long since elicited the fact that the Spy was a Sicilian Marquis who had been living at Palermo when my parents were there, and whose four children were exactly the same age as *their* four children. Soon afterwards his wife and all his children were swept away at one stroke by the cholera, and he was left utterly desolate. With characteristic Sicilian romance, he determined to create for himself a new family and a new interest in life by adopting the other family, which was exactly parallel to his own, and of which only the father had been removed—but adopting it by a mysterious bond, in which the difficulty of a constant surveillance should give entire occupation to his time and thought. When Italima heard this, after making inquires about him which proved satisfactory, she sent to the Spy to say that she thought it much better this secret surveillance should end, but that she should be happy to admit him as a real friend, and allow him to see as much as he liked of the family in which he took so deep an interest. But, though expressing great gratitude for this proposal, the Spy utterly declined it. He said that he had so long accustomed himself to the constant excitement of his strange life, that it would be quite impossible for him to live without it; that if ever an opportunity occurred of rendering any great service to the family whose fortunes he followed, he would speak to them, but not till then.

When I had been told this story, my sister and Italima took me out in the afternoon to drive in the park. As we were passing along the road by the Serpentine, my sister suddenly exclaimed, "There, look! there is the Family Spy," and, among those who walked by the water, I saw the tall thin grey figure she had described. We passed him several times, and he made such an impression upon me that I always knew him afterwards. My sister said, "If you look out at ten o'clock tonight, you will see him leaning against the railing of Grosvenor Square watching our windows,"—and so it was; there was the tall thin figure with his face uplifted in the moonlight.

In 1852 the extravagance of my two brothers Francis and William was already causing great anxiety to their mother. Francis, who had lately obtained his commission in the Life Guards through old Lord Combermere, had begun to borrow money upon the Gresford estate. William, who was in the Blues, with scarcely any fortune at all, had plunged desperately into the London season. When winter approached, their letters caused even more anxiety on account of their health than their fortunes: both complaining of cough and other ailments. One day, in the late autumn of 1852, my sister, coming into the dining room of the Palazzo Parisani, found her mother stretched insensible upon the hearthrug, with a letter open in her hand. The letter was from the new Sir John Paul, who had not in the least got over his first anger at his sister's change of religion,* and who wrote in the cruellest and harshest terms. He said, "Your eldest son is dying, it is quite impossible that you can arrive in time to see him alive. Your second son is also in a rapid decline, though if you set off at once and travel to England without stopping you may still be in time to receive his last words."

Palazzo Parisani was at once thrown into the utmost confusion, and all its inmates occupied themselves in preparing for immediate departure. Owing to the great number of things to be stowed away, it was, however, utterly impossible that they should leave before the next morning. Italima's state of anguish baffles description, for Francis was her idol. In the afternoon my sister, hoping to give her quiet, persuaded her to go out for an hour and walk in the gardens of the Villa Medici, where she would not be likely to meet anyone she knew. In the long arcaded bay-walks of the villa she saw a familiar figure approaching. It was the "Family Spy." He came up to her, and, to her amazement, he began to address her—he, the silent follower of so many years! He said, "The time has now come at which I can serve you, therefore I speak. This morning you received a letter." Italima started. "You are surprised that I know you have the letter, and yet I am going to tell you all that was in that letter," and he repeated it word for word. He continued—"I not only know all that was in that letter and the distress in which it has placed you, but I know all the circumstances under which that letter was written, and I know all that has happened to your sons since: I know all about your sons. Your son Francis was taken ill on such a day: he saw such and such doctors: he is already much better: there is no

* Italima and Esmeralda had converted to Catholicism.

danger: you may be quite easy about him. Your son William is not in danger, but he is really much the more ill of the two. Dr Fergusson has seen him, and a foreign winter is prescribed. It will not do for you to go to England yourself, but yet he is not well enough to travel alone. You have an old servant, Félix, who came to you in such a year, and who has been with you ever since. You must send him to fetch William, and here is a paper on which I have written down all the trains and steamers they are to travel by, both in going and returning." So saying, and having given the paper to Italima and bowing very low, the Family Spy retired. Italima went home. She acted entirely on the advice she had received. She un-packed her things and remained in her palazzo at Rome. She sent Félix, as the Spy had directed: he travelled according to the written programme, and in a fortnight he re-turned to Rome bringing William back with him. The Spy never spoke to any member of the family again.

It is anticipating, but I may mention here that when we went to Rome in 1857, I wondered if we should see the Family Spy. I spoke of it to my mother. As we passed through the Porta del Popolo, he was the first person who met us. I saw him very often that winter and again when I was at Paris with my sister in October, 1858. That winter my sister often saw him at Rome. The next year was marked by our great family misfortunes. My sister always expected that somehow or other he would come to the rescue of the lost fortunes, but he never did. Some time after she heard that he had died very suddenly about that time.

When I returned to my mother in the summer of 1852, she was at Eastbourne with Charlotte Leycester and very ill. It was the earliest phase of the strange hysteria with which I was afterwards so familiar—sudden flushings with a deathly chill over her face, and giddiness, sometimes followed by unconsciousness, occasionally by a complete apparent suspension of life, a death-like trance without breath or pulsation, lasting for hours, or even for many days together. It is a very rare illness, but it is known to doctors, and I believe it is called "Walking Coma." In this summer I first began the anxious watchings of first symptoms—the swelling of my mother's fingers around her rings, and then by a kiss searched if the alarming chill had already taken possession of her face. Happily, the heavenly state of mind in which she always lived took away from her the terror of these illnesses; the visions which beset her waking and sleeping were of all things good and beautiful: the actual trances themselves were to her a translation into heavenly places and to the companionship of the blessed, and for those who looked upon her, a transfiguration.

When my mother was able to move, it was decided that she must try foreign air, which then and often afterwards completely restored her to health for the time. It was settled that we should go to Heidelberg, and as her cousin Charlotte Leycester was to travel with her, I was able to precede her for a few days in the old Belgian towns, which, as I was then in the first enthusiasm about foreign travel, I looked upon as absolutely entrancing.

LETTER TO MY MOTHER. *Southgate, Oct. 12*—Mr Bradley is in nothing so extraordinary as in the education of his children. All the moral lessons to his little daughter Jessica are taken from reminiscences of his "poor dear first wife," who never existed. I am used to it now, but was amazed when I first heard little Jessie ask something about "your poor dear first wife, papa," and he took out a handkerchief and covered over both of their heads that no one might see them cry, which the little girl did abundantly over the touching story told her. Little Charlie's education was carried on in a similar way, only the model held up to him was a son of Mrs Bradley's by an imaginary first husband, who "died and is buried in Oxfordshire." Little Moses's mamma, "Mrs Jochebed Amram," is also held up as an effective example of Christian piety and patience, but Moses himself never touched their feelings at all.

On the 17th of November [1852] I went up to London for the funeral of the Duke of Wellington the following day. We had to set off at four o'clock next morning to reach our reserved seats in St. Paul's, though I do not think the service began till twelve. We were four hours in the long chain of carriages wending at a foot's pace towards St. Paul's. A number of curious cases of robbery occurred then. I remember one, of an old gentleman in a carriage before us who was leaning out of the carriage window with a pair of gold spectacles on his nose. A well-dressed man approached him between the two lines of carriages and said, "Sir, don't you know that you're very imprudent in leaning out of the carriage window on this occasion with such a very valuable pair of gold spectacles on your nose? An *ill-disposed* person might come up and whip off your spectacles like *this*"— and, suiting the action to the word, he whipped them off, and escaped between the opposite line of carriages, leaving the old gentleman without any chance of redress.

The last nine months of my stay at Southgate were less pleasant than the preceding ones, as Mr Bradley had ceased to like me, and, though he fully did his duty by me in work-time, plainly showed, out of working hours, that he would be very glad when the time came for our final separation. The change arose entirely from my resistance, backed up by Dr Vaughan at Harrow, to many of his absurd punishments. I was now nearly nineteen, and I offered to bear any amount of rational punishment he chose, but utterly refused to wear my coat inside out, and to run with a tin kettle tied to my coattail through the village, &c., which were the punishments he liked to impose.

But our final dispute came about in this way:—

My Latin prose was always the greatest stumbling block in my work, and I was inveterately careless over it, making the same mistakes over and over again. At last Bradley declared publicly, that for each of my commonest blunders, one of my companions should—kiss me! They thought it was great fun, but I declared I should not submit. The decree had a good effect so far, that for a very long time—a most unusually long time, the mistakes were evaded. At last, after about three weeks, a morning came when one of the mistakes occurred again. The fellow appointed to kiss me for this mistake was a big Scotchman named Buchan. Immediately the whole room was in motion, and Buchan in hot pursuit. I barricaded the way with chairs, jumped on the table, splashing right and left from the inkstands, but eventually I was caught and—kissed.

In a blind fury, scarcely knowing what I did, I knocked Buchan's head against the sharp edge of the bookcase, and, seizing a great Liddell and Scott Lexicon, rushed upon Bradley, who was seated unsuspecting in a low chair by the fire, and taking him unawares, banged him on the bald scalp with the Lexicon till I could bang no longer. Bradley, after this, naturally

said I must leave. I instantly fled over hedge and ditch fourteen
miles to Harrow, and took refuge with the Vaughans, and after a
day or two, Dr Vaughan, by representing the fatal injury it would
do me to be left tutorless just when I was going up to Oxford, persuaded Bradley to take me back and teach me as before. But this
he consented to do only on condition that he was never expected
to speak to me out of work-time, and he never did. My Southgate
life was hence-forth full of (in many ways well-deserved) petty
hardships, though they were made endurable, because the time in
which they had to be endured became every day more limited.

VI. OXFORD LIFE

JULIUS CHARLES HARE

AT NINETEEN, I WAS JUST beginning to feel something of the self-confidence which boys usually experience at thirteen, and, as I emancipated myself gradually from the oppressors of my boyhood, to yearn with eager longings for and sudden inexplicable sympathies towards friendship and confidence of companions of my own age. There was also a pleasure in feeling that henceforward, though I should always have to economize, I must have some money of my own, although a regular allowance was never granted at Oxford, or at any other time. It was partially the fact that I had no money to spend in my own way, and that my bills were always overlooked and commented upon, and partly that I had known no other young men except those whom I met at my private tutor's, which made me still very peculiar in dress as in voice and manner. I can see myself now—very shy and shrinking, arriving at Oxford in a rough "bear greatcoat," with a broad stripe down my trousers, such as was worn then, and can hear the shrill high tones in which I spoke.

TO MY MOTHER, *March 26 [1853].* It was nervous work walking in the cold morning down the High Street to University . . . . I knocked at the Dean's (Mr Hedley's) door. He took me to the Hall—a long hall, with long rows of men writing at a long table, at the end of which I was set down with pens, ink and paper. Greek translation, Latin compositions, and papers of arithmetic and Euclid were given me to do, and we were all locked in. I knew my work, and had done when we were let out, at half-past one, for twenty minutes. At the end of that time, Mr Hedley took me to the Master (Dr Plumptre). The old man sat in his study—very cold, very stern, and very tall. I thought the examination was over. Not a bit of it. The Master asked what books I had ever done and took down the names on paper. Then he chose Herodotus. I knew with that old man a mistake would be fatal, and I did not make it. Then he asked me a number of odd questions—all the principal rivers in France and Spain, the towns they pass through, and the points where they enter the sea; all the prophecies in the Old Testament in their order relating to the coming of Christ; all the relationships of Abraham and all the places he lived in. These things fortunately I happened to know. Then the Master arose and solemnly made a little speech—

"You have not read so many books, Mr Hare, not nearly so many books as are generally required, but in consideration of the satisfactory way in which you have passed your general examination, and in which you have answered my questions, you will be allowed to matriculate, and this, I hope, will lead you," &c., &c. But for me the moral lesson at the end is lost in the essential, and the hitherto cold countenance of Mr Hedley now smiles pleasantly.

Then a great book is brought out, and I am instructed to write

—"*Augustus Joannes Cuthbertus Hare, Armigeri filius.*" Then there is a pause. The Master and Dean consult how "born at Rome" is to be written. The Dean suggests, the Master does not approve; the Dean suggests again, the Master is irritated; the Dean consults a great folio volume, and I am told to write "*de urbe Roma civitate Italiae.*" When this is done, Mr Hedley stands up, the Master looks vacant, I bow and we go out.

At five o'clock, having got a cap and gown at the tailor's, I return to Mr Hedley, now very affable, who walks with me to Worcester, to the Vice-Chancellor. The servant at the door says, "A gentleman is matriculating." Mr Hedley says he is going to matriculate me. So we go in, and I write again in a great book and sign the Articles. I swear to abjure the Pope, and be devoted to the Queen, and kiss a Testament upon it. Then the Vice-Chancellor says, "Now attend diligently," and makes a little speech in Latin about obedience to the institutes of the University. Then I pay £3,10s and am free.

All through my first year at Oxford, Mr Jowett (afterwards Master of Balliol) continued to show me the utmost kindness, giving me extra work, and allowing me to bring the result to him in the evening. I had been so much neglected at Lyncombe, and so ill-grounded altogether in my boyhood that my passing all my examinations successfully was probably owing to this generous action of his. Honours at Oxford even in the History School, I never thought of. My mother would only have wondered what on earth I wanted them for, and, had I gained them, would have lamented them as terribly ensnaring.

I was profoundly grateful to Mr Jowett, but, being constantly asked to breakfast alone with him was a terrible ordeal. Sometimes he never spoke at all, and would only walk round the room looking at me with unperceiving, absent eyes as I ate my bread and butter, in a way that for a very nervous boy, was utterly terrific. Walking with this kind and silent friend was even worse: he scarcely ever spoke, and if, in my shyness, I said something at one milestone, he would make no response at all till we reached the next, when he would say abruptly, "Your last observation was singularly commonplace," and lapse into silence again.

The society of Mrs Gaskell the authoress was a great pleasure during this term at Oxford. I made great friends with her, and we kept up a correspondence for some time afterwards. Everybody liked Mrs Gaskell. I remember that one of the points which struck me most about her at first was not only her kindness, but her extreme courtesy and deference to her own daughters. While she was at Oxford, the subject of ghosts was brought forward for a debate at the Union; she wished to have spoken from the gallery, and if she had, would probably have carried the motion in favour of ghosts at once.

To MY MOTHER. *University College, Nov.18 [1853].*—I breakfasted the other day at Wadham with a most extraordinary man called R., whose arms and legs all straggled away from his body, and who holds up his hands like a kangaroo. His oddities are a great amusement to his friends, who nevertheless esteem him. One day a man said to him, "How do you do, R.?" and he answered, "Quite well, thank you." Imagine the man's astonishment at receiving next day a note—"Dear Sir, I am sorry to tell you that I have been acting a deceptive part. When I told you yesterday that I was quite well, I really had a headache; this has been on my conscience ever since."

The man was extremely amused, and showed the letter to a friend, who knowing R.'s frailties, said to him, "Oh, R., how could you act so wrongly as to call Mr Burton 'Dear Sir'—thereby giving him the impression that you liked him, when you know that you dislike him extremely?" So poor R. was sadly distressed, and a few days later Mr Burton received the following:—"Burton, I am sorry to trouble you again, but I have been shown that, under the mask of friendship, I have been for the second time deceiving you: by calling you Dear Sir, I may have led you to suppose I liked you which I never did, and never can do. I am, Burton, yours &c."

Among the remarkable persons whom I frequently saw in my earlier Oxford life was the venerable Dr (Martin Joseph) Routh, President of Magdalen, born 1755, who died in 1854, in his hundredth year. He would describe his mother as having known a lady who had met Charles II walking round the parks at Oxford with his dogs. He had himself seen Dr Johnson "scrambling up the steps of University." In him I myself saw a man of the type of Dr Johnson, and of much the same dress, and even ponderous manner of speaking. I remember Goldwin Smith once asking him how he did, and his replying, "I am suffering, sir, from a catarrhal cold, which, however, I take to be a kind provision of Nature to relieve the peccant humours of the system." His recollections of old Oxford extended naturally over the most immense period. George Dasent had told me that the President once asked him, "Did you hear, sir, of Gownsman's Gallows?"—"No, Mr President."—"What, sir, do you tell me, sir, that you never heard of

Gownsman's Gallows? Why, I tell you, sir, that I have seen two undergraduates hanged on Gownsman's Gallows in Holywell—hanged, sir, for highway robbery."

A few years before the President's death, when he was at Ewelme, his living in the country, his butler became insane and had to be sent away. When he was leaving, he asked to see the President once more, "to ask his blessing," as he said. The President received him in the garden, where the man, stooping as if to kiss his hand, bit it—bit a piece out of it. "How did you feel, Mr President," said Sir G. Dasent afterwards, "when the man bit your hand?"—"Why, at first, sir," said the President, "I felt considerably alarmed; for I was unaware, sir, what proportion of human virus might have been communicated by the bite; but in the interval of reaching the house, I was convinced that the proportion of virus must have been very small indeed: then I was at rest, but sir, I had the bite cauterized." It was often observed of Dr Routh that he never appeared on any occasion without his canonicals, which he wore constantly. Some ill-disposed undergraduates formed a plan which should force him to break this habit, and going under his window at midnight, they shouted "Fire!" The President appeared immediately and in the most terrible state of alarm, but in full canonicals.

It was only forty-eight hours before Dr Routh died that his powers began to fail. He ordered his servants to prepare rooms for Mr and Mrs Cholomondeley, who had been long since dead, and then they felt sure the end was come. They tried to get him upstairs to bed, but he struggled with the banisters as with an imaginary enemy. He then spoke of pedigrees, and remarked that a Mr Edwards was descended from two royal families: he just murmured something about the American war, and then he expired. He left his widow very ill provided for, but the college gave her a handsome income.

In the summer of 1854 a trip abroad for the Mother's health .... A most wearisome journey. A *voiturier* took us from Aix to Geneva, a place for which I conceived the most intense aversion, from its hot baking situation, and the illiberal and presumptuous "religion" of its inhabitants. At the Hotel des Étrangers, a house in a damp garden near the lake, we were seated almost alone at the little table d'hôte when we heard the most extraordinary hissing and rushing sound, like a clock being wound up, and a very little lady entered, who seemed to be impelled into the room, followed by her husband. On reaching her chair, several loud clicks resulted in her being lifted into it as by invisible power! It was Mrs Archer Clive, the then celebrated authoress of "Paul Ferroll," who had no legs, and moved by clock work.

My mother's sufferings from the heat led to our going from Geneva to Chamounix. On the way we slept at St. Martin. As I was drawing there upon the bridge, a little girl came to beg, but beggars were so common that I paid no attention to her entreaties, till her queer expression attracted me, and a boy who came up at the same time described her as an "*abandonée*," for her father was in prison, her sister dead, and her mother had deserted her and gone off to Paris. The child, who had scarcely an apology for being clothed, verified this in a touching and at the same time an elflike way—grinning and bemoaning her sorrows in the same breath. Charlotte Leycester gave her four sous, with which she was so enchanted that she rushed away, throwing her hands into the air and making every demonstration of delight, and we thought we should see no more of her. However, in going home, we found her under a wall on the other side of the bridge, where she showed us with rapture the bread she had been able to buy with the money which had been given her. An old woman standing by told us about her—how wonderfully little the child lived on, sleeping from door to door, and how extraordinary her spirits still were. It was so odd a case, and there was something so interesting in the child, that we determined to follow her, and see where she really would go to sleep. To our surprise, instead of guiding us through the village, she took her way straight up the woods on the mountainside, by a path which she assured us was frequented by wolves. It was very dark, and the place she led us to was most desolate—some châlets standing by themselves in the woods, almost at the foot of the mountain; the glass gone from the windows, which were filled up with straw and bits of wood. Meantime we had made out from the child that her name was Toinette, daughter of François Bernard, and that she once lived in the neighbouring village of Passy, where her home had been burnt to the ground, a scene which she described with marvellous gesticulations. She seemed to have conceived the greatest affection for Charlotte. When asked if she knew that it was wrong to lie and steal, she said, "Rather than steal I would have my head cut off, like the people in the prisons. I pray every day, and my prayer shall be always for you, Madame."

A great dog flew out of the cottage at us, but Toinette drove it away, and called out a woman who was standing in the doorway. The woman said she knew nothing of Toinette, but that she had implored to sleep there about three weeks before, and that she had slept there ever since; and then the child, caressing her and stroking her cheeks, begged to be allowed to do the same again.

The woman offered to go with us to another house, where the people knew the child better. On arriving, we heard the inmates at prayers inside, singing a simple litany in responses. Afterwards they came out to speak to us. They said it was but for a very small matter François Bernard was imprisoned, as he had only stolen some bread when he was starving, but that, if he came back, he could do nothing for Toinette, and as her uncles were idiots, there was nobody to take care of her: if we wished to do anything for her, we had better speak to the Syndic, who lived higher up the mountain; so thither we proceeded, with Toinette and all her female friends in our train.

It was a strange walk, by starlight through the woods, and a queer companionship of rough kindhearted people. Toinette, only seven years old, laughed and skipped over the stones, holding Charlotte's gown, and declaring she would never leave her. We had expected to find the magistrate living in a better house than the others, but it was like its neighbours—a little brown châlet by the side of a torrent. The Syndic was already in bed, but Madame, his wife, speedily got him up and we held a parley with him on the wooden staircase, all the other people standing below. He said that there were no workhouses, no orphan asylums, and that though it was a bad case, the commune had no funds; school did not open till October, and even if Toinette got work, there was no lodging for her at night. However, when Charlotte promised to clothe her, he was so much enchanted with the "*grandeur de sa charité*," that he said he would consult with the commune about Toinette. Meantime, in the morning Charlotte bought her some clothes, and settled something for her future; but before we left we saw that she must not be too much indulged, as she asked Charlotte, who had given her a frock, shoes, and a hat, to give her also some bonbons and a parasol!

We heard of Toinette Bernard for some years afterwards, and Charlotte Leycester sent annual remittances for her; but eventually she absconded and utterly disappeared like a waif.

Uncle Julius, whose health was rapidly declining, received my mother with many tears on our return. I have a vivid recollection of that first evening. My mother read "Bless the Lord, O my soul" at evening prayers, and said she always read that after a journey, with "He healeth all thy diseases"—so true of her. We went to Hastings for Uncle Julius's Charge to the clergy, which produced much enthusiasm amongst them, very different from his lengthy

HURSTMONCEAUX RECTORY

sermons in Hurstmonceaux, under which the whole congregation used quietly to compose themselves to sleep, probably well aware that they would not understand a word if they tried to attend. The effect was sometimes most ridiculous of the chancel filled with nodding heads, or of heads which had long since done nodding, and were resting on their elbows locked in fastest slumber. I believe Mrs Sherwood describes a similar scene in one of her stories. Aunt Esther and the curate would try in vain to keep themselves awake with strong lavender lozenges during Uncle Julius's endless discourses. And then "There's Mrs Hare asleep on one side of the Archdeacon and the curate on the other," the people would say, and he would go droning on with a sermon preached fifty times before. There were, however, days on which Uncle Julius would emerge from the vestry with clenched hands and his face full of pale enthusiasm, and then I would whisper to my mother, "Look, Uncle Julius is going to do Lady MacBeth!" There were no slumbers then, but rapt attention, as Uncle Julius in his most thrilling (and they were thrilling) tones went through the whole of the sleepwalking scene, wrung his hands over the pulpit-cushion, unable to wash out the "accursed spot" of sin. This was generally about once a year. Though Hurstmonceaux did not comprehend them, there are however, many fragments, especially similes, in Uncle Julius's ordinary parish sermons which will always have an effect, especially that of grief at a death—the heavy plunge when the person goes down, and the circles vividly apparent at first, then gradually widening, till they are lost and disappear altogether. And though they did not understand him, his parishioners loved Uncle Julius, for he always acted up to his own answer to a question as to the value of a living—"Heaven or hell, according as the occupier does his duty."

Uncle Julius had published a versified edition of the Psalms. He thought his Psalter would be adopted by the whole Church, but it was never used in a single church except Hurstmonceaux.

During the service, he had the oddest way of turning over the pages with his nose.

There certainly was a curious absence of ritual in the services at Hurstmonceaux. Yet one felt that Uncle Julius's whole heart was in the way he read the prayers. What was wanting arose from his personal characteristics, the same which made him always hopelessly unpunctual, which caused him to waste his mornings in hopeless dawdling just when there was most to be done, which so often sent him off for his afternoon walk just as the dinnerbell rang.

I insert a few paragraphs from my written winter journal. They scarcely give an idea of the stagnation of our Hurstmonceaux life.

Dec. 12 [1854].—A solemn tea-drinking of parish ladies at the Rectory. My mother very ailing, with trembling, and almost deaf.

Dec. 15—A bitter drive to Hailsham through the bleak ugly lanes. Mother very poorly, and unable to show interest in or comprehension of anything. Entirely thrown on my own resources.

Dec. 16—Intense cold and misery at church. Ill with this, and felt the great usual Sunday want of anything to do, as I did not like even to open any book which might offend Mother; but at last, finding "Arnold's Life" would not be taken ill, settled to that. Mother not able to speak or hear; felt the great solitariness of loneliness not alone, and longed to have some friend who would enter into my odd little trials—surely singular at twenty —but I never had one.

Dec. 17—Bitter cold and a great gale. Siberia can scarcely be colder than Hurstmonceaux. Went by Mother's wish to collect "Missionary Pence" from the poor. No words can say how I hate this begging system, especially from the poor, who loathe it, but do not dare to refuse when "the lady sends for their penny." Sat long time with Widow Hunnisett, and wondered how I shall ever endure it when I am in Orders, and have to sit daily in the cottages boring the people and myself.

We left Uncle Julius very feeble and ill at Hurstmonceaux. As soon as we reached London, my mother was attacked by severe bronchitis, and with this came one of her alarming phases of seeing endless processions passing before her, and addressing the individuals. Sometimes in the morning she was more worn than in the evening, having been what she called "maintaining conversation" all night long. In the hurry of after years, I have often looked back with surprise upon the stagnant *lull* of life in these winters, in which I scarcely ever left my mother, and, beyond chafing her limbs, reading to her, preparing remedies for all phases of her strange malady, scarcely did anything; yet always felt numb with fatigue when evening came, from the constant tension of undivided anxiety. It was very severe weather, and if I was ever able to go out, it was for a rush up Piccadilly and Regent Street, where I always enjoyed even the sight of human movement amongst the shivering blue-nosed people after the intensity of my solitude . . . .

My mother was never given to being alarmed about me at any time, but I think she must have had some anxieties this autumn [1854]; Oxford was so dreadfully unhealthy—suffering from a perfect "wave of cholera," while typhus fever and smallpox were raging in the lower parts of the town.

To My Mother. *Oxford, Oct. 23 [1854]*.—There was a special cholera service last night. It is very bad still, and the cases very rapid. Those taken ill at five die at seven, and for fear of infection are buried at seven the next morning.

Oct. 24—Typhus fever has broken out in the lower town in addition to everything else, and there are 1000 cases of smallpox, besides cholera. This morning I met two men at breakfast at Mr Jowett's. There was nothing to eat but cold mutton and some heavy bread called "Balliol bricks," but Mr Jowett was in his best humour, and though he would not utter a word himself, he assisted us into uttering a good many. He is certainly at once the terror and the admiration of those he wishes to be kind to; as for myself, I love him, though I often feel I would go round three streets any day to avoid him.

Jan. 23 [1855].—Before I was up, John came and said he thought there was a worse account from Hurstmonceaux. Soon Lea came, and I asked eagerly what it was. "It is over. He is gone. The Archdeacon is dead!" . . . . It was a long painful day in which it seemed almost sacrilegious to go about the ordinary work of life. Personally, however, I have only the regret for Uncle Julius which one feels for a familiar and honoured figure passing out of life. It is only "a grief without a pang." (Coleridge).

The weeks which succeeded my uncle's funeral were occupied by hard work at the Rectory for his widow, chiefly making a catalogue of the fourteen thousand volumes in the library, which she gave for the most part to Trinity College. Uncle Julius had intended them as a provision for her, to whom he had very little money to bequeath; but she chose thus to dispose of them and it was useless to contend with her. In the same way she decided upon giving away all the familiar pictures and sculptures, the former to the Fitzwilliam Museum at Cambridge. My mother felt parting as I did with all these beautiful inanimate witnesses of our past lives—the first works of art I had known, the only ones which I then knew intimately. They have not been much valued at Cambridge, where the authorship of most of the pictures has been questioned; but whoever they were by, to us, who lived with them so much, they were always delightful.

The installation of Lord Derby as Chancellor and the reception of Disraeli (then still a dandy in ringlets, velvet waistcoat, and prominent gold chains) made the "Commemoration" of this year especially exciting; though my pleasure in it was damped by the sudden news of the failure of Sir John Paul's bank in the Strand, and fear for its effect upon my "real mother" and sister, who lost about two thousand a year by this catastrophe, though it was not this cause which involved them in the irretrievable ruin that afterwards befell them. I have always thought that Sir John Paul must have been rather mad. After he had done his best to ruin all his family, and had totally ruined hundreds of other people, he said very complacently, "This is the Lord's doing, and it is marvellous in our eyes."

The longer I lived at Oxford, the more I learnt how little I could believe anything I heard there. Connected with a college of which many of the members belonged to the *lower* upper classes of society, I had peculiar opportunities for observing how often young men thought it worthwhile to pretend to a position and acquaintances which did not belong to them. One instance of this is too extraordinary to be omitted. From the very beginning of February, certain men in Hall (the great place for gossip and scandal) had spoken constantly of a certain Mrs Fortescue, who had come to reside in Oxford, an exceedingly clever person and very highly connected. The subject did not interest me in the least, but still I heard of her so often, that I could not help being familiar with the name. Gradually her acquaintance seemed to extend; men said, "I don't *exactly* know Mrs Fortescue, but my family do"—or "My friend So-and-So means to introduce me," and so on. Mrs Fortescue's witty sayings also were frequently repeated and commented upon. After some months it was said that Mrs Fortescue was going to give a ball, for which there was anxiety to procure invitations—some men "had them, but did not mean to go,"—others were "sure to have them." As I did not wish to go, the subject was of very slight importance to me.

Within a week of the alleged date of Mrs Fortescue's ball, my friend P. came late at night to see me. He said, "I have a dreadful thing to tell you. I have a secret to reveal at which you will be aghast.... *I am Mrs Fortescue!*" Early in the year, observing how apt men were to assume intimacies which they did not possess, he and one or two other friends had agreed to talk incessantly of one person, a wholly imaginary person, and, while "making her the fashion," see if, very soon, a number of men would not pretend to be intimate with her. Dozens fell into the trap. In a certain class of men, every one was afraid of being behind his neighbour in boasting of an intimacy, etc., with one who was praised so highly. They even pretended to have received invitations to the imaginary ball. But the trick had assumed much greater dimensions than ever was intended at first; many people had been duped whose fury at the discovery would be a serious matter; many Oxford ladies had been asked to the ball, and, in fact, there was nothing to be done *now* but to go through with the whole drama to the end—the ball must take place! P. was quite prepared for the emergency of having to represent Mrs Fortescue, but positively refused to go through it alone. His object was to implore me to help him out by appearing in some assumed character. This I for a long time refused, but at length assented to get up all the statistics of the neighbouring great house of Nuneham, and to arrive as Miss Harcourt, an imaginary niece of Lady Waldegrave, just come from thence. I was well acquainted with the best Oxford dressmaker, with whom one of my friends lodged, and she undertook to make my dress; while various styles of hair were tried by another person, who undertook that department, to see which produced the most complete disguise.

When the evening of the ball arrived, I took care to reach "Wyatt's Rooms" very early. Only a number of men and a very few ladies were there, when "Miss Harcourt—Miss Amy Leighton" were shouted up the staircase, and I sailed up (with another undergraduate, who represented my somewhat elderly companion) in a white tulle dress trimmed with a little gold lace and looped up with blue cornflowers, a wreath (wreaths were worn then) of the same, and a blue opera-cloak. Mrs Fortescue, an elderly handsome woman, quite on the *retour*, dressed in crimson satin, came forward to meet me and kissed me on both cheeks, and I was introduced to a lady—a *real* lady—by whom I sat down. It is impossible to detail all the absurdities of the situation, all the awkward positions we were thrown into (Mrs Fortescue had engaged her servants, being then in morning toilette, days before). Suffice it to say that the guests assembled, and the ball and the supper afterwards went off perfectly, and gave boundless satisfaction. I only refused to dance, pretending to have sprained my ankle in coming down in the train some days before; but I limped round the room on the arm of my own doctor (who never discovered me) between the dances, and examined the pictures on the walls. Mrs Fortescue was inimitable. The trick was never discovered at the time, and would still be a secret, but that a friend, to whom I had revealed the story on promise of *strict secrecy*, repeated it long afterwards to P.'s elder brother.

In June my mother visited me at Oxford on her way to West Malvern. Frequently we went to see the Miss Ragsters, two remnants of the oldest families in Worcestershire, who, at a great age, were living, very poor, in a primitive farmhouse, with their one servant Betty—"the girl" they always called her, who still wore a pinafore, though she had been in their service forty-seven years.

JOURNAL. *Lime, Dec. 23 [1855].*—

The dear Mother says her great wish is that I should study—drink deep, as she calls it—in Latin and Greek, for the strengthening of my mind. It is quite in vain to try to convince her that college lectures only improve one for the worse, and that I might do myself and the world more good by devoting myself to English literature and diction, the one only thing in which it is ever possible that I might ever distinguish myself. Oh, how I wish I could become an author! I begin so now to thirst after distinction of some kind, and of that kind above all others: but I know my mind must receive quite a new tone first, and that my scattered fragments of sense would have to be called into an unanimous action to which they are quite unaccustomed.

The Talmud says that "there are four kinds of pupils—the sponge and the funnel, the strainer and the sieve; the sponge is he who spongeth up everything; and the funnel is he that taketh in at this ear and letteth out at that: the strainer is he that letteth go the wine and retaineth the dross; the sieve is he that letteth go the bran and retaineth the fine flour." I think I have begun at least to *wish* to belong to the last.

Soon after this was written we went to London. At Grosvenor Crescent I often had the opportunity of seeing people of more or less interest, for my Aunt Kitty was a capital talker, as well as a very wise and clever thinker. Macaulay often dined with her, and talked to a degree which made those who heard him sympathise with Sydney Smith, who called him "that talking machine" and declared that, when ill, he dreamt he was chained to a rock and being talked to death by Macaulay or Harriet Martineau.

In returning to Oxford in 1857, I terribly missed my constant companions hitherto—I may mention Godfrey Lushington (then of All Souls) as an acquaintance of whom I saw much at this time, and whom I have always liked and respected exceedingly, though our paths in life have not brought us often together since. It was very difficult to distinguish him from his twin brother Vernon; indeed, it would have been impossible to know them apart, if Vernon had not, fortunately for their friends, shot off some of his fingers.

In March [1857] I was proud to receive my aunt, Mrs Stanley, with all her children, Mrs Grote, and several others, at a luncheon in my rooms in honour of Arthur Stanley's inaugural lecture as

Professor of Ecclesiastical History, in which capacity his lectures, as indeed all else concerning him, were subjects of the greatest interest to me, my affection for him being that of a devoted younger brother.

I was enchanted with Mrs Grote, whom De Tocqueville pronounced "the cleverest woman of his acquaintance," though her exterior—with a short waist, brown mantle of stamped velvet, and huge bonnet, full of full-blown red roses—was certainly not captivating. Sydney Smith always called her "Grota," and said she was the origin of the word grotesque. Mrs Grote was celebrated for having never felt shy. She had a passion for discordant colours, and had her petticoats always arranged to display her feet and ankles, of which she was excessively proud. At her own home of Burnham she would drive out with a man's hat and a coachman's cloak of many capes. She had an invalid friend in that neighbourhood, who had been very seriously ill, and was still intensely weak. When Mrs Grote proposed coming to take her for a drive, she was pleased, but was horrified when she saw Mrs Grote arrive in a very high dogcart, herself driving it. With great pain and labour she climbed up beside Mrs Grote, and they set off. For some time she was too exhausted to speak, then she said something almost in a whisper. "Good God! don't speak so loud," said Mrs Grote, "or you'll frighten the horse: if he runs away, God only knows when he'll stop."

On the occasion of this visit at Oxford, Mrs Grote sat with one leg over the other, both high in the air, and talked for two hours, turning with equal facility to Saffi on Italian Literature, Max Muller on Epic Poetry, and Arthur on Ecclesiastical History, and then plunged into a discourse on the best manure for turnips and the best way of forcing Cotswold mutton, with an interlude first upon the "harmony of shadow" in watercolour drawing, and then upon rat-hunts at Jemmy Shawe's—a low public-house in Westminster. Upon all these subjects she was equally vigorous, and gave all her decisions with the manner and tone of one laying down the laws of Athens.

I did not often meet Mrs Grote in after life, but when I did, was always on very cordial terms with her. She was, to the last, one of the most original women in England, shrewd, generous, and excessively vain. I remember hearing that when she published her Life of her husband, Mr Murray[*] was obliged to insist upon her suppressing one sentence, indescribably comic to those who were familiar with her uncouth aspect. It was—"When George Grote and I were young, we were equally distinguished by the beauty of our persons and the vivacity of our conversation!" Her own true vocation, she always declared, was that of an opera-dancer.

In my final (History and Law) Schools I had passed with great ease, and had for some time been residing at Oxford as a Bachelor, having taken my degree. But as one friend after another departed, the interest of Oxford had faded. I left it on the 13th of June 1857, and without regret.

* John Murray, the publisher.

VII. FOREIGN LIFE

DOLCEACQUA

IN JUNE, 1857 WE LEFT Lime for a long residence abroad.

JOURNAL. *Aug. 6*—Throughout our travels we have perpetually fallen in with two solitary ladies. We asked where they were going. "Oh, where is it?" said the younger lady; "I quite forget the name of the place; something very long, I know."—"Oh, Constantinople, my dear, that's the name, and then we go to a place they call Smyrna, and then to Algeria; for you see we've been to Rome and Naples, and if you don't mind travelling, it's just the same thing whether you go to one place or another."

In Rome naturally one of my first visits was to Mrs Hare and my sister, whom I found established on the first floor of the Palazzo Parisiani. "Italima" liked my coming and going, and was very angry if I did not come, though she never professed any maternal affection for me. I often found myself in difficulties between my two mothers. My adopted mother would sometimes take an alarm that I was going too often to Italima, and would demand my presence just on the particular occasion when "Italima" had counted on it; in which case I always gave way to her. And indeed, as a rule, I always spent all my time with my mother, except about two evenings in the week when I went to Italima and the Palazzo Parisiani.

Whilst we were at Naples my mother lost her gold watch. We believed it to have been stolen as we were entering the Museo Borbonico, and gave notice to the police. They said they could do nothing unless we went to the King of Thieves, who could easily get it back for us: it would be necessary to make terms with him. So a *ragazaccio* ("a rascal of a boy") was sent to guide us through one of the labyrinthine alleys on the hill of St Elmo to a house where we were presented to the King of Thieves. He mentioned his terms, which we agreed to, and he then said, "If the watch has been stolen anywhere within the twelve miles round Naples, you shall have it in twenty-four hours." Meanwhile the watch was found by one of the *custodes* of the Museo at the bottom of that bronze vase in which you are supposed to hear the roaring of the sea; my mother had been stooping down to listen, and the watch had fallen in. But the story is worth mentioning, as the subserviency of the police to the King of Thieves was characteristic of public justice under Ferdinand II.

About the 10th of June we settled at Lucca baths, in the pleasant little Casa Bertini, a primitive house more like a farmhouse than a villa, on the steep hillside above the Grand Duke's palace, a charming little garden of oleanders and apple trees at the back, with views down into the gorge of the river, and up into the hilly cornfields, which were always open to us.

This summer at Lucca was altogether the greatest halt in my life I had ever known. We seemed so removed from the world, and I was more free from family snubbings than I had ever been before. But all through the time we were there, I had been far from well, and the doctor who was consulted declared that I could not survive the severities of an English winter. In spite of this, my mother never flinched in her determination to return, for having once taken the impression (without the remotest reason) that I had a tendency to Roman Catholicism, she had far greater terror of what she considered as danger to my soul than danger to my body.

When we left the Bagno di Lucca on the 2nd of August, I left it in despair. Behind us was a quiet, peaceful and far from useless life, encircled by troops of friends, and supplying the literary and artistic occupations in which I began to feel that I might possibly in time be able to distinguish myself. Before us was the weary monotony of Hurstmonceaux, only broken by visits from or to relatives, by most of whom I was disliked, if not positively ill-treated. I also felt sure that all the influence of my aunts would be used with my easily guided mother to force upon me the most uncongenial of employments, which she was only too certain to allow them to advocate as "especially desirable for Augustus, because they *were* uncongenial!" I was also at the time in more than usual disgrace, because disgust at the sham Christians, sham Evangelicals, sham Protestants, with whom for years I had been thrown, had induced me to avow my horror of Ordination. In every way I felt myself unfitted for it.

We were a few days at Turin. The society there was then, as it is still, the very climax of stagnation. One of its most admired ornaments was a beautiful young Contessa la Mormora. She did nothing all day, absolutely nothing, but sit looking pretty, with her chin leaning upon her hand. Her mother-in-law was rather more energetic than herself, and hoping to rouse her, left a new *Journal des Modes* upon her table. Some days after, she asked what she thought of it. "Alas!" said the young Countess, with her beautiful head still leaning upon her hand, "I have been so much occupied, that I never have found time to look into it." In all my acquaintance since with Italian ladies, I have always found the same, that they are all intensely occupied, but that it is in doing —nothing.

A great contrast to the Italians at Turin was Mr Ruskin, whom we saw constantly. He was sitting all day upon a scaffold in the gallery, copying bits of the great picture by Paul Veronese. My mother was very proud of my drawings at the time and gave them to him to look at. He examined them all very carefully and said nothing for some time. At last he pointed out one of the cathedrals at Perugia as "the least bad of a very poor collection." One day in the gallery I asked him to give me some advice. He said, "Watch me." He then looked at the flounce in the dress of a maid of honour of the Queen of Sheba for five minutes, and then he painted one thread; he looked for another five minutes, and then he painted another thread. At the rate at which he was work-ing he might hope to paint the whole dress in ten years: but it was a lesson as to examining what one drew well before drawing it.

During the winter we were absent at Rome, our house of Lime was lent to Aunt Esther and Mrs Alexander. Two cabinets con-tained all our family Manuscripts, which Aunt Esther knew that I valued beyond everything else. Therefore, she forced both the cabinets open and destroyed the whole—all Lady Jones's jour-nals and letters from India, all Bishop Shipley's letters—every letter, in fact, relating to any member of the Hare family. She replaced the letters to my adopted mother from the members of her own family in the front of the cabinets and thus the fact that they had nothing behind them was never discovered until we left Hurstmonceaux, two years later. When we asked about it, Aunt Esther only said, "Yes, I did it; I saw fit to destroy them." It was a strange and lasting legacy to bequeath, and I think I cannot be harsh in saying that only a very peculiar temperament could construe such an act into "right-doing."

VIII. Tales and Excursions

The Oakwalk, Holhurst

Upon returning to England in the winter of 1858, I felt more bitterly than ever the want of sympathy which had formerly oppressed me. Though I had the most idolatrous love for my dearest mother, and the most over-anxious wish to please her, there was then none of the perfect friendship between us, the easy interchange of every thought, which there was in later years; for she was still so entirely governed by her sisters-in-law as scarcely to have any individuality of her own. Often, often, did she pain me by suspecting my motives and questioning my actions, even when I was most desirous of doing right; and from the long habit of being *told* that I was idle and ignorant, that I cared for nothing useful, and that I frittered away my life, she had grown to believe it, and constantly assumed that it was so. Thus all my studies were embittered to me. I was quite sure that nothing I did would be appreciated, so that it never seemed worthwhile to do anything, and I became utterly deficient in that cheerfulness of disposition which is the most important element in all private success.

At this time all the intellectual impetus I received, and without which I should have fallen into a state of stagnation, came from the house of my aunt, Mrs Stanley. Her grace, ease and tact in society were unrivalled. At her house, and there alone, I met people of original ideas and liberal conversation. In this conversation, however, I was at that time too shy to join, and I was so dreadfully afraid of my aunt, who, with the kindest intentions, had a very cold unsympathetic manner in private, that—while I always appreciated her—I was unable to reap much benefit from her society. Perhaps my chief friend was my cousin Arthur Stanley, whom I was not the least afraid of, and whom I believe to have been really fond of me at this time; also, though he had a very poor opinion of my present powers and abilities, he did not seem, like other people, to despair of my future.

It was owing to the kindness of my cousin Arthur and that of Albert Way that I obtained from John Murray, the publisher, the employment of my next two years—the "Handbook of Berks, Bucks, and Oxfordshire."

The commission to undertake this Handbook was one which I hailed with rapture. The work was in every respect welcome to me . I knew nothing then of the mercantile value of my labour. I did not know (and I had no one to inform me) that I was giving away the earnest work of two years for a pitiful sum, which was not a tenth of its value, and which was utterly insufficient to meet its expenses: ten guineas for a sheet, containing twenty-four pages of the close double-columned type of Murray's "Handbooks."

The style of my writing was to be as hard, dry and incisive as my taskmaster. It was to be a mere catalogue of facts and dates, mingled with measurements of buildings, and irritating details as to the "E.E.," "Dec.," or "Perp." architecture even of the most insignificant churches, this being the peculiar hobby of the publisher. No sentiment, no expression of opinion was ever to be allowed; all description was to be reduced to its barest bones, dusty, dead and colourless. In fact, I was to produce a book which I knew to be utterly unreadable, though correct and useful for reference. Many a paper struggle did I have with John Murray the third— for there has been a dynasty of John Murrays in Albemarle Street—as to the retention of paragraphs I had written.

A house which I was frequently invited to use as a center for my excursions was that of my father's first cousin Penelope, Mrs Warren, who was living at Worting, near Basingstoke, in the old home left to her by Lady Jones. It was in a most dreary, cold, wind-stricken district, and was especially selected on that account by Lady Jones, because of its extreme contrast to the India she abominated. It was on one of my early visits at Worting that I first made acquaintance with my cousin Harriet, Mrs Thornton, niece of Mrs Warren. One of Mrs Thornton's stories, which I have often repeated since, is so curious as to deserve insertion here.

M. de Sartines had been brought up by an old friend of his family who lived in Picardy. The château of his old friend was the home of his youth, and the only place where he felt sure that all his failings would be overlooked and all his fancies and wishes would be considered.

While he was absent from France on diplomatic service, M. de Sartines heard with great grief that his old friend was dead. In losing him, he lost not only the friend who had been as a second father, but the only home which remained to him in France. He felt his loss very much—so much, indeed, that for many years he did not return to France at all, but spent his time of leave in traveling in Italy and elsewhere.

Some years after, M. de Sartines, finding himself in Paris, received a letter from the nephew of his old friend, who had succeeded to the Picardy property. It was a very nice letter indeed, saying how much he and his wife wished to keep up old family ties and connections, and that though he was well aware that it would cost M. de Sartines much to revisit the château so tenderly connected with memories of the dead, still, if he could make that effort, no guest would be more affectionately welcomed, and that he and his wife would do their utmost to make him feel that the friendship which had been held had not passed away, but was continued to another generation. It was so nice a letter that M. de Sartines felt that he ought not to reject the hand of friendship stretched out in so considerate and touching a manner, and though it certainly cost him a great effort, he went down to the château in Picardy.

His old friend's nephew and his wife received him on the doorstep. Everything was prepared to welcome him. They had inquired of former servants which room he had occupied and how he liked it arranged, and all was ready accordingly. They had even inquired about and provided his favourite dishes at dinner. Nothing was wanting which the most disinterested solicitude could effect.

When M. de Sartines retired to his room for the night, he was filled with conflicting emotions. The blank which he felt in the loss of his old friend was mingled with a grateful sense of the kindness he had received from the nephew. He felt he could not sleep, or would be long in doing so; but having made up a large fire, for it was very cold weather, he went to bed.

In process of time, as he lay wakefully with his head upon the pillow, he became aware of the figure of a little wizened old man hirpling towards the fire. He thought he must be dreaming, but, as he listened, the old man spoke—"*Il y a longtemps que je n'ai vu un feu, il faut que je me chauffe.*" *

The blood of M. de Sartines ran cold within him as the figure turned slowly round towards the bed and continued in trembling accents—"*Il y a longtemps que je n'ai vu un lit, il faut que je me couche.*" **

But every fibre in M. de Sartines' body froze as the old man, on reaching the bed, drew the curtains, and seeing him, exclaimed—"*Il y a longtemps que je n'ai vu M. de Sartines, il faut que je l'embrasse.*" §

M. de Sartines almost died of fright. But fortunately he did not quite die. He lived to know that it was his old friend himself. The nephew had got tired of waiting for the inheritance; he had imprisoned his uncle in the cellar, and had given out his death, and had a false funeral of a coffin filled with stones. The invitation to his uncle's friend was a *coup de théâtre*: if any suspicions had existed, they must have been lulled forever by the presence of such a guest in the château. But on the very day on which M. de Sartines had arrived, the old gentleman had contrived to escape from his cell, and wandering half imbecile about the house, made his way to the room where he remembered having so often been with his friend, and found there his friend himself.

M. de Sartines saw the rightful owner of the castle reinstated, and the villainy of the wicked nephew exposed; but the old man died soon afterwards.

* "It has been a long time since I have seen a fire; I must warm myself."
** "It has been a long time since I have seen a bed; I must lie down."
§ "It has been a long time since I have seen M. de Sartines; I must kiss him."

Mrs Thornton described how old Mr Thornton had been staying in Somersetshire with Sir Thomas Acland, when he heard two countrymen talking together. One of them said to the other, who was trying to persuade him to do something, "Wal, noo, as they say, 'shake an ass and go.'" Mr Thornton came back and said to Sir Thomas, "What very extraordinary proverbial expressions they have in these parts. Just now I heard a man say 'shake an ass and go'—such a very extraordinary proverbial expression." "Well," said Sir Thomas, "the fact is there are a great many French expressions lingering in this neighbourhood: that meant *'Chacun à son goût!'*" *

I visited Fritwell Manor, a most picturesque old house. Fritwell is a haunted house, and was inhabited by two families. When the Edwardes lived there in the summer, no figure was seen, but stains of fresh blood were constantly found on the staircase. When the Grants lived there for hunting in the winter, there was no blood, but the servants who went down first in the morning would meet in the staircase an old man in a grey dressing-gown, bleeding from an open wound in the throat. It is said that Sir Baldwin Wake, a former proprietor, quarrelled with his brother about a lady of whom they were both enamoured, and giving out that he was insane, imprisoned him till real madness ensued. His prison was at the top of the house, where a sort of large human dog-kennel

* "Each to his own taste."

still exists, to which the unfortunate man is said to have been chained.

LETTER TO MOTHER. *June 16 [1859].*—I have enjoyed a visit to the Henry Leycesters at White Place, which lies low in the meadows. Little Mrs Leycester is a timid shrinking creature, who daily becomes terribly afraid of the domestic ghost (a lady carrying her head) as evening comes on. "Imagine, my feelings, Mr Hare," she says, "my awful position as a wife and a mother, when my husband is away, and I am left alone in the long evenings with *her*."

After we parted at Paris in the autumn of 1858, Italima and my sister Esmeralda, as usual, spent the winter at Rome, returning northward by the seat of the war in Lombardy. Alas! A terrible cloud of misfortune was gathering over them . . . .

When Mrs Hare and my sister arrived at Geneva in June 1859, though their fortunes had suffered very considerably by the Paul bankruptcy, they were still in possession of a large income, and of every luxury of life. To save the trouble of taking a villa, they engaged an excellent suite of apartments in the Hôtel de la Metropole, where they intended remaining for the greater part of the summer.

Soon after her arrival, Italima (Mrs Hare) wrote to her banker for money, and was much astonished to hear from him that she had overdrawn her account by £150. Knowing that she ought at that season to have plenty of money in the bank, she wrote to her attorney, Mr B. (who had the whole management of her affairs), to desire that he would pay the rest of the money due into Coutts', and that he would send her £100 immediately. She had no answer from Mr B., and she wrote again and again, without any answer. She was not alarmed, because Mr B. was always in the habit of going abroad in the summer, and she supposed that her letters did not reach him because he was away. Still, as she really wanted the money, it was very inconvenient.

One day Italima received a letter from her eldest son Francis, who said that he knew she would not believe him, but that Mr B. was a penniless bankrupt, and that she would receive no more money from him. She did not believe Francis a bit, still the letter made her anxious and uncomfortable: no money had come in answer to her repeated letters, and there were many things at Geneva to be paid for. They paid their bills at Geneva, and left for Paris on the night train.

Straight from London Bridge Station they drove to Mr B.'s office. He was there, and apparently delighted to see them. "Well, Mr B., and pray why have you sent me no money?" asked Italima. "Why, I've sent you quantities of money," said Mr B., without a change of countenance. "If you write to Messrs. O. and L., the bankers at Geneva, you will find it's all there. I have sent you money several times," and he said this with such perfect *sang-froid* that they believed him. Italima then said, "Well now, Mr B., I should wish to see the mortgages," because from time to time he had persuaded her to transfer £46,000 of her own fortune from other securities to mortgages on a Mr Howell's estate in Cornwall. Mr B. replied, "Do you know, when you say that, it would almost seem as if you did not quite trust me."—"That I cannot help," said Italima, "but I should wish to see the mortgages."—"There is no difficulty whatever," said Mr B.; "you

could have seen them last year if you had wished: today you cannot see them because they are in the Bank, and the Bank is closed,
but you can fix any other day you like for seeing them,"—and
they fixed the following Wednesday.

When the Wednesday came on which they were to see the
mortgages, Italima was not well, and she said to my sister, "I am
quite glad I am not well, because it will be an excuse for you to
go and fetch the mortgages, when we can look them over quietly
together." My sister went off to Lincoln's Inn, but before going
to Mr B., she called at the house of another lawyer, whom she
knew very well, to ask if he had heard any reports about Mr B. "I
pray to God, Miss Hare, that you are safe from that man," was all
he said. She rushed on to the office. Mr B. was gone: everything
was gone: there were no mortgages: there was no Mr Howell's
estate: there was no money: £60,000 was gone: there was absolutely nothing left whatever.

Never was ruin more complete! Italima and Esmeralda had
nothing left: not a loaf of bread, not a penny to buy one—nothing.

It was too true; he had taken everything. The marriage settlement was in favour of the younger children, I being one of the
three who would have benefited. Some years before, Mr B. had
been to Italima and persuaded her to give up £2000 of my brother
William's portion, during her life, in order to pay his debts. On
her assenting to this, Mr B. had subtly entered the whole sum
mentioned in the settlement, instead of £2000, in the deed of
release, and the two trustees had signed without a question, so
implicit was their faith in Mr B., who passed not only for a very
honourable, but for a very religious man. Mr B. had used the
£2000 to pay William's debts, and had taken all the rest of the
money for himself. About Italima's own fortune he had been

even less scrupulous. Mr Howell's estate in Cornwall had never existed at all. Mr B. had taken the £46,000 for himself; there had been no mortgages, but he had paid the interest as usual, and the robbery had passed undetected. He had kept Italima from coming upon him during the last summer by cutting off her supplies, and all might have gone on as usual if Italima had not insisted upon seeing the mortgages.

Her despair and misery were terrible to witness. She did nothing all day but lament and wail over her fate, and was most violent to my sister, who bore her own loss with the utmost calmness and patience. Nothing could exceed Lady Williamson's kindness to them. She pressed them to stay on with her, and cared for them with unwearied generosity during the first ten months of their destitution. Many other friends offered help, and the Liddell cousins promised an annual subscription for their maintenance.

It was just before Easter 1860, that I was first told that we should have to leave our dear home at Hurstmonceaux. Many years before, there had been an alarm, and my mother would then have bought the Lime property, but that the price asked was so greatly above its value, and no other purchasers came forward. So she was satisfied to go on renting Lime and the surrounding fields for a small sum. Thus it was inevitable that at Michaelmas we must leave our dear home, and though I had suffered much at Hurstmonceaux, and though our position there as a ruined family was often a dismal one, yet we felt that nothing could ever replace what Lime itself was, where every plant was familiar, and every tree had its own personal reminiscence. And there was also the great difficulty of finding a new home within our small means, and yet large enough to house our many books and pictures.

All through the summer of 1860 we were occupied in considering our new home. We sent for all the London agents' lists of places to be let or sold south of the Humber, and many of these, in Kent, Surrey, Berks, Bucks, Oxfordshire, Hampshire, Hertfordshire, I went to see, either with or without my mother. If she were not with me, I wrote to her long accounts, always concluding with saying, "They are not like Holmhurst, not in the least like Holmhurst,"—Holmhurst being the ideal place in the unwritten novels which my mother and I had been accustomed to narrate to each other in our long journeys abroad. My being difficult to satisfy gave the aunts an unusual handle for abuse, and plentifully did they bestow it upon me. "What can it signify whether you have a view or not? No one but you would care to waste your time in always looking out of the window," &c., &c. Especially was indignation roused by my refusing to consider an old house which the Stanleys were determined on our taking in Oxfordshire —Hazeley Court—and which was to be had very cheap because no servants could be persuaded to stay there on account of a frightful apparition which was supposed to haunt it.

At last we almost despaired of finding any place to suit us. Just then a neighbour sent us a Hastings paper with a very humble advertisement marked, "At Ore, a house, with thirty-six acres of land, to be let or sold." "What a horrible place this must be," I said, "for which they cannot find one word of description;" for the very ugliest places we had seen had often been described in the advertisements as "picturesque manorial residences," "beautiful villas with hanging woods," etc. But my mother rightly thought that the very simple description was perhaps in itself a reason why we should see it, and after breakfast we set off in the little carriage. It was a drive of about fourteen miles. Long before we could arrive at Ore, we passed under a grey wall over-hung by trees. "It looks almost as if there might be a Holmhurst inside that wall," I said. Then we reached a gate between two clipped yew-trees, and a board announced, "This house is to be let or sold." We drove in. It was a lovely day. An arched gateway

THE ARSON STEPS, HOLMHURST

was open towards the garden, showing a terrace, vases of scar-let geraniums, and a background of blue sea. My mother and I clasped each other's hands and simultaneously exclaimed—"This is Holmhurst!"

The house was let then, and we were refused permission to see the inside, but my mother bought the property at once: she was as sure as I was that we should never like any other place as well.

My "Handbook" (nominally Murray's) of Oxfordshire, Buckinghamshire and Berkshire had been published during our winter absence in France; my little book "A Winter in Mentone" appeared soon after our return. The "Winter at Mentone" fell perfectly flat, but Murray was so pleased with the laudatory notices which followed the appearance of the Handbook, that he asked me to select any other counties I liked. I chose Durham and Northumberland, and after the middle of July [1861] went there for three months. In undertaking these counties, I again assented to an arrangement by which I was never repaid for my work; but the work was one which I liked extremely, bringing me in contact with endless interesting persons.

LETTER TO MOTHER. *Doncaster, July 24 [1861].*—The people here are a perpetual amusement to Kate, they are so quaint and original. Kate said to an old man, "What are you so low about, my man?" "Why," he said, "what wi' faith, and gas, and balloons, and steam-ingines a-booming and a-fizzling through t'warld, and what wi' t'arth a-going round once in twenty-four hours, I'm fairly muzzled and stagnated."

I have been to call on the daughters of "Presence-of-Mind Smith," who was Dean of Christ Church, and to the close of his life used to tell this story of himself. "In my life," he said, "there has been one most fortunate incident. A friend of mine persuaded me to go out with him in a boat upon a lake. I did not wish to go, but he persuaded me, and I went. By the intervention of Providence, I took my umbrella with me. We had not been long on the lake when the violence of the waves threw my friend out of the boat drowning, and he sank. Soon, as is the case with drowning persons, he came up again, and clutched hold of the side of the boat. Then such, providentially, was my presence of mind, that I seized my umbrella and rapped him violently on the knuckles till he let go. He sank, and I was saved."

Streatlam Castle, Sept. 27 [1861].—This is the oddest house I ever was in! Everything is arranged for you, from the moment you get up till the moment you go to bed, and you are never allowed to deviate from the rules laid down: I even write this in time stolen from the half-hour for dressing. We are called at eight, and at ten march in to breakfast with the same procession as at dinner, only at this meal "Madame Bowes"—Mary Eleanor Bowes, 9th Countess of Strathmore—does not appear, for she is then reclining in a bath of coal-black acid, which "refreshes her system," but leaves her nails black. After breakfast we are all set down to employments appointed for the morning. At twelve Madame appears, having painted the underlids of her jet-black eyes with belladonna. At two the bell rings for luncheon, and we are fetched if not punctual to an instant. At three we are all sent out driving (the coachman having exact orders where to take us) immense drives (24 miles today) in an open barouche and pair. At seven we dine in great splendour, and afterwards we sit in the oak drawing room and talk about our ancestors!

The town of Barnard Castle is most picturesque, with a ruined castle of the Baliols. Dickens, in early life, used frequently to come down and stay there with some young artist friends of his.

The idea of "Humphrey's Clock" first sprung from Humphrey, the watchmaker in the town, and the picture in the beginning of the book is of the clock over the door of his shop. While at Barnard Castle, Dickens heard of the school at Bowes which he afterwards worked up as Dotheboys Hall. Many of these schools, at £15 and £20 a year, existed at that time in the neighbourhood, and were principally used for the sons of London tradesmen, who, provided their sons got a moderate education, cared little or nothing what became of them in the meantime. Dickens went over to see the school at Bowes, and was carefully shown over it, for they mistook him for a parent coming to survey it, with a view of sending his son there. Afterwards the school was totally ruined. At one of Mr Bowes's elections, the Nicholas Nickleby or former usher of the school, who was then in want of a place, wrote to him to say in what poverty he was. He had "formerly been living with Mr Shawe at Bowes, and they had been happy and prosperous, when Mr Dickens's misguided volume, sweeping like a whirlwind over the schools of the North, caused Mr Shawe to become a victim to paralysis, and brought Mrs Shawe to an untimely grave."

I cannot remember whether it was in this or the preceding winter that I spent an evening with Dr Lushington, the famous judge, who having been born in the beginning of 1782, and preserving evergreen all the recollections of his long life, was one of the most delightful of men. I took the opportunity of persuading Dr Lushington to tell me himself the most celebrated of his stories. I wrote it down at once.

"There was once, within my memory, an old gentleman who lived in Kent, and whose name, for very obvious reasons, I cannot mention, but he lived in Kent. He was a very remarkable old man, and chiefly because in the whole course of his very, very long life—for he was extremely old—he had never been known on any single occasion to want presence of mind; he had always done exactly the right thing, and he had always said exactly the right word, at exactly the right moment. The old gentleman lived alone. That is to say, he had never married, and he had no brother or sister or other relation living with him, but he had a very old housekeeper, a very old butler, a very old gardener—in fact, all the old-fashioned retinue of a very old-fashioned household, and bound together by mutual respect and affection, the household was a very harmonious one.

"Now I must describe what the old gentleman's house was like. Upstairs, there was a very long passage, which ended in a blank wall. At the end of the passage, on the left, was a dressing-room, and on the right was a bedroom, the room in which the old gentleman himself slept. The bedroom was entered by a very heavy swing-door, which could only be opened from the inside—that is to say, the old gentleman carried the key upon his watch-chain, and let himself in and out. When he wished house-maids or other persons to go in or out, he left the door open; but when he was inside and shut the door, no one could come in unless he opened the door to them. People may say 'it was very eccentric;' it *was* very eccentric: but the old gentleman was very peculiar; it was the way he chose to live: at any rate, it was a fact. Through the bedroom, opposite the door into the passage, was another door which led into the plate-room. This was also a very heavy swing-door, which could only be opened from the outside, and very often in summer the old gentleman would set it open at night, because he thought it gave more air to the bedroom. Everything depends upon your attending to and understanding the geography of these rooms. You see they were all en suite cross-wise. If you stood in the plate-room, and all the doors were open, you would see the dressing-room, and vice versa.

"One morning when the old gentleman came down to breakfast, he found upon his plate a note. He opened it, and it contained these words—'Beware, you are in the hands of thieves and robbers.' He was very much surprised, but he had such presence of mind that he threw the note into the fire and went on buttering his toast, having his breakfast. Inwardly he kept a sharp lookout upon all that was going on. But there was nothing special going on whatever. It was very hot summer weather; the old gardener was mowing the lawn, the old housekeeper cooked the dinner, the old butler brought it in: no, there was nothing whatever especial going on.

"That night, when the old gentleman went to bed, he took particular care to examine his room, and to see that his heavy swing-door was well fastened, so that no one could come in to disturb him. And when he had done this, he went to bed and fell asleep, and slept very well till the next morning, for nothing happened, nothing whatever.

"When the next morning came, he rang his bell for his hot water as usual, but nobody came. He rang, and rang, and rang again, but still nobody came. At last he opened his bedroom door, and went out down the passage to the head of the staircase, and called to the butler over the banisters. The butler answered. 'Why did you not attend to my bell?' said the old gentleman. 'Because no bell rang,' answered the butler. 'Oh, but I have rung very often,' said the old gentleman; 'go downstairs again, and I will pull the bell again; watch if it rings.' So the butler went downstairs, and the old man pulled the bell, but no bell rang. 'Then,' said the old gentleman, 'you must send for the bell-hanger at once; one cannot live with broken bells; that sort of thing cannot be allowed to go on in the house,'—and he dressed and went down to breakfast.

"While he was eating his breakfast, the old gentleman found he had forgotten his pocket-handkerchief, and went up to his room to get it. And such was the promptitude of that old-fashioned household, that the village being close to the house, and the bell-hanger living in the village, the master's orders had already been obeyed, and the bell-hanger was already in the room, standing on a ladder, arranging the new wire of the bell. In old-fashioned houses, you know, the bell wires come through the wall and go round the top of the room, so that you can see them, and so it was in this house in Kent. You do not generally perhaps observe how many wires there are in your room, but it so happened that, as he lay in bed, the old gentleman had observed those in his, and there were three wires. Now he looked, and there were four wires. Yes, there was no doubt there were four wires going round his room. 'Now,' he said, 'now I know exactly what is going to happen,' but he gave no outward sign of having discovered anything and he went down and finished his breakfast.

"All that day everything went on as usual. It was a dreadfully hot day in July—very sultry indeed. The old gentleman was subject to bad nervous headaches, and in the afternoon he pretended to be not quite so well. When dinnertime came, he was very suffering indeed. He spoke of it to the butler. He said, 'It is only one of my usual attacks; I have no doubt it is the weather. I shall be better tomorrow; but I will go to bed early.' And towards half-past nine he went upstairs. He left the door of the bedroom ajar, so that anyone could come in; he set the door of the plate-room wide open, for the sake of more air to the bedroom, and he went to bed. When he was in bed, he rang the bell, the new bell that the bell-hanger had put up that morning. The butler came. The old gentleman gave some orders about horses for the next day, and then said, 'Do not disturb me in the morning. I had better sleep off my headache; I will ring when I want to get up. You can draw the curtains round the bed, and then shut the door.' So the butler drew the curtains round the bed, and went out, shutting the door after him.

"As soon as the old gentleman heard the footsteps of the butler die away down the passage, he dressed himself completely from head to foot; he took two loaded pistols and a blunderbuss. He stealthily opened the heavy swing-door of the bedroom. He let himself out into the dark passage. He shut the bedroom door behind him. It fastened with a click; he could not go in himself any more, and he crossed the passage, and stood in the dark dressing-room with the door open.

"It was still very early and eleven o'clock came, and nothing happened; and twelve came and nothing happened; and one o'clock came and nothing happened. And the old gentleman—for he was already very old—began to feel very much exhausted, and he began to say to himself, 'Perhaps after all I was wrong! Perhaps after all it is a hallucination; but I will wait till two o'clock.'

"At half-past one o'clock there was a sound of stealthy footsteps down the passage, and three figures passed in front of him and stood opposite the bedroom door. They were so near that he could have shot them every one; but he said to himself, 'No, I'll wait, I'll wait and see what is going to happen.' And as he waited, the light from the dark lantern which the first man carried fell upon their faces, and he recognised them. And the first figure was the butler, and the second figure was the bell-hanger, and the third figure, from having been long a magistrate on a London bench, he recognised as the most notorious ruffian of a well-known London gang. He heard the ruffian say to the butler, 'I say, it's no use mincing this kind of thing: no use doing this kind of thing by halves: better put him out of the way at once, and go on to the plate afterwards.'—'Oh no,' said the butler, 'he has been a good master to me; I'll never consent to that. Take all he has; he'll never wake, not he; but you can't do him any harm; I'll never consent to that.' And they wrangled about it for some time, but at last the butler seemed to get the better, and the ruffian had to consent to his terms.

"Then exactly what the old gentleman had expected happened. The butler, standing on tiptoe, could just reach the four wires of the bells, which came through into the low passage above the bedroom door. As the butler reached the lowest of the wires, and by leaning his weight upon it, pulled it downwards, it was seen that the wire was connected with the bolt of the door on the inside; the bolt rolled up, and the heavy swing-door of the bedroom, of which the hinges were well oiled for the occasion, rolled open. 'There,' said the butler, as they passed into the room, 'master always sleeps like that. Curtains drawn all round the bed. He'll not hear anything, not he.' And they all passed in through the open door of the plate-room. The old man waited till they were entirely occupied with the plate-chest, and then he slipped off his slippers, and, with a hop, skip, and a jump, he darted a-cross the room, and—bang! they were all caught in a trap. He banged to the heavy swing-door of the plate-room, which could only be opened from the outside.

"Having done that—people may believe it or not, but I maintain that it is true—the old man had such presence of mind, that he undressed, went to bed, and slept soundly till the next morning. Even if this were not so, till the next morning he did not send for the police, and the consequence was that when he did send for the police, and the door was opened, the following horrible scene revealed itself: the ruffian had tried to make a way of escape through the roof, had stuck fast and was dreadfully mangled in the attempt: the bell-hanger had hung himself from the ceiling: and the butler was a drivelling idiot in the corner, from the horror of the night he had gone through."

JOURNAL. *Mainsforth, April 24 [1862].*—Sitting alone with Miss Robinson, just now, she talked much of Sir Walter Scott.

"I knew Sir Walter Scott very well: to hear him talk was like hearing history with all the disagreeable parts weeded out. I often dined with him in Edinburgh. I went with my Sister Surtees to his house just after his first paralytic seizure. We found him dreadfully altered, and he described to us all that had happened. 'I was sitting with Sophy, when I was taken,' he said, 'and I could not speak; so I ran upstairs into the drawing room, where there were several ladies in the room, and there I soon became insensible and could not be roused. I remember it as if it were today,' he said; 'they all began to beel, and they made such a tiran, you can scarcely imagine it. I did not wish to frighten them any more, so I did not say what I felt, but I'll tell you what it was, Mrs Surtees —*I shook hands with death.*'

"Lady Scott was brought up in France. She was a very frivolous person—very exceedingly. The first time I dined with them, I sat next to her, and she wore a brocaded silk gown which she told me cost two hundred guineas. 'Dear me, Lady Scott,' I said, 'but is that not a very large price?'—'Yes,' she replied, 'but that's what my dressmaker charges *me*.' People never knew what present to give to Sir Walter; so, when they wished to make a present, they gave ornaments to Lady Scott, and she would come down to a common dinner with her arm quite covered with bracelets. What more she could have worn if she went to court, I cannot imagine. She never entered into Sir Walter's pursuits at all.

"Walter was the old piper, and a very fine-looking person he was. He used to walk about the gallery on the outside playing the pibroch on the bagpipes. He could not have done it in the room, it was so deafening. Sir Walter liked it because it was national."

LETTER TO MOTHER. *Westgate Street, Newcastle, May 6 [1862].* — Yesterday afternoon I came here, to the old square dark red brick house of the Claytons, who are like merchant-princes in New-castle, so enormous is their wealth, but who still live in the utmost simplicity in the old-fashioned family house in this re-tired shady street . . . .

May 7—How amused my mother would be with this quaintest

of families, who live here in the most primitive fashion, always treating each other as if they were acquaintances of the day, and addressing one another by their full titles, as "Miss Anne Clayton, will you have the goodness to make the tea?"— "Mr Town-Clerk of Newcastle, will you have the kindness to hand me the toast?" &c. Miss Anne is a venerable lady with snow-white hair, but her brother Matthew, who is rather older, is convinced that she is one of the most harum-scarum young girls in the world, and is continually pulling her up with "Miss Anne Clayton, you are very inaccurate,"—"Miss Anne Clayton, be careful what you say,"—"Miss Anne Clayton, another inaccuracy,"—while the poor old sister goes on her own way without minding a bit . . . . This evening old Mr Matthew has been usually extraordinary, and very fatiguing—talking for exactly two hours about his boot-makers, Messrs Hoby and Humby, whence they came, what they had done, and how utterly unrivalled they were. "Miss Anne Clayton," he said at the end, "I hope you understand all I've been saying. Now wait before you give an opinion, but above all things, Miss Anne Clayton, don't, don't be inaccurate."

In June I was at Chartwell in Kent, when Mr Colquhoun told me the following story, from personal knowledge both of the facts and persons:—

"On awaking one morning, Mr Rutherford of Egerton (in Roxburghshire) found his wife dreadfully agitated, and asked her what was the matter. 'Oh,' she said, 'it is something I really cannot tell you, because you could not possibly sympathise with it.'— 'But I insist upon knowing,' he said. 'Well,' she answered, 'if you insist upon knowing, I am agitated because I have had a dream which has distressed me very much. I dreamt that my aunt, Lady Leslie, who brought me up, is going to be murdered; and not only that, but in my dream I have seen the person who is going to murder her:—I have seen him so distinctly, that if I met him in any town of Europe, I should know him again.'—'What bombastical nonsense!' said Mr Rutherford; 'you really become more and more foolish every day.'—'Well, my dear,' said his wife, 'I told you that it was a thing in which you could not sympathise, and I did not wish to tell you my dream.'

"Coming suddenly into her sitting-room during the morning, Mr Rutherford found his wife still very much agitated and distressed, and being of choleric disposition, he said sharply, 'Now do let us have an end once for all of this nonsense. Go down into Fife and see your aunt, Lady Leslie, and then, when you have found her alive and quite well, perhaps you will give up having these foolish imaginations for the future.' Mrs Rutherford wished no better; she put a few things into a hand bag, she went to Edinburgh, she crossed the Firth of Forth, and that afternoon at four o'clock she drove up to Lady Leslie's door. The door was opened by a strange servant. It was the man she had seen in her dream.

"She found Lady Leslie well, sitting with her two grown-up sons. She was exceedingly surprised to see her niece but Mrs Rutherford said that having that one day free, and not being able to come again for some time, she had seized the opportunity of coming for one night; and her aunt was too glad to see her to ask many questions. In the course of the evening Mrs Rutherford said, 'Aunt, when I lived at home with you, whenever I was to have an especial treat, it was that I might sleep in your room. Now I am only here for one night; do let me have my old child's treat over again: I have a special fancy for it;' and Lady Leslie was rather pleased than otherwise. Before they went to bed, Mrs

Rutherford had an opportunity of speaking to her two cousins alone. She said, 'You will be excessively surprised at what I ask, but I shall measure your affection for me entirely by whether you grant it: it is that you will sit up tonight in the room next to your mother's, and that you will tell no one.' They promised, but they were very much surprised.

"As they were going to bed, Mrs Rutherford said to Lady Leslie, 'Aunt, shall I lock the door?' and Lady Leslie laughed at her and said, 'No, my dear; I am much too old-fashioned a person for that,' and forbade it. But as soon as Mrs Rutherford saw that Lady Leslie was asleep, she slipped out of bed and turned the lock of the door. Then, leaning against the pillow, she watched, and watched the handle of the door.

"The reflection of the fire scintillated on the round brass handle of the door, and, as she watched, it almost seemed to mesmerise her, but she watched still. Suddenly the speck of light seemed to appear on the *other* side; some one was evidently turning the handle of the door. Mrs Rutherford rang the bell violently, her cousins rushed out of the next room, and she herself threw the door wide open, and there, at the door, stood the strange servant, the man she had seen in her dream, with a covered coal-scuttle in his hand. The cousins demanded why he was there. He said he thought he heard Lady Leslie's bell ring. They said, 'But you do not answer Lady Leslie's bell at this time in the night,' and they insisted upon opening the coal-scuttle. In it was a large knife.

"Then, as by sudden impulse, the man confessed. He knew Lady Leslie had received a large sum for her rents the day before, that she kept it in her room, and that it could not be sent away till the next day. 'The devil tempted me,' he said, 'the devil walked with me down the passage, and unless God had intervened, the devil would have forced me to cut Lady Leslie's throat.'

"The man was partially mad—but God had intervened."

LETTER TO MOTHER. *Weeping Cross, Stafford, August 21 [1862].*—
Miss Sarah Salt met me at the Stafford station and drove me here
—a moderate-sized house, simply furnished, but with the luxury of a cedar wood ceiling, which smells delicious. Out of a
window seat in the low comfortable library rose the thin angular
figure of Harriet Salt, speaking in the subdued powerless way
of old. She had a huge cat with her, and an aunt—rather a pretty
old lady. "What is your aunt's name?" I said afterwards to Miss
Sarah. "Oh, Aunt Emma."—"Yes, but what is her other name?
What am I to call her?"—"Oh call her Aunt Emma; she would
never know herself by any other name."—"And what do you do
when your Aunt Emma Petit is here too?"—"Oh, she is only
Aunt Emma, and this is the other Aunt Emma; so when Aunt
Emma from Lichfield is here, and we want this one, we say,
'Other Aunt Emma, will you come here?'"

At seven the clergyman and his wife came to dinner. I took in
the aunt, a timid old lady, who seldom ventured a remark, and
then in the most diffident manner. This was her first—"I think I
may say, in fact I believe it has been often remarked, that Holland is a very flat country. I went there once, and it struck me
that the observation was correct." In the evening Miss Sarah
looked at my drawings, and said, "Well, on the whole, considering that they are totally unlike nature, I don't dislike them quite

so much as I expected." We breakfasted this morning at half-past seven, summoned by a gong; Miss Sarah having said, "At whatever hour of the day or night you hear that gong sound, you will know that you are expected to appear somewhere." She presided at the breakfast-table with a huge tabby-cat seated on her shoulder. "Does not that cat often tear your dress?" I asked. "No," she replied, "but it very often tears my face," and went on pouring out the tea.

LETTER TO MOTHER. *Ripley Castle, August 28 [1862].*—In coming down to dinner, I found a tall distinguished-looking lady upon the staircase, with whom I made friends at once: Lady Georgiana Grey. In the evening something was said about many ghost stories being the result of a practical joke. Lady Georgiana Grey, who had been sitting quietly, suddenly rose—awful almost with her white face and long black velvet dress—and exclaimed, "If any one ever *dared* to play a practical joke upon me, *all* my fortune, *all* my energies, my whole *life* would be insufficient to work my revenge." And she swept out of the room. They say it is because of the Grey story about a head. Lady Georgiana first saw the head, when she was in bed in Hanover Square, in the autumn of 1823. She rushed for refuge to her mother's room where she remained all night. Lady Grey desired her on no account to mention what she had seen to her father. But a fortnight later Lord Grey came into the room where Lady Georgiana was sitting with her mother and sister, much agitated, saying that he had just seen a head rolling towards him.

Wallington, Sept. 24 [1862].—Opening from the enclosed courtyard, which now forms a great frescoed hall in the centre of this house of Wallington, are endless suites of huge rooms, only partly carpeted and thinly furnished with ugly last-century furniture, partly covered with faded tapestry. The last of these is "the ghost-room," and Wallington is still a haunted house: awful noises are heard all through the night; footsteps rush up and down the untrodden passages; wings flap and beat against the windows; bodiless people unpack and put away their things all night long, and invisible beings are felt to breathe over you as you lie in bed. I think my room quite horrid, and it opens into a long suite of desolate rooms by a door which has no fastening, so I have pushed the heavy dressing-table with its weighty mirror, &c., against it to keep out all the nasty things that might try to come in. Old Lady Trevelyan was a very wicked woman and a miser: she lived here for many years, and is believed to wander here still: her son, Sir Walter, has never been known to laugh.

Sir Walter is a strange-looking being, with long hair and moustache, and an odd careless dress. He also has the reputation of being a miser. He is a great teetotaller, and inveighs everywhere against wine and beer: I trembled as I ran the gauntlet of public opinion yesterday in accepting a glass of sherry. Lady Trevelyan is a great artist. She is a pleasant, bright little woman, with sparkling black eyes, who paints beautifully, is intimately acquainted with all the principal artists, imports baskets from Madeira and lace from Honiton, and sells them in Northumberland, and always sits upon the rug by preference.

There is another strange being in the house. It is Mr Wooster, who came to arrange the collection of shells four years ago, and has never gone away. He looks like a church-brass incarnated, and turns up his eyes when he speaks to you, till you see nothing but the whites. He also has a long trailing moustache, and in all things imitates, but caricatures, Sir Walter. What he does here nobody seems to know; the Trevelyans say he puts the shells to rights, but the shells cannot take four years to dust.

St. Michael's Vicarage, Alnwick, Oct. 4 [1862].—I have been kindly received here by the Court Granvilles: he is a fiery, impetuous little man; she (Lady Charlotte) a sister of the Duke of Athole. We went again to dinner—only Sir Cresswell Cresswell, the famous judge, there, and Lady Alvanley . . . . Sir Cresswell was most amusing in describing how, when a lady was being conveyed in a sedan-chair to a party at Northumberland House, the bottom fell out, and, as she shouted in vain to make her bearers hear, she was obliged to run as fast as she could all the way through the mire inside the shell of the chair.

Several more visits brought me home at the end of November with an immense stock of new material, which I arranged in the next few months in "Murray's Handbook of Durham and Northumberland"—work for which neither Murray nor any one else gave me much credit, but which cost me great labour and into which I put my whole heart.

IX. Home Life with the Mother

AMALFI

When I returned from the North in the winter of 1862-63, I was shocked to find how much a failure of power, which I had faintly traced in the summer, had increased in my dearest mother. I inwardly vowed never again to undertake anything which should separate me from her. Some work which might be done at home would doubtless turn up, and meanwhile I had constant employment in the service and watchings which scarcely ever permitted me to be away from her side.

At Christmas my mother suffered terribly, and was so liable to a sudden numbness which closely threatened paralysis, that by day and night remedies had always to be prepared and at hand. The doctors agreed that it was absolutely necessary she should go abroad. This gave rise to terrible anxiety. All my difficulties were enormously added to by different members of the family insisting that my mother ought to stay at home, and that I knew it, but "dragged her abroad for my own pleasure and convenience." On February 16 we left home, and proceeded to Nice, where we spent the spring—my mother recovered rapidly and entirely.

We left home again for Italy on the 26th of October. In those days there was no railway across the Mont Cenis, but my mother enjoyed the *vetturino* journey along the roads fringed with barberries. Beyond this, travelling became difficult, owing to the floods. At Piacenza, we were all ejected from the train, and forced to walk along the line for a great distance, and then to cross a ford, which made me most thankful that my mother was tolerably well at the time.

At the station of Ficulle near Orvieto, where the railway to the south came to an end altogether at that time, the floods were out all over the country, and there were no carriages—everything being quite disorganised. We arrived at a miserable little station, scarcely better than a small open shed, in torrents of rain, at twelve o'clock in the day and had to wait till the same hour of the day following, when carriages would arrive from Orvieto. After some time my mother was conveyed to a wretched little inn, but it was necessary for someone to remain to guard the luggage, and knowing what a fearful hardship it would be considered by our cross-grained manservant, John Gidman, I remained sitting upon it, without any food except a few biscuits, in pitch darkness at night, and with the swelching rain beating down upon my miserable shed, for twenty-four hours. It was a very unpleasant experience.

One day in the spring, mother and I drove to our favourite spot of the Acqua Acetosa, and walked in the sun by the muddy Tiber. When we came back, we found news that Aunt Esther was dead. She had never recovered from a violent cold which she caught when lying for hours in pouring rain, upon her husband's grave. Her death was characteristic of her life, for, with the strongest sense of duty and a determination to carry it out to the uttermost, no mental constitution can possibly be imagined more happily constructed for self-torment than hers. My mother grieved for her loss, and I grieved that my darling had sorrow. How many years of heartburnings and privation are buried for ever out of sight in that grave! *Resquiscat in pace.* I believe that I have entirely forgiven all the years of bitter suffering that she caused me. "He who cannot forgive others, breaks the bridge over which he must pass himself: for every man hath need to be forgiven," was a dictum of Lord Herbert of Cherbury.

As we returned through Rome we stayed at the Palazzo Parisani, and much enjoyed the luxury of the large cool rooms, where we lived chiefly on ricotta and lettuces. One day as we came in, the porter gave us a black-edged letter. It was the news that poor "Italima" was released from all her sorrows.

After Italima's death, Esmeralda had moved from Bryanston Street to a house in Duke Street, Manchester Square, which was kept by Mrs Thorpe, the faithful and devoted maid of Italima's old friend Mrs Chambers. Here my sister had every comfort, and might have had rest, but one day her brother William came to visit her, and broke a blood vessel while he was in the house. His wife was sent for, and for several weeks he hovered between life and death; indeed, he never really recovered from this attack, though he was able to be moved in a month and lived for more than three years. The fatigue of her brother's illness entirely prostrated Esmeralda, who was already terribly shaken in health by the fatigue of the strange watchings, enjoined by Catholicism, which followed her mother's death.

In November, three suits in Chancery were suddenly decided in her favour. By two of these, my sister recovered £8000 of her mother's fortune; by the third she secured £3000 from the trustees who had signed away her mother's marriage settlement. During the summers of 1864 and 1865 I was often with my sister in London. At her house I now, at least on one occasion, met each of my brothers, but we never made the slightest degree of real acquaintance; indeed, I doubt if I should have recognized either of them if I met him in the street.

When my eldest brother, Francis, came of age, he had inherited the old Shipley property of Gresford in Flintshire, quantities of old family plate, &c., and a clear £3000 a year. He was handsome and clever, a good linguist and a tolerable artist. But he had a love of gambling, which was his ruin, and before he was seven-and-twenty [October 1857] he was in the Queen's Bench, without a penny in the world, with Gresford sold—Hurstmonceaux sold—his library, pictures, and plate sold, and £53,000 of debts. After Francis was released in 1860, he went to join Garibaldi in his Italian campaign, and being a brave soldier, and, with all his faults, devoted to military adventure and impervious to hardships, he was soon appointed by the Dictator as his aide-de-camp. He fought bravely in the siege of Capua. His especial duty, however, was to watch and follow the extraordinary Contessa della Torre, who rode with the troops, and by her example incited the Italians to prodigies of valour. Of this lady Francis said —

"The Contessa della Torre was exceedingly handsome. She wore a hat and plume, trousers, boots, and a long jacket. She was foolhardy brave. When a shell exploded by her, instead of falling on the ground like the soldiers, she would stand looking at it, and making a cigarette all the time. The hospital was a building surrounding a large courtyard, and in the centre of the court was a table where the amputations took place. By the side of the surgeon who operated stood the Contessa della Torre, who held the arms and legs while they were being cut off, and when they were severed, chucked them away to join others on a heap close by. There were so many, that she had a heap of arms on one side of her and a heap of legs on the other. The soldiers, animated by her example, often sang the Garibaldian hymn while their limbs were being taken off, though they fainted away afterwards.

"When the war was over, the Contessa della Torre retired to Milan. Her first husband, the Count della Torre, she soon abandoned; her second husband, Signor Martino, a rich banker, soon abandoned *her*. Lately she has founded a Society for the Conversion of the Negroes of Central Africa, of which she appointed herself patroness, secretary, and treasurer; and, obtaining an English Clergy List, wrote in all directions for subscriptions. Of course many clergy took no notice of the appeal, but a certain proportion responded and sent donations, which it is needless to say were *not* applied to Central Africa."

After the siege of Capua, Francis was very ill with a violent fever at Naples, and then remained there for a long time because he was too poor to go away.

It may seem odd that I never mentioned my second brother, William, in these memoirs, but the fact is, that after he grew up, I never saw him for more than a few minutes. It is one of the things I regret most in life that I never made acquaintance with William. I believe now that he was misrepresented to us and that he had many good qualities; and I often feel, had he lived till I had the means of doing so, how glad I should have been to have helped him, and how fond I might have become of him. At Eton he was an excessively good looking boy, very clever, very mischievous, and intensely popular with his companions. He never had any fortune, so that it was most foolish of his guardian (Uncle Julius) to spend £2000 which had been bequeathed to him by "the Bath Aunts," in buying him a commission in the Blues. I only once saw him whilst he was in the army, and only remember him as a great dandy, but I must say that he had the excuse that everything he wore became him. After he left the army he was buffeted about from pillar to post, and lived no one knows where or how. Our cousin Lord Ravensworth was very kind to him, and so was old Lady Paul; but to Hurstmonceaux or Holmhurst he was never invited, and he would never have been allowed to come. I have often thought since how very odd it was that when he died, neither my mother nor I wore the slightest mourning for him; but he was so entirely outside our life and thoughts, that somehow it would never have occurred to us. He had, however, none of the cold self-contained manner which characterised Francis, but was warm hearted, cordial, affection-ate, and could be most entertaining. After his mother's great mis-fortunes he went to Spain on some temporary appointment, and at Barcelona nearly died of a fever, through which he was nursed by a lady who had taken an extraordinary fancy to him; but on his return, when it was feared he would marry her, he took everyone by surprise in espousing the very pretty portionless daughter of a physician at Clifton.

X. English Pleasures and Roman Trials

Le Puy

I WENT TO NORTH WALES to pay a visit to our cousinhood at Bodryddan, which had been the home of my grandmother's only brother, the Dean of St Asaph. As an ecclesiastical dignitary, Dean Shipley would certainly be called to account in our days. He was devoted to hunting and shooting, and used to go up for weeks together to a little public-house in the hills above Bodryddan, where he gave himself up entirely to the society of his horses and dogs. He had led a very fast life before he took orders, and he had a natural daughter by a Mrs Hamilton, who became the second wife of our grandfather; but after his ordination there was no further stain upon his character.

As a father he was exceedingly severe. He never permitted his daughters to sit down in his presence, and he never allowed two of them to be in the room with him at once, because he could not endure the additional talking caused by their speaking to one another. His daughter Anna Maria had become engaged to Captain Dashwood, a very handsome young officer, but before the time came at which he was to claim her hand, he was completely paralysed, crippled, and almost imbecile. Then she flung herself upon her knees, imploring her father with tears not to insist upon her marriage with him; but the Dean sternly refused to relent, saying she had given her word, and must keep to it.

She nursed Captain Dashwood indefatigably till he died, and then she came back to Bodryddan and lived there with her aunt Mrs Yonge, finding it dreadfully dull, for she was a brilliant talker and adored society. At last she went abroad with her aunt Louisa Shipley, and at Corfu she met Sir Thomas Maitland, who gave her magnificent diamonds and asked her to marry him. But she insisted on coming home to ask her father's consent, at which the Dean was quite furious. "Why could you not marry him at once?"—and indeed, before she could get back to her lover, he died!

After the death of Mrs Yonge, Mrs Dashwood lived at Cheltenham, a rich and clever widow, and had many proposals. To the disgust of her family, she insisted upon accepting Captain Jones, who had been a neighbour at Bodryddan, and was celebrated for his fearfully violent temper. The day before the wedding it was nearly all off, because, when he came to look at her luggage, he insisted on her having only one box, and stamped all her things down into it, spoiling all her new dresses. He made her go with him for a wedding tour all over Scotland in a pony-carriage, without a maid, and she hated it; but in a year he died.

Then she insisted on marrying the Rev G. Chetwode, who had had one wife before and had two afterwards— an old beau, who used to comb his hair with a leaden comb to efface the grey. On her death he inherited all she had—diamonds, £2000 a year, all the fine pictures left her by Mr Jones, and all those Landor had collected for her in Italy.

But to return to Dean Shipley .... The Dean was much interested in the management of his estate, but he insisted that every detail should pass through his own hands. For instance, when he was absent in London, a number of curious images and carvings in alabaster were discovered under the pavement at Bodryddan: news was immediately sent to him, but he desired that everything should be covered up, and remain till he came home. On his return, he put off the examination from time to time, till, on his death, the place was forgotten and now no one is able to discover it.

I went to stay at Dalton Hall in Lancashire, to visit Mrs Hornby, a cousin of my Aunt Penrhyn. A sister-in-law of Mrs Hornby —a Mrs Bayley—was staying at Dalton when I was there. She told me, first hand, a story of which I have heard many distorted versions. I give it in her words:

"My sister, Mrs Hamilton (née Armstrong) was one night going to bed, when she saw a man's foot project from under the bed. She knelt down then and there by the bedside and prayed for the wicked people who were going about—for the *known* wicked person especially—that they might be converted. When she concluded, the man came from under the bed and said, 'I have heard your prayer, ma'am, and with all my heart I say Amen to it;' and he did her no harm and went away. She heard from him years afterward, and he was a changed man from that day."

Apropos of the growth of a story by exaggeration, Mrs Bayley said:—

"The first person said, 'Poor Mrs Richards was so ill that what she threw up was almost like a black crow.' The second said, 'Poor Mrs Richards was so ill; it was the most dreadful thing, she actually threw up a black crow.' The third said, 'Poor Mrs Richards has the most dreadful malady: it is almost too terrible to speak of, but she has already thrown up . . . three black crows.'"

In the autumn of 1867, my mother was terribly ill, so that our journey abroad was a very anxious one to look forward to. I tried, however, to face it quite cheerily.

JOURNAL. *Nice, Nov. 17 [1867].*—So far all our troubles and anxieties are past, and the sweet Mother certainly not the worse, perhaps rather better for all her fatigues. It is an extraordinary case, to be one day lying in a sort of vision on the portals of another world, the next up and travelling.

Pisa, Dec. 1—We left Nice on the 21st and slept at Mentone. The second day, at Loiano I was left behind. I went just outside the hotel to draw, begging my mother and Lea to pick me up as they went by. The carriage passed close by me and they did not see me. At first I did not hurry myself, thinking, when they did not find me, that they would stop for me a little further on; but seeing the carriage go on and on, I ran after it as hard as I could, shouting at the pitch of my voice; but it never stopped, and I quite lost sight of it in the narrow streets of one of the fishing villages before reaching Finale. At Finale I was in absolute despair at their not stopping, which seemed inexplicable, and I pursued mile after mile, footsore and weary, through the grand moun-

tain coves in that part of the Riveria and along the desolate
shore to Noli, where, just as night closed in, I was taken up by
some people driving in a little carriage, on the box of which, in a
bitter cold wind, I was carried to Savona, where I arrived just as
our heavy carriage with its inmates was driving into the hotel. It
was one of the odd instances of my dear mother's insouciance, of
her "happy-go-lucky" nature : "they had not seen me, they had
not looked back; no, they supposed I should get on somehow;
they knew I always fell on my legs." And I was perfectly conscious that if I had not appeared for days, my mother would have
said just the same.

Rome, 44 Piazza di Spagno, Dec. 29—We moved here on the
20th to a delightfully comfortable apartment, which is a perfect
sun-trap. On Saturday I was constantly restless, with a sense of
fire near me, but could discover nothing burning in the apartment. I had such a strong presentiment of fire that I refused to go
out all day. When Lea came in with my tea at 8 p.m., I told her
what an extraordinary noise I continually heard—a sort of rushing
over the ceiling, which was of strained canvas—but she thought
nothing of it. Soon after she was gone, a shower of sparks burst
into the room and large pieces of burning wood forced their
way through a hole in the ceiling.

Shouting to Lea, I rushed up to the next floor, and rang violently and continuously on the bell, shouting, "*Fuoco, fuoco*;"
but the owners of the apartment were gone to bed and would not
get up; so, without losing time, I flew downstairs, roused the
porter, sent him off to fetch Ferdinando Manetti, who was re-
sponsible for our apartment, and then for the *pompieri*. Meantime,
the servants of Miss Robertson, who lived below us, had come
to our help, and assisted in keeping the fire under with sponges

of water, while Lea and I rushed about securing money, valuables, drawings, &c., and then, dragging out our great boxes, began rapidly to fill them. Mother was greatly astonished at seeing us moving in and out with great piles of things in our arms, but did not realize at once what had happened. I had just arranged for her being wrapped up in blankets and carried through the streets to Palazzo Parisani, when the *pompieri* arrived. From that time there was no real danger. They tore up the bricks of the floor above us, and poured water through upon the charred and burning beams, and a cascade of black water and hot bricks tumbled through together into our drawing room.

XI. ESMERALDA

ANNE F. M. L. HARE
'ESMERALDA'

THE WINTER OF 1866-67 WAS chiefly passed by my sister at the house of Mrs Alfred Montgomery at Ifield near Crawley, where Esmeralda and her aunt for many months shared in the house-keeping. For Esmeralda had been induced to regard Mrs Montgomery as a religious martyr, and her impressionable nature was completely fascinated by her hostess. While at Ifield, a fatal web was drawn each day more closely by her Catholic associates, by which Esmeralda was induced to entrust large sums to her brother Francis for speculation. Her unworldly nature was persuaded to consent to this means of (as Francis represented) largely increasing her income, to employ in assisting various religious objects. Esmeralda never knew or had the faintest idea of the sum to which her speculations amounted. She was beguiled on from day to day by two evil advisers and her heart being in other things, was induced to trust and believe that her worldly affairs were in the hands of disinterested persons.

During the winter an alarming illness attacked my brother Francis. He was my brother by birth, though I had seldom ever seen him, and scarcely ever thought about him . . . till this winter when my sister mentioned his refusing to go to live with her in Grosvenor Street and of his putting her to the unnecessary expense of paying for lodgings for him. Here he caught cold, and one day, unexpectedly, Dr Squires came to tell Esmeralda that he considered him on the point of death. She flew to his bedside and remained with him all through the night.

After this Esmeralda wrote to us (to Rome) that the condition of Francis was quite hopeless, and that her next letter must contain the news of his death. What was our surprise, therefore, when the next letter was from Francis himself (who had never written to us before), not merely saying that he was better, but that he was going to be married immediately to a person with whom he had long been acquainted. At the time of this marriage, Esmeralda went away into Sussex, and afterwards, when she returned to London, she never consented to see Mrs Francis Hare.

My sister's cheque-books of the last year of her life show that during that year alone her brother Francis had received £900 from her, though her income at the most did not exceed £800. He had also persuaded Esmeralda to take a house called "Park Lodge" in Paddington, with an acre and a half of garden. The rent was certainly low, and the arrangement, as intended by Esmeralda, was that her brother should live in two or three rooms of the house, and the rest should be let furnished. But tenants never came, and Francis lived in the whole of the house, after furnishing it expensively and sending in the bills to his sister, who paid them in her fear lest anxiety about money matters might make him ill again.

In the beginning of May, Esmeralda was very ill with an attack like that from which she had suffered at Dijon several years before. Having been very successfully treated then in France, she persuaded her aunt to obtain the direction of a French doctor. The remedy which this doctor administered greatly increased the malady. At half-past four in the morning of May 25 the most mysterious black sickness had come on, and could not be arrested. Dr Squires, summoned in haste, says that he arrived exactly as a clock near Grosvenor Square struck five. He saw at once that the case was quite hopeless, still for three hours he struggled to arrest the malady. At the end of that time, Esmeralda suddenly said, "Dr Squires, this is very terrible, isn't it?"—"Yes," he replied, throwing as much meaning as possible into his voice, "it is indeed *most* terrible." Upon this Esmeralda started up in the bed and said, "You cannot possibly mean that you think I shall not recover?" Dr Squires said, "Yes, I am afraid it is my duty to tell you that you cannot possibly recover now." —"But I do not feel ill," exclaimed Esmeralda; "this sickness is very terrible, but still I do not feel ill."—"I cannot help that," answered Dr Squires, "but I fear it is my duty to tell you that it is quite impossible you can live."

After a pause she said, "Tell me how long you think it possible I should live." Dr Squires said, "You might live two days, but it is quite impossible that you should live longer than that."

My sister then made a very simple will, leaving everything to her (Protestant) aunt Miss Paul, except her interest in Park Lodge and a chest of plate which she left to Francis, and her claims to a portrait by Sir Joshua Reynolds, which she left to me . . . . About nine o'clock in a loud and clear voice, she called "Auntie," and instantly fell back and died.

Upon that night and all succeeding nights until the funeral, the three maids persistently refused at night to go upstairs, saying they had seen a spirit there and they remained all through the night huddled up together in a corner of the kitchen. If they had the opportunity, they always made mysterious hints of poison, and of Esmeralda's death having been caused by unnatural means. They talked a great deal, saying that Miss Hare herself said in her last moments, "I am poisoned and I die of poison." In consequence of the servants' certain conviction that my sister had been poisoned, Mrs Fitz-Gerald was most anxious, before my return to England, for a post-mortem examination, but Francis violently opposed this, and he carried his point.

The opinion that my sister's death was caused by poison was shared by many of those who came to see her after her death. Three eminent physicians gave it as their opinion that hers were the usual symptoms and appearances induced by corrosive poison.

On the day before the funeral, I saw Mrs Fitz-Gerald, who was in the inner drawing room, after looking into a blotting-book, suddenly burst into tears. "Oh," she said, "the whole mystery is revealed now; it is all quite plain; you may see what it was that killed your sister," and she held up a letter from Francis, written on the Friday evening before her death—a cruel letter, telling her in the harshest terms that she was totally ruined, that she might sell the house and her plate, and all else she possessed, for she had nothing whatever to live upon; but that, as he did not wish her to starve, she and her aunt might come to live *with his wife.* It was Esmeralda's peculiar habit, when she was ill or suffering, to put letters aside and not read them till she felt better; it is therefore possible that she did not open this letter till Monday, when it gave the final blow . . . . Always afterwards, when others spoke of poison, I said, "There were strange signs of poison, and many people think she was poisoned, but it is my firm conviction that she did not die of poison, but *of a broken heart—a heart broken by her brother Francis.*"

In October my sister possessed £12,000 clear, besides a great quantity of plate, diamonds and other valuables, and the house in Grosvenor Street paid for and clear from debt, as well as the property in the Palazzo Parisani at Rome. At the time of her death she possessed, interest and principal combined, £216, and debts to a considerable amount, while the diamonds and plate seemed to have disappeared several days afterwards. I found a pawn-ticket from Attenborough for £120 upon diamonds. I afterwards found a pawn-ticket for £100 upon plate; later I found a third ticket for £82 upon some diamond earrings. Attenborough told me that Francis had brought his sister there at different times and placed the plate and diamonds in pawn.

On June 9 I received a letter from Mary Stanley saying that some friends had come up to her at a party and spoken of the cruel way in which Mr (Francis) Hare had been treated by his Protestant relations. They said that Mrs Montgomery (one of Esmeralda's Catholic friends) had asserted that the doors of the house in Grosvenor Street were forcibly closed upon Mr and Mrs Francis Hare during Miss Hare's illness, and that she was influenced in her last moments to cancel a will in which she had left all her money to her brother Francis; also that neither Francis nor his wife were then allowed to enter the house or to see their aunt, and that they had nothing to live upon, owing to their having been disinherited by Miss Hare who supported them during her life.

On June 11 Mary Stanley came down to Holmhurst and vehemently urged my writing to Mrs Montgomery in defense of Mrs Paul. On June 12 I yielded to her repeated solicitations and wrote—Mary Stanley and my adopted mother looking over the

letter and approving it sentence by sentence. When it was finished, Mary Stanley said, "That letter is perfect: you must not
alter a word: it could not be better."

In the third paragraph I wrote, "Francis and his wife are *not*
allowed by the lawyer's direction, to see my aunt until the whole
terrible story of my sister's sudden death is cleared up . . ." I
pointed out in an earlier paragraph that in her previous will my
sister had not even mentioned Francis's name.

In less than a week from the time of my sending the letter to
Mrs Montgomery, I received one from a lawyer who had long
been mixed up with Francis's affairs, stating that unless I at
once withdrew and apologized for every part of that letter, an
action for libel would be brought against me. Knowing that
Francis was utterly insolvent, my family and I treated this as an
idle threat, and declining any correspondence with the person
in question, referred him to my solicitor.

The action for libel was declared, an action which openly
avowed its object, to extort £5000. I did all I could to save family scandal by offering to withdraw the letter altogether. My
solicitor made every possible offer on my part, but was always
answered that they must have "pecuniary compensation." On
Tuesday, July 28, the Roman Catholic lawyer asked for permission to fix the day for the trial. This courtesy was not refused. He
fixed the day instantly and summoned his witnesses, but he did
not let us know till Saturday, August 1, that the trial was to be on
Monday August 3, when, owing to the want of a London post on
Sunday, it was most difficult, almost impossible, to summon our
witnesses. On Saturday, August 1, the announcement came
that the trial would take place at Guildford on Monday the 3rd.

On Monday morning, Mary Stanley and I drove early to the

Waterloo Station to go down to Guildford. There were so many passengers for the trial that a special train was put on. The heat of that day was awful, a broiling sun and not a breath of air. We had a little room to meet in at the hotel. Almost immediately I was hurried by my solicitor to the room where our senior counsel, the great Hawkins, was breakfasting at the end of a long table. He complained of the immense mass of evidence he had had to go through. He said—what I knew—that such a trial must expose terrible family scandals—that it would be a disgrace not to snatch at any chance of bringing it to a close—that probably the judge would give it for private investigation to some other Queen's counsellor—that, in fact, it was never likely to *be* a trial.

When I came down from Mr Hawkins, Mary Stanley and I were taken to court. There were so many cases to be tried, that ours could not come on for some time. We were given places on the raised dais behind the judge and there we all sat waiting through many hours. In that intensely hot weather, the courthouse, with its high timber roof and many open windows, was far cooler than the outer air, and we did not suffer from the heat. But the judge, Baron Martin, whom I have heard described as far more at home on a racecourse than on the judgment-seat, was suffering violently from diarrhoea, was most impatient of the cases he had to try, and at last snatched his wig from his head and flung it down on the ground beside him.

About three o'clock in the afternoon we were assured that it was quite impossible our case could be brought on that day, as there were still so many others to be tried, and we were advised to go out and rest. So Mary Stanley and I went back to the hotel and remained there in a cool room. Presently, to our horror, a messenger came running down from the court and said, "Your case is on, and has been on twenty minutes already." We rushed to the court and found the whole scene changed. All the approaches to the court were crowded, literally choked up with witnesses and Roman Catholic spectators. The court itself was packed to overflowing.

When I was brought in, all seemed to be confusion, every one speaking at once; Mr Hawkins was in vain trying to put in a word, the judge was declaiming that he would have an end of the trial, while Serjeant Parry for the prosecution was in a loud voice reading the letter to Mrs Montgomery and giving his comments upon it. The utmost excitement prevailed in court. Almost everyone stood up. Mr Hawkins urged me, "Are your adopted family prepared to pay what the Roman Catholics claim?"— "Certainly not."—"Then you must submit to a verdict."—"I leave it in your hands." So I wrote on a bit of paper, "Say no more than this. I withdraw anything that may be legally taken as libelous in the letter to Mrs Montgomery." Then Mr Hawkins again stood up and said that he was in a position to withdraw the letter—if it contained any libelous statements to apologise for them. At the same time "his client could not submit to be told that he had either acted maliciously or invented anything: he was absent from England at the time of his sister's death and had throughout acted entirely upon information he had received from those upon the spot."

"I will have an end of this, gentlemen," exclaimed the judge— "I give a verdict for forty shillings."

"Make it ten guineas, my Lord," shouted the Roman Catholic lawyer, who had previously interrupted Serjeant Parry by saying, "We will have money, we will have money." "There shall be an end of this, gentlemen," said the judge; "I give a verdict for forty shillings," and he walked out of the court. And so this painful ordeal came to an end. It was not till afterwards that I was aware that the verdict of forty shillings obliged me to pay the costs of both sides—£199 to my lawyer, and £293 to the Roman Catholic lawyer, which was afterwards reduced by a taxing-master to £207, 9s, 1d.

On August 7, Monsignor Paterson wrote a long letter to Mary Stanley, explanatory of his conduct in the affair. It contained the following remarkable passage: —

"A day or two after Miss Hare's death, which took me quite by surprise, I went to her house, and there saw Sister Pierina, who told me she had been summoned, and found Miss Hare actually dying; that she seemed very suffering, and had some difficulty in resigning herself to the will of God. I remember also hearing that she expressed distress at some conduct on the part of Mr Francis Hare, and I thought that other expressions used implied a suspicion on her part of some kind of *foul play*. Of course, had I taken this *au sérieux*, it would have made a great impression, but I set it down, after a moment's reflection, as a random (perhaps almost delirious) expression, such as people who are very ill sometimes use with very little meaning at all."

Strange certainly that an eminent Roman Catholic priest should call at his friend's house, hear that she had died suddenly, and that she had said on her deathbed that she died from "foul play," and yet be able so easily to dismiss the subject from his mind!

Soon after the trial I wrote a long account of the whole proceedings to Archbishop Manning. His answer was very kind but very evasive—"Miss Hare's death was most sad . . . the trial must have been most painful," he "sympathised deeply," &c., but without giving a direct opinion of any kind.

It was not till some months later that I became acquainted with a secret which convinced me that, though my sister's end was probably hastened by the conduct of her brother Francis, yet poison was the original cause of her death. When we next visited Pisa, Madame Victoire told me how, when my sister was a little girl of six years old at Paris, she and her own little girl, Victoria Ackermann, were sitting on two little stools doing their needle-work side by side. Suddenly there was a terrible outcry. Little Anna Hare had swallowed her thimble. The whole house was in consternation, doctors were summoned in haste, the child was given emetics, was held upside down, everything was done that could be done to bring the thimble back, but it was too late. Then the doctors inquired what the thimble was like, and on seeing the thimble of the little Victoria, who had received one at the same time, were satisfied that it was not dangerous, as the thimble being of walnut-wood, would naturally dissolve with time, and they gave medicines to hasten its dissolution.

But, in the midst of the confusion, came Mrs Large, the nurse, who confessed with bitter tears that, owing to her folly, the thimble was not what it was imagined to be. She had not liked to see the child of the mistress with the same thimble as the child of the maid, and had given little Anna one with a broad band which looked like gold but was really copper. When the doctors heard this, the accident naturally assumed a serious aspect, and they redoubled their efforts to bring back the thimble. But everything failed; the wooden thimble dissolved with time, but the copper band remained. Gradually, as Esmeralda grew stronger, the accident was forgotten by all but her mother, Mrs

Large, and Madame Victoire, who observed from time to time, in childish illnesses of unusual violence, symptoms which they alone could recognise, but which were such as would arise through slight injury from poison of verdigris.

As my sister grew, the copper ring grew also, attenuated to the minutest thread, but encircling her body. From time to time she was seriously affected by it, but her mother could not bear it to be spoken of, and her repulsion for the subject communicated itself to Esmeralda herself. She was warned to evade a damp climate or the use of vegetables. When she was seized with her violent illness at Dijon, the symptoms were all such as would be caused by poison of verdigris. She then went to Pisa, where Madame Victoire was alarmed by what she heard, and insisted upon the best advice being procured, and a medical examination. The doctors who saw her, even then spoke to Madame Victoire of her state as very serious, and requiring the most careful watching. When Esmeralda went to Rome to the canonisation in the summer of 1867, she returned by Pisa.

The faithful Madame Victoire then sent for a famous medical professor of the University of Bologna to meet her, and insisted upon her being examined by him. He afterwards told Madame Victoire privately that though, by intense care, Miss Hare might live for many years, her life, in case of accident, hung on a thread, and that it was highly improbable that she would live long, for that the copper ring was beginning to tell very seriously upon her constitution, and that when she died it would probably be suddenly of black sickness, with every appearance of poison —poison of verdigris. And so it was.

One of the principal actors in the scene at Guildford was soon after called to account before a higher tribunal than any that earth can afford. On the 18th of November [1868] I received (at Rome), to my great surprise, a letter from Madame Flora Limosin, of the Hôtel de Londres at Pisa (Victoire's youngest daughter), saying that Francis was about to arrive there from Hyéres. He had been sent away from England some time before, having then £80 in his possession. Whether this sum was obtained by a Roman Catholic subscription, I have never been able to learn, but from this time the Roman Catholic conspirators ceased to help him: he had failed as the instrument for which they required him, and they now flung him aside as useless. His folly at Guildford, in lending himself to their designs, has also alienated the whole of his own family, even to the most distant degrees of relationship. Not knowing where to turn, he could only think of two persons who would receive him in his destitution. His mother's faithful maid Madame Victoire and her daughter Flora were still living at Pisa, and to them, when he had only £20 left, he determined to make his way. On landing at Spezia, though even then in a dying state, he would not enter a hotel, because he felt that if he entered it he would never have strength to leave it again, and he sat for hours upon his luggage on the platform of the station till the train started. For the sake of their old companionship in childhood, and of the kindness she had received from my father, Flora Limosin not only received Francis, but also the person to whom he was married, and gave them some quiet rooms opening upon the garden of the Hôtel de Londres, where he was nursed by the faithful friends of his infancy. He was attended by Padre Pastacaldi, who administered to him the last offices of the Church, and says that he died penitent, and sent me a message hoping that I forgave him for all that had passed at

Guildford. He died on the 27th of November, utterly destitute, and dependent upon the charity of his humble friends. He was buried by them in a corner of the Campo Santo at Pisa, near their own family burial place, where the letters F. H. in the pavement alone mark the resting place of Francis George Hare, the idolised son of his mother.

XII. Dreadful Floods
and the Last of the Mother

ANTONIO, PISA, DURING THE FLOOD

SEPT. 10 [1869].—WE have all been to luncheon at Carham, one of the well-known haunted houses: the "Carham light" is celebrated and constantly seen. We asked old Mrs Compton of eighty-three, who lives there now, about the supernatural sights of Carham. "Och," she said, "and have ye niver heard the story of the phantom carriage? We have just heard it this very morning: when we were waiting for you, we heard it drive up. We are quite used to it now. A carriage drives quickly up to the door with great rattling and noise, and when it stops, the horses seem to paw and tear up the gravel. Strange servants are terribly frightened by it. One day when I was at luncheon I heard a carriage drive up quickly to the door: there was no doubt of it. I told the servant who was in waiting to go out and see who it was. When he came back I asked who had come. He was pale as ashes. Oh, he said, it's only the phantom coach.

"And then there is the Carham light. That is just beautiful! It is a large globe of fire in the shape of a full moon: I have seen it hundreds of times. It moves about in the woods, and sometimes settles on one place. The first time I saw it I was driving from

Kelso and I saw a great ball of fire. I said to the driver, 'What is that?'—'Oh, it's just the Carham light,' he said. When Dick (her son-in-law) came in, he said he did not believe it; but that night it came—bright as ever. All the gentlemen went out into the woods to examine it; but it moved before them. They all saw it, and they were quite convinced: it has never been explained."

We left home in 1869 on the 14th of October. On December 10 occurred the terrible floods of the Arno.

LETTER. *Pisa, Dec. 11 [1869].*—On the last three days the Mother has been very ill. On Thursday she had an attack of fainting, and seemed likely to fall into one of her long many days' sleep. The rain continued day and night in torrents. Yesterday made it three weeks since we arrived, and in that time there had been only two days in which the rain had not been ceaseless. The Arno was much swollen; I saw it on Thursday, very curious, up to the top of the arches of the bridge.

Yesterday from the passage window I saw a volume of muddy water slowly pouring down the street, not from the Arno, but from towards the railway station. I meant to go and see the water nearer but before I could reach the main entrance, in half a minute the great heavy waves of the yellow flood were pouring into the courtyard and stealing into the entrance hall.

It was as suddenly as that it came upon us.

The scene for the next half-hour baffles all description. The servants rushed about in distraction: Lea, pale as ashes, thought and cried that our last moment was come; and all the time the yellow heavy waters rose and rose, covering first the wheels of the omnibus, the vases, the statues in the garden, then up high into the trees. Inside, the carpets were rising and swaying on the water, and in five minutes the large pieces of furniture were beginning to crash against each other.

I had rushed at the first alarm to the *garde meuble,*[*] and (how I did it I cannot imagine) dragged our great box to the stairs: it was the only piece of luggage saved from the ground floor. Then I rushed to the *salle-à-manger*, and shouting to Flora to save the money in her bureau, swept all the silver laid out for dinner into a tablecloth, and got it safe off. From that moment it was a *sauve qui peut*. I handed down rows of teapots, jugs, sugar-basins, &c., to the maids, who carried them away in lapfuls: in this way also we saved all the glass, but before we could begin upon the china, the water was up to our waists and we were obliged to retreat, carrying off the tea-urns as a last spoil. The whole family, with Amabile and all the old servants, were now down in the water, but a great deal of time was wasted in the belief that a poor half-witted Russian lady was locked into her room and drowning, and in breaking open the door; but when at last a panel of the door was dashed in, the room was found full of water and all its contents swimming about, but the lady was . . . gone out for a walk!

As I was coming in from the lower rooms to the staircase with a load of looking-glasses, a boat crashed in at the principal entrance, bringing home the poor lady and two other English, who had been caught by the flood at the end of the street, and had

[*] Furniture storage place.

been for some time in the greatest peril: the boatmen having declined to bring them the few necessary steps until they had been paid twenty francs, and then having refused altogether to bring a poor Italian who had no money to give them. At this moment Madame Victoire insisted on taking the opportunity of the boat to return to her own house. It was a dreadful scene, all the women in the house crying and imploring her to stay, but she insisted on embarking. She did not arrive without hairbreadth escapes. When she reached her own house, the current was so strong, and the boat was dashed so violently against the walls, that it was impossible for her to be landed; but the flood was less violent beneath her larger house which is let to the Marchese Guadagna, from which sheets were let down from the upper windows, and she was fastened to them and raised: but when she reached the grille of the first-floor windows, and was hanging halfway, the current carried away the boat, and at the same moment the great wall opposite S. Antonio fell with an awful crash. However, the Guadagna family held tight to the sheets, and Madame Victoire was landed at last, though she fell insensible on the floor when she entered the window.

The walls were now falling in every direction with a dull roar into the yellow waters. The noise was dreadful—the cries of the drowning animals, the shrieks of the women, especially of a mother whose children were in the country, wringing her hands at the window of an opposite house. The water in our house was rising so rapidly that it was impossible to remain longer on the side towards the principal staircase, and we fled to the other end, where Pilotte, a poor boy in the service, lay dangerously ill, but was obliged to get up from his bed, and, though quite blind from ophthalmia, was far more useful than anyone else. Still we saved an immense number of things, and I was able to cut down pictures, &c., floating on a sofa as if it were a boat. The great difficulty in reaching the things was always from the carpet rising, and making it almost impossible to get out of the room again. It was about half-past 5 p.m. when we were obliged to come out of the water, which was then terribly cold and above the waist.

Meantime the scene in the street was terrible. The missing children of the woman opposite were brought back in a boat and drawn up in sheets; and the street, now a deep river, was crowded with boats, torches flashing on the water, and lights gleaming in every window. All the thirty poor hens in the henhouse at the end of the balcony were making a terrible noise as they were slowly drowned, the ducks and pigeons were drowned too, I suppose, being too frightened to escape, and many floated dead past the window. The garden was covered with cushions, chairs, tables, and ladies' dresses, which had been washed out of the lower windows. There was great fear that the omnibus horse and driver were drowned, and the Limosins were crying dreadfully about it; but the man was drawn up late at night from a boat, whose crew had discovered him on the top of a wall, and at present the horse exists also, having taken refuge on the terrace at the end of the garden, where it is partially above water. The street was covered with furniture, great carved wardrobes being whirled down to the Arno like straws. The cries of the drowning animals were quite human.

All this time my poor sweet mother had been lying perfectly still and patient, but about 6 p.m., as the water had reached the highest step of the lower staircase and was still mounting, we had our luggage carried up to the attics, secured a few valuables in case of sudden flight (as no boat would have taken luggage), and began to get Mother dressed. There was no immediate danger, but if another embankment broke, there might be at any moment, and it was well to be prepared. Night closed in terribly—pouring rain again, a perfectly black sky, and waters swelling round the house: every now and then the dull thud of some falling building, and, from beneath, the perpetual crash of the furniture and floors breaking up in the lower rooms. Mother lay down dressed, most of the visitors and I walked the passages and watched the danger marks made above water on the staircase, and tried to comfort the unhappy family, in what, I fear, is their total ruin. It seemed as if daylight would never come, but at 6 a.m. the water was certainly an inch lower.

It was strange to return to daylight in our besieged fortress. There had been no time to save food, but there was one loaf and a little cheese, which were dealt out in equal rations, and we captured the drowned hens as the aviary broke up, and are going to boil one of them down in a tiny saucepan, the only cooking utensil saved. Everyone has to economise the water in their jugs (no chance of any other), and most of all their candles . . . . How we are ever to be delivered I cannot imagine. The railways to Leghorn, Spezia, and Florence must all be under water.

Dec. 14—It seems so long now since the inundation began and we were cut off from everyone: it is impossible to think of it as only three days.

Nothing can be more dreadful than the utter neglect of the new Government and of the municipality here. They were fully warned as to what would result if Pisa was not protected from the Arno, but they took no heed, and ever since the dikes broke they have given no help, never even consenting to have the main drains opened, which keeps us still flooded, refusing to publish lists of the drowned, and giving the large sums sent for distribution in charity into the hands of the students, who follow one another, giving indiscriminately to the same persons, whilst others are starving. On Saturday night there ceased to be any immediate alarm: the fear was that the Arno might break through at the Spina, which still stands, and which, being so much nearer, would be far more serious to us. The old bridge is destroyed. All through that night the Vicomte de Vauriol and the men of the house were obliged to watch on the balconies with loaded pistols, to defend their property floating in the garden from the large bands of robbers who came in boats to plunder, looking sufficiently alarming by the light of their great torches. The whole trousseau of the Vicomtesse is lost, and her maid has 4000 francs in her box, which can still be seen floating open . . . . But the waters are slowly going down. Many bodies have been found, but there are still many more beneath the mud. In the lower rooms of this house the mud is a yard deep, and most horrid in quality, and the smell of course dreadful. I spend much of my time at the window in hooking up various objects with a long iron bed-rod—bits of silver, teacups, even books—in a state of pulp.

Dec. 19—My bulletin is rather a melancholy one, for my poor mother has been constantly in bed since the inundation, and cannot now turn or move her left side at all. I have also been very ill myself, with no sleep for many days, and agonies of neuralgia from long exposure in the water. However, I get on tolerably, and have plenty to take off my thoughts from my own pain in

attending to Mother and doing what I can for the poor Limosins
. . . . In the quarter near this seventy bodies have been found in
the mud, and as the Government suppresses the number and
buries them all immediately, there are probably many more. Our
friends at Rome have been greatly alarmed about us.

Dec. 27—Mother has been up in a chair for a few hours daily,
but cannot yet be dressed. The weather is horrible, torrents of
rain night and day—quite ceaseless, and mingled with snow,
thunder, and lightning. It is so dark even at midday, that Mother
can see to do nothing, and I very little. The mud and smell would
prevent our going out if it were otherwise possible. It has indeed
been a dismal three months, which we have all three passed
entirely in the sickroom, except the four days I was away. . . .Still
the dear Mother says "we shall have time to recount our miseries
in heaven when they are over; let us only recount our mercies
now."

LETTER. *33 Via Gregoriana, Rome, Jan. 19 [1870].*—You will
have heard from others of our misfortunes at Pisa, of Mother's
terrible illness, and my wearing pains, and in the midst of all this
our awful floods, the Arno bursting its banks and overwhelming
the unhappy town with its mud-laden waves.

When the real danger to life once subsided and the poor
drowned people had been carried away to their graves, and the
water had changed into mud, it was a strange existence, and we
had still six weeks in the chilled house with its wet walls, and
an impossibility of going out or having a change. However, there
is a bright side to everything, and the utter isolation was not
unpleasant to me. I got through no end of writing work, having
plenty also to do in attending on my poor mother; and you know
how I can never sufficiently drink in the blessedness of her

sweet companionship, and how entirely the very fact of her existence makes sunshine in my life, wherever it is.

All the time of our incarceration I have employed in writing from the notes of our many Roman winters, which were saved in our luggage, and which have been our only material of employment. It seems as if "Walks in Rome" would some day grow into a book. Mother thinks it presumptuous, but I assure her that though of course it will be full of faults, no book would ever be printed if perfection were waited for. And I really do know much more about the subject than most people, though of course not half as much as I ought to know.

On Friday we had a terrible catastrophe. In the evening at the hotel the poor Mother fell violently on her head on the hard stone floor and was dreadfully hurt. For some hours the Mother was quite unconscious, and she can still see nothing, and I am afraid that it will be some days before any sight is restored, but all is going on well . . . .

Do you know, I am going to renounce the pomps and vanities of the world this winter and not "go out" at all. I have often found that it has rather fatigued Mother even to *hear* of my going out, and it is far easier to give a thing up altogether than partially. In the daytime I can see people.

LETTER. *Jan. 31*—We have had another anxious week, though once more all is going on well. On Monday the Mother was well enough to see visitors, but that night was in terrible suffering, and the next day had a slight paralytic seizure followed by long unconsciousness; but all was accounted for the next morning when we found the roof white with snow. She continued in great suffering till Friday, when the weather suddenly changed to *scirocco* and she at once rallied.

Rome, March 20 [1870].—Mother has had many sad nights, always worse than her days, without rest even for a minute. From four to ten p.m. the nervous spasms in the paralyzed arm are uncontrollable, and she can only endure them by holding tight to my arm or Lea's.

April 3—The Mother goes on slowly, but I hope has not had an unpleasant week. She never seems to find the time long, and always looks equally placid and happy. Physically she is certainly more comfortable now she is entirely in bed. Her chief trouble is from the returning vitality of the poor arm; the muscles knot all round it, and move on slowly by a quarter of an inch at a time, as the life advances; passing the shoulder was agony, and I dread the passing the elbow. Meantime, the rest of the arm is an independent being, acting by its independent muscular action, and is obliged to be constantly watched, as it will sometimes lay its heavy weight upon her chest, once clutched her by the throat and nearly strangled her, at others annoys her by stealing her pocket-handkerchiefs! She has been able to hear a psalm and some prayers read aloud every evening, and occupies herself with her own inexhaustible stores of mental hymns and verses incessantly.

April 10—My dear Mother is much the same.... The paralysed arm is quite useless, and has a separate and ungovernable individuality. This is why she can never be left alone. Its weight is like a log of lead, and sometimes it will throw itself upon her, when no efforts of her own can release her. Odd as it sounds, her only safe moments are when the obstreperous member is tied up by a long scarf to the post of Lea's bed opposite and cannot injure her. Mentally, she is always happy and quiet, and I believe that she never feels her altered life a burden. She repeats constantly her hymns and verses, for which her memory is wonderful, but she has no longer any power of attention to reading and to consecutive ideas. All names of persons and places she remembers perfectly.

Aug. 8 [1870].—Back at Holmhurst.—It is inexpressibly touching to me how Mother now seems to have an insight into my past feelings which she never had before, and to understand and sympathise with childish sufferings which she never perceived at the time, or from which she would have turned aside if she had perceived them. Today, after her dinner, she said most touchingly, watching till everyone went away and calling me close to her pillow—"I want to make my confession to you, darling. I often feel I have never been half tender enough to you. I feel it now, and I should like you to know it. You are such a comfort and blessing to me, dearest, and I thought perhaps I might die suddenly, and never have told you so. I cannot bear your being tied here, and yet I do not know how I could do without you, you are so great a blessing to me."

LETTER. *Sunday morning, Nov. 13 [1870].*—My darling Mother has entered into the real life.

Maria Hare
Nov. 22, 1798.
Nov. 13, 1870.

Until the
Daybreak.

XIII. My Solitary Life

AUGUSTUS ABOUT 1871.

MY MOTHER HAD LONG THOUGHT and latterly often said, that it was impossible I could long survive her: that when two lives were so closely entwined as ours, one could not go on alone. She had often even spoken of "when we die." . . . . It was partly owing to the strong impression in her mind that I could not survive her that my mother had failed to make the usual arrangements for my future provision. As she had never allowed any money to be placed in my name, I had—being no legal relation to her—to pay a stranger's duty of 10 per cent on all she possessed, and this amounted to a large sum, when extended to a duty on every picture, even every garden implement, &c. Not only this, but during her lifetime she had been induced by various members of the family to sign away a large portion of her fortune and in the intricate difficulties which arose I was assured that I should have nothing whatever left to live upon beyond £60 a year, and the rent of Holmhurst (fortunately secured) if it could be let. I was urged by the Stanleys to submit at once to my fate, and to sell Holmhurst; yet I could not help hoping for better days, which came with the publication of "Walks in Rome."

That was not the only trouble that pressed upon me at this time. It will be recollected that, in my sister's death bed will, she had bequeathed to me her claim to a portrait by Sir Joshua Reynolds. It was the very fact of this bequest which in 1871 made my poor Aunt Eleanor (Miss Paul) set up a counter claim to the picture, which was valued at £2000.

Five-and-twenty years before, the picture had been entrusted for a time to Sir John Paul, who unfortunately, from some small vanity, allowed it to be exhibited in his own name instead of that of the owner. But I never remember the time when it was not at Hurstmonceaux after 1845, when it was sent there. Uncle Julius bequeathed the portrait with all else he possessed, to his widow, who transferred the picture at once to my adopted mother.

But the strongest point against us was that somehow or other, *how* no one should explain, the picture had been allowed to remain for more than a year in the hands of Sir John Paul, and he had exhibited it. Though the impending trial about the picture question was very different from that at Guildford, the violent animosity displayed by my poor aunt made it most painful, in addition to the knowledge that she (who had inherited everything belonging to my father, mother, and sister, and had dispersed their property to the four winds of heaven, whilst I possessed *nothing* which had belonged to them) was now trying to seize property to which she could have no possible moral right, though English law is so uncertain that one never felt sure to the last whether the fact of the picture having been exhibited in Sir John Paul's name might not weigh fatally with both judge and jury.

For the whole month of November [1871] I was in London, expecting the trial every day, but it was not till the evening of the 6th of December that I heard it was to be the next morning in the law court off Westminister Hall. The court was crowded. My counsel, Mr Pollock, began his speech with a tremendous exordium. "Gentlemen of the jury, in a neighbouring court the world is sitting silent before the stupendous excitement of the Tichborne trial: gentlemen of the jury, *that* case pales into insignificance— pales into the most *utter* insignificance before the thrilling interest of the present occasion. On the narrow stage of this domestic drama, all the historic characters of the last century and all the literary personages of the present seem to be marching in a solemn procession." And he proceeded to tell the really romantic history of the picture—how Benjamin Franklin saw it painted, &c. I was called into the witness box and examined and cross-examined for an hour by Mr H. James. As long as I was in the region of my great-uncles and aunts, I was perfectly at home, and nothing in the cross-examination could the least confuse me. Then the counsel for the opposition said, "Mr Hare, on the 20th of April 1866 you wrote a letter, &c.: what was in that letter?" Of course I said I could not tell. "What do you think was in that letter?" So I said something, and of course it was exactly opposite to the fact.

As witnesses to the fact of the picture having been at the Rectory at the time of the marriage of my Uncle Julius, I had subpœnaed the whole surviving family of Mrs Julius Hare, who could witness to it better than anyone else, as they half-lived at Hurstmonceaux Rectory after their sister's marriage. Her two sisters, Mrs Powell and Mrs Plumptre, took to their beds, and remained there for a week to avoid the trial, but Dr Plumptre and Mr (F. D.) Maurice had to appear, and gave evidence as to the picture having been at Hurstmonceaux Rectory at the time of their sister's marriage in 1845, and having remained there afterwards during the whole of Julius Hare's life. Mr George Paul was then called, and took an oath that, till he went to America in 1852, the picture had remained at Sir John Paul's; but such is the inattention and ignorance of their business which I have always observed in lawyers, that this discrepancy passed absolutely unnoticed.

The trial continued for several hours, yet when the court adjourned for luncheon I believed all was going well. It was a terrible moment when afterwards Judge Mellor summed up dead against us. I had made admissions which I had really previously forgotten, but which were most dangerous, as to the difficulty which I then felt in establishing our claim to the picture. These weighed with Judge Mellor, and had the jury followed his lead, our cause would have been ruined. The jury demanded to retire, and were absent for some time. Miss Paul, who was in the area of the court, received the congratulations of all her friends, and I was so certain that my case was lost, that I went to the solicitor of Miss Paul and said that I had had the picture brought to Sir Lefevre's house in Spring Gardens and that I wished to give it up as soon as ever the verdict was declared, as if any injury happened to it afterwards, a claim might be made against me for £2000.

Then the jury came back and gave a verdict for . . . the defendant! It took everybody by surprise, and it was the most triumphant moment I ever remember. All the Pauls sank down as if they were shot. My friends flocked round me with congratulations.

The trial took the whole day, the court sitting longer than usual on account of it. The enemy immediately applied for a new trial, which caused us much anxiety, but this time I was not required to appear in person. The second trial took place on the 6th of January, 1872, before the Lord Chief Justice, Judge Blackburn, Judge Mellor, and Judge Hannen, and after a long discussion, was given triumphantly in my favour, Judge Mellor withdrawing his speech made at the former trial, and stating that, after reconsideration of all the facts, he rejoiced at the decision of the jury.

As both trials were gained by me, the enemy had nominally to pay all the costs, but still the expenses were most heavy. It was just at the time when I was poorest, when my adopted mother's will was still in abeyance. There were also other aspirants of the picture, in the shape of the creditors of my brother Francis, who claimed as representing my father. It was therefore thought wiser by all that I should assent to the portrait being sold, and be content to retain only in its place a beautiful copy which had been made for me by the kindness of my cousin Madeline Shaw-Lefevre. The portrait by Sir Joshua Reynolds was sold at Christie's in the summer of 1872 for £2200 and is now in the National Gallery of America at New York.[*]

In November [1872] I went to stay at Bretton near Wakefield, a great house in the Black Country, built by the famous "Madam Beaumont," who followed the example of her ancestors in making an enormous fortune by her skillful management of her lead-mines. It is recorded that when Mr Pitt was dining with her, and all her magnificent plate was set out, she exclaimed, with pardonable pride, "That is all the lead-mines," when he replied, "Oh, really, I thought it was silver," and would talk on, to her great annoyance, and never allow her a moment to explain.

Dec. 13 [1872].—I arrived at Hatfield in the dark.

* It is not clear what A.H. is referring to here. The Metropolitan Museum of Art in New York was founded in 1870 and opened at its present site in 1880.

Lady Salisbury showed us the house. In the drawing-room, over the chimney-piece, is a huge statue of James I of bronze. It is not fixed, but supported by its own weight. A ball was once given in that room. In the midst of the dancing someone observed that the bronze statue was slowly nodding its head, and gave alarm. The stampede was frightful. All the guests fled down the long gallery.

My book "Wanderings in Spain" came out in the autumn of 1872, and met with more enthusiastic reception from the public than anything I have ever written. Three editions were called for in six weeks, but there the sale ended. This was so for a long time. Then in about ten years several more editions were called for in rapid succession. One can never anticipate how it will be with books.

The unusual success which was attending my "Walks in Rome," and the many notes which I already possessed for a similar work in the neighbourhood, made me devote my time to "Days Near Rome" and in January [1873] I left England to make Rome a center from whence to revive my recollection of the towns I had already visited in the Campagna and its surrounding mountains, and to examine and sketch those I had not yet seen.

At one of my lectures at the Palace of Cæsars a curious thing happened. We were about forty in number, and I had taken my company all over the palace, explaining and telling the story of the different rooms as we went. Finally as was my habit, I assembled them on the slope towards the Forum for a sort of recapitulation and final discourse on all we had seen. I had observed a stranger who had attached himself to our party looking more and more angry every minute, but the "why" I could not understand. When I had concluded, the stranger stepped forward, and in a very loud voice he addressed the whole party—"Gentlemen and ladies, it is not my habit to push myself forward, and it is excessively painful to me to do it on the present occasion; but there are some things which no gentleman ought to pass unnoticed. All that this person has been telling you about the Palace of the Cæsars, he has had the effrontery to relate to you as if it were his own. You will be astounded, gentlemen and ladies, to hear that it is taken, word for word—word for word, without the slightest acknowledgement, from Mr Hare's 'Walks in Rome'!"

I went on to Florence, where I found two old friends of my childhood—Ann-Emilia and Kate Malcolm. I remember the latter telling me, on this occasion, of a friend of hers who was one day sitting at the end of her terrace at a retired watering-place, and heard a bride and bridegroom talking together beneath. "My dear," said the bridegroom, "I think it would not be unpleasant if a friend were to turn up this evening."—"My dear," retorted the bride, "I should be thankful to see even an enemy."

With the Malcolms I saw much of Sir James Lacaita. He was very full of convents and their abuses. He told me that he had personally known a nun who was forced into a convent to prevent her from marrying the man she loved; but he made a silken ladder, and, by bribing the gardener, got it fixed to her window. The nun escaped, but was in such a hurry to descend, that she slid down the cords, cut open both her hands, and bore the marks all of her life. Her lover was rich, had relays of horses, and they escaped to Sicily, were married at once, and had eleven children. Lacaita also told me:

"A beautiful girl of good family was left £6000 by her father, on condition that she did not enter a convent. To prevent her doing so, he ordained that the money should revert to her brother in case of her becoming a nun.

"The girl hated the very idea of a convent, but the brother made a compact with an abbess to give her a third of the girl's fortune if they could force her to take the veil. She resisted vigorously, though the brother's wife ill-treated her in every possible way, and she had no other home. She possessed a lover, who professed great devotion, but never would come to the point. At last the time came when the brother had arranged for her to go to the convent. Her treatment was such that she had no other course. Her lover came and pitied her. She implored him; she knelt at his feet; she stretched out her hands; she said, 'You know you can save me;' but he feared the priests, the Church, and her brother too much. As she knelt there, her sister-in-law opened the door. Then her horror at her position was so great, she at once declared that she would take the veil: she only wished the event hurried on.

"At last the day of the sacrifice arrived. Lacaita was present. The bride came in, in her wedding splendour, *fière,* * darting defiance at them all; but Lacaita said he never should forget the shriek she gave when all was over and the grille closed upon her.

"The remorse of the lover began at once: he never spoke to a woman for twenty years: then he—married!"

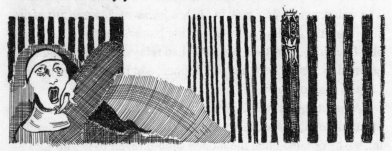

* Proud, haughty.

XIV. The Vampire of Croglin Grange and Other Stories

LADY WATERFORD.

I spent June 1873 in London. At luncheon at Lady Marion Alford's I met Mr Carlyle, who went off into one of his characteristic speeches. "That which the world torments me in most is the awful confusion of noise. It is the devil's own infernal din all the blessed day long, confounding God's warks and His creatures—a truly awfu' hell-like combination, and the warst of a' is a railway whistle, like the screech of ten thousand cats and ivery cat of them all as big as a cathedral."

Ford Castle, Oct. 18 [1873].—Lady Waterford talked to us of old Lady Balcarres the severe mother, who, when one of her little boys disobeyed her, ordered the servants to fling him into the pond in front of the house. He managed to scramble out again; she bade them throw him in a second time, and a second time he got out, and, when she ordered it a third time, he exclaimed in his broad Scotch accent, "Woman, wad ye droun yer ain son?"

Speaking of complexions—"My grandmother used to say," said

Mrs Fairholme, "that beauty 'went out' with open carriages. 'Why, you are just like men, my dear,' she said, 'with your brown necks, and your rough skins, and your red noses. In our days it was different; young ladies never walked, ate nothing but white meat, and never washed their faces. They covered their faces with powder, and then put cold cream on, and wiped it off with flannel: that was the way to have a good complexion.'"

"I think it was Henri III," said Lady Waterford, "who used to go to sleep with raw veal chops on his cheeks, and to cover his hands with pomade, and have them tied up to the top of the bed by silk cords, that they might be white in the morning."

Ruby Castle, Nov. 1 [1873].—The first morning I was here, as I was walking on the terraced platform of the castle with Lady Chesham, she talked of the silent Cavendishes, and said it was supposed to be the result of their ancestor's marriage with Rachel, Lady Russell's daughter; that after her father's death she had always been silent and sad, and that her descendants had been silent and sad ever since. Lord Carlisle and his brother were also silent. Once they travelled abroad together, and at an inn in Germany, slept in the same room, in which there was also a third bed with the curtains drawn round it. Two days after, one brother said to the other, "Did you see what was in that bed in our room the other night?" and the other answered, "Yes." This was all that passed, but they had both seen a dead body in the bed.

In Wilton Crescent I saw Mrs Leycester, who was just from Cheshire. She said:—

"A brother of Sir Philip Egerton had lately been given a living in

Devonshire, and went to take possession of it. He had not been long in his rectory before, coming one day into his study, he found an old lady seated there in an armchair by the fire. Knowing no old lady could really be there, and thinking the appearance must be the result of an indigestion, he summoned all his courage and boldly sat down upon the old lady, who disappeared. The next day he met the old lady in the passage, rushed up against her, and she vanished. But he met her a third time, and then, feeling that it could not always be indigestion, he wrote to his sister in Cheshire, begging her to call upon the Misses Athelstan, sisters of the clergyman who had held his living before, and say what he had seen. When they heard it, the Misses Athelstan looked inexpressibly distressed and said, 'That was our mother: we hoped she would be at rest.'"

About "ghost stories" I always recollect what Dr Johnson used to say—"The beginning and end of ghost stories is this, all argument is against them, all belief is for them."

The success of "Walks in Rome" and the great pleasure which I had derived from the preparation of my "Days Near Rome" made me undertake, in the spring of 1874, the more ambitious work of "Cities of Northern and Central Italy," in preparation for which I left England at the end of January.

JOURNAL. *Florence, May 4* —General von Raasloff is here, and says that a friend of his in going to China received endless commissions for things he was to bring home, but that only one of the people who gave them sent money for the things they wanted. On his return, this commission was the only one he had fulfilled. His disappointed friends upbraided him, and he said, "You see it was very unfortunate, but when we were nearing China, I spread out all my different commissions on the deck that I might examine them, and I put the money for each on the paper to which it belonged: and—it was very unfortunate, but my attention was called away for an instant, and behold a great gust of wind had come, and all those commissions which were not weighted by money had been blown far out to sea, and I never saw them again."

Mademoiselle von Raasloff told me that—

"Count Piper, an ancestor of the present Count Piper, was a very determined gambler. Being once at one of his desolate country estates, he was in perfect despair for someone to play with him, but he was alone. At last, in a fit of desperation, he said, 'If the Devil himself were to come to play with me, I should be grateful.' Soon a tremendous storm began to rage, during which a servant came in and said that a gentleman overtaken by night was travelling past, and implored shelter. Count Piper was quite enchanted, and a very gentlemanlike man was shown in. Supper was served, and then Count Piper proposed a game of cards, in which the stranger at once acquiesced. Count Piper won so enormously, that he felt quite ashamed, and at last he proposed their retiring. As they were leaving the room, the stranger said, 'I am very much concerned that I have not sufficient money with me to pay all my debt now; however, I shall beg you to take my ring as a guarantee, which is really of greater value than the money, and which has very peculiar properties, one of which is that as long as you wear it, all you possess is safe from fire.' The Count took the ring, and escorting the stranger to his room, wished him good-night. The next morning he sent to inquire after him: he was not there, his bed had not been slept in, and he never was heard of again. Count Piper wore the ring, but after some time, as it was very heavy and old-fashioned, he took it off and put it away. The next morning came the news that one of his finest farmhouses had been burnt down. And so it always is in that family. The descendants of Count Piper always have to wear the ring, and if ever they leave it off for a single day, one of their houses on one of their great estates is burnt."

In returning from Italy I spent the rest of the summer in London. June 24 [1874] I dined with Lord Ravensworth at Percy's Cross. Captain Fisher told me that —

When Mr Macpherson of Glen Truim was dying his wife had gone to rest in a room looking out over the park, and sat near the window. Suddenly she saw lights as of a carriage coming in at the distant lodge-gate, and calling to one of the servants, said, "Do go down; someone is coming who does not know of all this grief." But the servant remained near the house, they saw it was a hearse drawn by four horses and covered with figures. As it stopped at the porch door, the figures looked up at her, and their eyes glared with light; then they scrambled down and seemed to disappear into the house. Soon they reappeared and seemed to lift some heavy weight into the hearse, which then drove off at full speed, causing all the stones and gravel to fly up at the windows. Mrs Macpherson and the butler had not rallied from their horror and astonishment, when the nurse watching in the next room came in to tell her that the Colonel was dead.

Captain Fisher told us this really extraordinary story connected with his own family:—

"Fisher may sound a very plebeian name, but this family is of very ancient lineage, and for many hundreds of years they have possessed a very curious old place in Cumberland, which bears the weird name of Croglin Grange. The great characteristic of the house is that never at any period of its very long existence has it been more than one storey high, but it has a terrace from which large grounds sweep away towards the church in the hollow and a fine distant view.

"When, in lapse of years, the Fishers outgrew Croglin Grange in family and fortune, they were wise enough not to destroy the long-standing characteristic of the place by adding another storey to the house, but they went away to the south, to reside at Thorncombe near Guilford, and they let Croglin Grange.

"They were extremely fortunate in their tenants, two brothers and a sister. They heard their praises from all quarters. To their poorer neighbours they were all that is most kind and beneficent, and their neighbours of a higher class spoke of them as a most welcome addition to the little society of the neighbourhood. On their part the tenants were greatly delighted with their new residence. The arrangement of the house, which would have been a trial to many, was not so to them. In every respect Croglin Grange was exactly suited to them.

"The winter was spent most happily by the new inmates of Croglin Grange, who shared in all the little social pleasures of the district, and made themselves very popular. In the following summer, there was one day which was dreadfully, annihilatingly hot. The brothers lay under the trees with their books, for it was too hot for any active occupation. The sister sat in the verandah and worked, or tried to work, for, in the intense sultriness of that summer day, work was next to impossible. They dined early, and after dinner they still sat out in the verandah, enjoying the cool air which came with evening, and they watched the sun set, and the moon rise over the belt of trees which separated the grounds from the churchyard, seeing it mount the heavens till the whole lawn was bathed in silver light, across which the long shadows from the shrubbery fell as if embossed, so vivid and distinct were they.

"When they separated for the night, all retiring to their rooms on the ground floor (for, as I said, there was no upstairs in that house), the sister felt that the heat was still so great that she could not sleep, and having fastened her window, she did not close the shutters—in that very quiet place it was nót necessary—and, propped against the pillows, she still watched the wonderful, the marvellous beauty of that summer night. Gradually she became aware of two lights, two lights which flickered in and out in the belt of trees which separated the lawn from the churchyard, and as her gaze became fixed upon them, she saw then emerge, fixed in a dark substance, a definite ghastly something, which seemed every moment to become nearer, increasing in size and substance as it approached. Every now and then it was lost for a moment in the long shadows which stretched across the lawn from the trees, and then it emerged larger than ever, and still coming on—on. As she watched it, the most uncontrollable horror seized her. She longed to get away, but the door was close to the window and the door was locked on the inside, and while she was unlocking it, she must be for an instant nearer to it. She longed to scream, but her voice seemed paralysed, her tongue glued to the roof of her mouth.

"Suddenly, she never could explain why afterwards, the terrible object seemed to turn to one side, seemed to be going round the house, not to be coming to her at all, and immediately she jumped out of bed and rushed to the door, but as she was unlocking it, she heard scratch, scratch, scratch upon the window, and saw a hideous brown face with flaming eyes glaring in at her. She rushed back to the bed, but the creature continued to scratch, scratch, scratch upon the window. She felt a sort of mental comfort in the knowledge that the window was securely fastened on the inside. Suddenly the scratching sound ceased, and a kind of pecking took place. Then, in her agony, she became aware that the creature was unpicking the lead! The noise continued, and a diamond pane of glass fell into the room. Then a long bony finger of the creature came in and turned the handle of the window, and the window opened, and the creature came in; and it came across the room, and her terror was so great that she could not scream, and it came up to the bed, and it twisted its long bony fingers into her hair, and it dragged her head over the side of the bed, and— it bit her violently in the throat.

"As it bit her, her voice was released, and she screamed with all her might and main. Her brothers rushed out of their rooms, but the door was locked on the inside. A moment was lost while they got a poker and broke it open. Then the creature had already escaped through the window, and the sister, bleeding violently from a wound in the throat, was lying unconscious over the side of the bed. One brother pursued the creature, which fled before him through the moonlight with gigantic strides, and eventually seemed to disappear over the wall into the churchyard. Then he rejoined his brother by the sister's bedside. She was dreadfully hurt and her wound was a very definite one, but she was of strong disposition, not given either to romance or superstition, and when she came to herself she said, 'What has happened is most extraordinary and I am very much hurt. It seems inexplicable, but of course there is an explanation, and we must wait for it. It will turn out that a lunatic has escaped from some asylum and found his way here.' The wound healed and she appeared to get well, but the doctor who was sent for to her would not believe that she could bear so terrible a shock so easily, and insisted that she must have a change, mental and physical; so her brothers took her to Switzerland.

"Being a sensible girl, when she went abroad, she threw herself at once into the interests of the country she was in. She dried plants, she made sketches, she went up mountains, and as autumn came on, she was the person who urged that they should return to Croglin Grange. 'We have taken it,' she said, 'for seven years, and we have only been there one; and we shall always find it difficult to let a house which is only one storey high, so we had better return there; lunatics do not escape every day.' As she urged it, her brothers wished nothing better, and the family returned to Cumberland. From there being no upstairs in the house, it was impossible to make any great change in their arrangements. The sister occupied the same room, but it is unnecessary to say she always closed her shutters, which, however, as in many old houses, always left one top pane of the window uncovered. The brothers moved, and occupied a room together exactly opposite that of their sister, and they always kept loaded pistols in their room.

"The winter passed most peacefully and happily. In the following March the sister was suddenly awakened by a sound she remembered only too well—scratch, scratch, scratch upon the window, and looking up, she saw, climbed up to the topmost pane of the window, the same hideous brown shrivelled face, with glaring eyes, looking in at her. This time she screamed as loud as she could. Her brothers rushed out of their room with pistols, and out of the front door. The creature was already scudding away across the lawn. One of the brothers fired and hit it in the leg, but still with the other leg it continued to make way, scrambled over the wall into the churchyard, and seemed to disappear into a vault which belonged to a family long extinct.

"The next day the brothers summoned all the tenants of Croglin Grange, and in their presence the vault was opened.. A horrible scene revealed itself. The vault was full of coffins; they had been broken open, and their contents, horribly mangled and distorted, were scattered over the floor. One coffin alone remained intact. Of that the lid had been lifted, but still lay loose upon the coffin. They raised it, and there, brown, withered, shrivelled, mummified, but quite entire, was the same hideous figure which had looked in at the windows of Croglin Grange, with the marks of a recent pistol-shot in the leg; and they did—the only thing that can lay a vampire. They burnt it."

JOURNAL. *Highcliffe, June 30 [1874].*—It is delightful to be here again . . . Lady Waterford talked of a visit she had had at Ford from Mr Wayte, the new Rector of Norham, who told her that a few nights before, his curate, Mr Simon, had been obliged to go to fetch some papers out of the vestry at night. When he opened the church door, the moonlight was streaming in at the west window, and the middle of the nave was in bright light, but the side aisles were dark. He walked briskly down the middle of the church to the vestry, and, as he went, was aware that a figure dressed in white was sitting motionless in the corner of one of the pews in the aisle. He did not stay, but went into the vestry to get his papers, and, as he returned, he saw that the figure was still in the same place. Much agitated, he did not go up to it, but hurried home, and waited for daylight, when he returned at once to the church. The figure was still there, and did not move as he approached. When he uncovered its face, he saw that it was a dead body. The body had been found in the Tweed the day before, and the finders had not known what to do with it, so they had wrapped it in a sheet, and set it up in the church.

JOURNAL. *Powderham Castle, Oct. 4*—A week here has been most delightful. The wife of a neighbouring clergyman was very seriously ill of a strange and mysterious complaint. It was observed that her worst attacks always came on after her husband had administered the Sacrament to her. Mr O., who was attending her, studied her case very much, and came to the conclusion that, if the peculiar symptoms she exhibited came from unnatural causes, they could only be produced by a single and very rare drug. Forthwith he set himself to find out if there was any place in the neighbourhood where that drug was sold, and at last he did find it. He asked at the place if they had sold any of it. "Oh, yes; to the parson at——; he bought some yesterday." As Mr O. was going home he met the clergyman himself. He stopped him and said, "I have just found out that yesterday you bought some drugs at M.; now if Mrs X. is worse tomorrow, I shall know what has caused it." That afternoon the clergyman went down to the shore to bathe, and he never returned. He was known to be a splendid swimmer, and he was seen to swim far, far out to sea.

Stone Hall, Plymouth, Oct. 13—Another pleasant family home! I came on Monday to the George Edgecumbes. The late Lord Mount Edgecumbe lived here for many years, quite helpless from rheumatic gout. It was his mother who was buried alive and lived for many years afterwards. It was known that she had been put into her coffin with a very valuable ring upon her finger, and the sexton went in after the funeral, when the coffin was put into the vault, to get it off. He opened the coffin, but the ring was hard to move and he had to rub the dead finger up and down. This brought Lady Mount Edgecumbe to life, and she sat up. The sexton fled, leaving the doors of the vault and church open. Lady Mount Edgecumbe walked home in her shroud, and appeared in front of the windows. Those within thought it was a ghost. Then she walked in at the front door. When she saw her husband, she fainted away in his arms. This gave her family time to decide what should be done, and they settled to persuade her it had been a terrible delirium. When she recovered from her faint, she was in her own bed, and she ever believed it had been a dream.

On Monday we went in the Admiral's steam-pinnace to Cotohele. Up steep woods we walked to Cotohele, an unaltered old house, with gate-tower, courtyard, chapel, armour-hung hall and dark tapestried bedrooms. Within the entrance are ever-fresh stains like blood, which you can mop up with blotting paper. Sir Richard Edgecumbe went out, bidding the porter, on peril of his life, to let no one in without a password. To prove his obedience, he came back himself and demanded entrance. The porter, recognizing his master's voice, let him in, upon which Sir Richard cleft open his skull with his battle-axe as he entered. The so-called blood forms a dark pool, and looks as if it had been spilt yesterday. Some say it is really a fungus which only grows where blood has been shed, and that the same existed on the site of the scaffold on Tower Hill.

Abbots Kerswell, Oct. 26—I have been very glad to see this place—my cousin Marcus Hare's home. Two more days at Powderham. Lady Waterford said, "Now I must tell you a story.

IN THE WALKS, HOLMHURST.

Somers came to Highcliffe this year. He was suffering so much from a piece of the railroad that had got into his eye and he was in great pain but he was just as pleasant as ever. The next day he insisted on going off to Lymington to see Lord Warwick, who was there and who had been ill; and it was an immense drive, and when he came back, he did not come down, and Pattinson said, 'Lord Somers is come back, but he is suffering so much pain from his eye that he will not be able to have any dinner.' So I went up to sit with him. He was suffering great pain, and I wanted him not to talk, but he said, 'Oh no; I have got a story quite on my mind and I must tell it you.' And he said that when he got to Lymington, he found Lord Warwick ill in bed, and he said, 'I am so glad to see you, for I want to tell you such an odd thing that has happened to me. Last night I was in bed and the room was quite dark (this old-fashioned room of the inn at Lymington which you now see). Suddenly at the foot of the bed there appeared a great light, and in the middle of the light the figure of Death just as it is seen in the Dance of Death and other old pictures—a ghastly skeleton with a scythe and a dart; and Death balanced the dart, and it flew past me, just above my shoulder, close to my head, and it seemed to go into the wall; and then the light went out and the figure vanished. I was as wide awake then as I am now, for I pinched myself hard to see, and I lay awake for a long time, but at last I fell asleep. When my servant came to call me in the morning, he had a very scared expression of face, and he said, "A dreadful thing has happened in the night, and the whole household of the inn is in the greatest confusion and grief, for the landlady's daughter, who slept in the next room, and the head of whose bed is against the wall against which your head now rests, has been found dead in her bed." ' "

Nov. 9—Lady Waterford, Miss Lindsay, and I walked to distant plantations to see some strange grass, which, from being surrounded by water at times, had been matted together so that it formed a thick trunk, and branched out at the top like a palmtree, with the oddest effect. Lady Waterford talked of an old woman she knew, whose husband was very ill, dying in fact. One day when she went to see him, she found his wife busy baking cakes, and she—the old woman—said that as he was dying she was getting them ready for his funeral. Going again some days later,

Lady Waterford found the man still alive, and she could not resist saying to the woman that she thought her cakes must be getting rather stale. "Yes, that they are," said the wife; "some folks are so inconsiderate."

Hutton, Yorkshire, Nov. 30 [1874].—I came here yesterday, arriving in the dark. There is a Mr Stover here who is amusing. An uncle of his lives in a haunted house at Biddick. One day when he came in from shooting, he hung his hat on a pole-screen, and sat down by the fire to read his newspaper. Presently, looking over his paper, he saw, to his amazement, his hat on the top of the screen nodding at him. He thought he must be dreaming, but watched, and it certainly nodded again. He got up and walked round it, when it seemed still. Then he sat down again and watched it, and it nodded again, and not only that, but the screen itself seemed to be moving bodily towards him. He watched it, and it certainly crossed part of the pattern of the carpet: of this there could be no doubt. Then he could bear it no longer, and he rushed at the screen and knocked it over. Underneath was his tame tortoise.

Ripley Castle, Dec. 12 [1874].—I found here Count and Countess Bathyany, people I am very glad to see . . . . A story which Countess Bethyany told from personal knowledge was that of Sir Samuel Romilly.

Lord Grey and his son-in-law, Sir Charles Wood, were walking on the ramparts of Carlisle. The rampart is there still. It is very narrow, and there is only one exit; so if you walk there, you must return as you came. While they were walking, a man passed them, returned, passed them again, and then disappeared in front of them over the parapet, where there was really no means of exit. There was a red scarf round his throat. "How very extraordinary! And how exactly like Sir Samuel Romilly!" they both exclaimed. At that moment Sir Samuel Romilly had cut his throat in a distant part of England.

We have tea in the evening in the oak room in the tower, where Miss Ingilby has often had much to say that is interesting, especially this story.

A regiment was lately passing through Derbyshire on its way to fresh quarters in the North. The Colonel, as they stayed for the night in one of the country towns, was invited to dine at a country-house in the neighbourhood, and to bring any one he liked with him. Consequently he took with him a young ensign for whom he had taken a great fancy. They arrived and it was a large party, but the lady of the house did not appear till just as they were going in to dinner, and when she appeared, was so strangely *distraite* and preoccupied that she scarcely attended to anything that was said to her. At dinner, the Colonel observed that his young companion scarcely ever took his eyes off the lady of the house, staring at her in a way which seemed at once rude and unaccountable. It made him observe the lady herself, and he saw that she scarcely seemed to attend to anything said by her neighbours on either side of her, but rather seemed, in a manner quite unaccountable, to be listening to someone or something behind her. As soon as dinner was over, the young ensign came to the Colonel and said, "Oh, do take me away: I entreat you to take me away from this place." The Colonel said, "Indeed your conduct is so very extraordinary and unpleasant, that I quite agree with you that the best thing we can do is to go away;" and he made the excuse of his young friend being ill, and ordered their carriage. When they had driven some distance the Colonel asked the ensign for an explanation of his conduct. He said that he could not help it: during the whole of dinner he had seen a terrible black shadowy figure standing behind the chair of the lady of the house, and it had seemed to whisper to her, and she to listen to it. He had scarcely told this, when a man on horseback rode rapidly past the carriage, and the Colonel, recognising one of the servants of the house they had just left, called out to know if anything was the matter. "Oh, don't stop me, sir," he shouted; "I am going for the doctor: my lady has just cut her throat."

Dec. 27—I have been staying at Brighton with old Mrs Aïdé, who looks like Cinderella's godmother or some other good old fairy. I heard this curious story:—

The Princess Dolgorouki had been a great heiress and was a person of great wealth and importance. One day she was driving through a village near S. Petersburg, when she heard the clear glorious voice of a young girl ringing through the upper air from a high window of one of the poor houses by the wayside. So exquisitely beautiful was the voice, that the Princess stopped her carriage to listen to it, and, when it ceased, the Princess sent into the house to inquire who the singer had been. "Oh," they said, "it is one of your own serfs: it is the girl Anita;" and they brought the singer out, a sweet, simple, modest-looking girl of sixteen, and at the bidding of the Princess she sang again, quite simply, without any shyness, in the road by the side of the carriage. The Princess was greatly captivated by her, and finding that she was educated beyond most of those in her condition of life, and being at that time in want of a reader in her palace at S. Petersburg, she took her to live with her, and Anita occupied in her house a sort of intermediate position, arranging the flowers, and reading when she was wanted. Gradually the Princess became very fond of her, and gave her masters, under whom she made such astonishing progress, that she became quite a well-educated young lady, while her glorious voice formed the great attraction to all parties at the Dolgorouki Palace.

The Princess Dolgorouki never foresaw what actually happened, that when her son returned from "the grand tour," which young men made then, and found a very beautiful, interesting girl domesticated with his mother, he would fall in love with her. When she saw that it was so, she said to her son that she had a great regard for the girl and could not have her affections tampered with, so that he had better go away again. The young prince answered that he had no idea whatever of tampering with the girl's affections, that he loved her and believed that she loved him, and that he meant to marry her.

On hearing this the fury of the Princess knew no bounds. She tried to reason with her son, and when she found him perfectly impracticable, she expelled him from her house and got him sent to France. She also sent for the parents of Anita, and told them that they must look out at once for a suitable person for her to marry, for that she must be married before Prince Dolgorouki returned. She said that she had no complaint to make of the girl, and that she would help her to make a good marriage by giving her a very handsome dowry; all that she required was that she should be married at once. Before leaving, however, Prince Dolgorouki had found means to be alone for a few minutes with Anita, and had said to her, "I know my mother well, and I know that as soon as I am gone she will try to insist upon your marriage. She will not consider you, and will sacrifice you to the fulfilment of her own will. Have faith, however, in me, hold out, and believe that, however impossible it may seem, I shall be able at the last moment to save you."

The bridegroom whom Anita's father found was a certain Alexis Alexandrovitch, a farmer near their village and a person in a considerably higher position than their own. He was rich, he was much esteemed, he was greatly in love with Anita, but he was vulgar, he was hideous, he was almost always drunk, and Anita hated him. He came to her father's house and proposed. She refused him, but he persisted in persecuting her with his attentions, and her own family tried to force her consent by ill-treatment, half-starved her, cut her off from all communication with others and from all her usual employments, and shut her up in a room at the top of the house.

At last, when the girl's position was becoming quite untenable and her courage was beginning to give way, Prince Dolgorouki contrived to get a note conveyed to her. He said, "I know all you are suffering; it is impossible that you can go on like this. Pretend to accede to their wishes. Accept Alexis Alexandrovitch, but believe that I will save you at the last moment."

So Anita said to her father and mother that she gave in to their wishes, that she would marry Alexis Alexandrovitch. And the wedding day was fixed and the wedding feast was prepared. And the old Princess Dolgorouki gave not only a very handsome dowry, but a very splendid set of peasant's jewellery to the bride. She did not intend to be present at the ceremony herself, but she would send her major-domo to represent her.

The wedding day arrived, and the bride went with her family to the church, which was darkened, with candles burning everywhere. And Alexis Alexandrovitch also arrived, rather more drunk than usual. The church was thronged with people from end to end, for the place was within a drive of S. Petersburg, and it was fine weather, and hundreds of persons who remembered Anita and had admired her wonderful voice at the Dolgorouki Palace drove out to see her married. According to the custom of the Greek Church, the register was brought to be signed before the ceremony. He signed his name "Alexis Alexandrovitch," and she signed her name "Anita." And the sermon began, and the crowd pressed thicker and thicker round the altar, and there was a constant struggle to see. And the service went on, and the crowd pressed more closely still, and somehow in the press the person who stood next to Anita was not Alexis Alexandrovitch, and the service went on, and Anita was married, and then the crowd opened to let the bridal pair pass through, and Anita walked rapidly down the church on the arm of her bridegroom, and it was not Alexis Alexandrovitch, and it was Prince Dolgorouki. And a carriage and four was waiting at the church door, and the bridal pair leapt into it and were whirled rapidly away.

The old Princess Dolgorouki sent at once to stop them at the frontier, but the flight had been so well arranged that she was too late. Then she swore (having everything in her own power) that she would cut off her son without a penny, and that she would never see him again. Happy in each other's love, however, the young Prince and Princess Dolgorouki lived at Paris, where, though they were poor, Anita's wonderful voice could always keep them from want. There, their two children were born. Four years elapsed, and they heard nothing from their Russian home. Then the family lawyer in S. Petersburg wrote to say that the old Princess Dolgorouki was dead. Whether she had repented of disinheriting her son and had destroyed her will before her death, or whether she had put off making her unjust will till it was too late, no one ever knew. The will of disinheritance was never found, and her son was the heir of all his mother's vast estates.

The young couple set out with their children for Russia to take possession, but it was in the depth of winter, the Prince was very delicate, and the change to the fierce cold of the north made him very ill, and at some place on the frontier—Wilna, I think—he died. The unhappy widow continued her journey with her children to S. Petersburg, but when she arrived, the heir-at-law had taken possession of everything. "But I am here; I am the Princess Dolgorouki," she said. "No," was the answer; "you have been residing for four years with Prince Dolgorouki, but the person you married was Alexis Alexandrovitch, and the register in which you both signed your names before your marriage exists to prove it." A great lawsuit ensued, in which the young widow lost almost all the money she had, and eventually she lost her lawsuit too, and retired in great penury to Warsaw, where she maintained herself and her children by singing and giving music lessons.

But at Warsaw, as at Paris, her beauty and gentleness, and the patience with which she bore her misfortunes, made her a general favourite. Amongst those who became devoted to her was a young lawyer, who examined into the evidence of the trial which had taken place, and then, going to her, urged her to try again. She resisted, saying that the case was hopelessly lost, and besides, that she was too poor to reopen it. The lawyer said, "If you regain the vast Dolgorouki inheritance, you can pay me something: it will be a drop in the ocean to you; but if the lawsuit fails I shall expect no payment." So she let him try.

Now the lawyer knew that there was no use in contending against the register, but he also felt that as—according to his view—

in the eyes of God his client had been Princess Dolgorouki, there was no harm in tampering with that register if it was possible. It was no use, however, to alter it, as hundreds of witnesses existed who had seen the register as it was, and who knew that it contained the name of Alexis Alexandrovitch as the husband of Anita, for the trial had drawn attention to it from all quarters. It was also most difficult to see the register at all, because it was now most carefully guarded. But at last there came a time when the young lawyer was not only able to see the register, but when for three minutes he was left alone with it. And he took advantage of those three minutes to do what?

He scratched out the name, or part of the name of Alexis Alexandrovitch, and he wrote the name of Alexis Alexandrovitch over again.

Then when people came and said, "But here is the register—here is the name of Alexis Alexandrovitch," he said, "Yes, there is certainly the name of Alexis Alexandrovitch, but if you examine, you will find that it is written over something else which has been scratched out."

And the case was tried again, and the young widow was reinstated in the Dolgorouki property, and she was the grandmother of the present Prince Dolgorouki.

Heckfield Place, Aug. 13 [1875].—I went with Lord Selborne and Miss Palmer to Strathfieldsaye. The Duke of Wellington, dressed like a poor pensioner, received us in his uncomfortable room, where Lord Selborne, who has a numismatical mania, was glad to stay for two hours examining coins. Meanwhile the Duke, finding we were really interested, took Miss Palmer and me upstairs, and showed us all his relics. It was touching to see the old man, who for the greater part of his lifetime existed in un-loving awe of a father he had always feared and been little no-ticed by, now, in the evening of life, treasuring up every rem-iniscence of him and considering every memorial as sacred.

One day the great Duke was much surprised by receiving a letter which read as follows:—"Being in the neighbourhood, I venture to ask permission to see some of your Grace's best breeches. C. London." He answered to the Bishop of London that he had great pleasure in assenting to his request, though he must confess it had given him very considerable surprise. London House was thrown into confusion. The note was from Loudon, the great gardener, and "breeches" should have been read "beeches."

Oct. 4 [1875].—A most charming visit to Lady Mary Egerton at Mountfield Court. Mr Charles Newton of the British Musem is here, who is always charming, with ripple of pleasantest anecdote and kindly, genial manners. He says:—

General Skenk had a monkey and a parrot, which hated each other. One day he imprudently went out, leaving them alone to-gether in a room. When he came back, the monkey was sitting in his armchair, bleeding profusely, and looking very sheepish and ashamed of himself, while the floor was covered with feathers. The parrot had disappeared, but while General Skenk was looking for any further remains of it, out from under a sofa walked a perfectly naked bird, and said, "What a hell of a time we've had!"

Mr Newton was at a spiritual seance. An old man of the party was told that the spirit manifested was his wife, upon which he said:—

"Is that you, 'Arriet?"

"Yes, it's me."

"Are you 'appy, 'Arriet?"
"Yes, very 'appy."
"'Appier than you were with me, 'Arriet?"
"Yes, much 'appier."
"Where are you, 'Arriet?"
"In 'ell."

XV. London Walks and Society

My three thick volumes of the "Cities of Northern and Central Italy" appeared in the autumn of 1875, a very large edition (3000 copies) being printed at once. They were immediately the subject of a violent attack from Mr Murray, who saw in them rivals to his well-known red Handbooks. A most virulent and abusive article appeared upon my work in the *Athenaeum*, accusing me, amongst other things, of having copied from Murray's Handbooks without acknowledgment, and quoting, as proof, passages relating to Verona in both books, which have the same singular mistake. It was certainly a curious accident which made me receive the proof-sheets of Verona when away from home on a visit at Tunbridge Wells, where the only book of reference accessible was Murray's "Handbook of Northern Italy," which I found in the house, so that the mistakes in my account of Verona *were* actually copied from Murray's Handbook, to which I was indebted for nothing else whatever, as I had for years found Murray's Handbooks so inefficient, that I had never bought or made any use of them.

Mr Murray further took legal proceedings against me, because in one of my volumes I had mentioned that the Italian Lakes were included in his Swiss rather than his Italian Handbooks: this having been altered in recent years, but having been the case in the only volume of his Handbooks I had ever possessed. On all occasions, any little literary success I met with excited bitter animosity from Mr Murray.

Another curious attack was made upon me by the eccentric Mr Freeman, the historian of the Norman Conquest. He had published in the *Saturday Review* a series of short articles on the Italian cities, which I always felt had never received the attention they deserved owing to the unpopularity of the dogmatic and verbose style in which they were written. Therefore, really with the idea of doing Mr Freeman a good turn, I had rather gone out of my way to introduce extracts from his articles where I could, that notice might thus be attracted to them—an attention for which I had already been thanked by other little-read authors, as, whatever may be the many faults of my books, they have always had a large circulation. But in the case of Mr Freeman, knowing the singular character of the man, I begged a common friend to write to his daughter to mention my intention and ask her, if her father had no objection to my quoting from his articles, to send me a list of them (as they were unsigned), in order that I might not confuse them with those of another person. By return of post, I received, without comment from Miss Freeman, a list of her father's articles, and I naturally considered this as equivalent to his full permission to quote from them. I was therefore greatly surprised, when Mr Freeman's articles appeared soon afterwards in a small volume, to find it introduced with a preface the whole object of which was, in the most violent manner, to accuse me of theft. I immediately published a full statement of the circumstances under which I had quoted from Mr Freeman in sixteen different newspapers. Mr Freeman answered in the *Times* by repeating his accusation, and in the *Guardian* he added, "Though Mr Hare's conduct was barefaced and wholesale robbery, I shall take no further notice of him till he has stolen something else."

I need scarcely say that, as soon as possible thereafter, I eliminated all reference to Mr Freeman, and all quotations from his works, from my books.

JOURNAL. *Charlton Hall, June 17 [1876].*—Andover told of an American who never was on time for anything in his life, was unpunctual for everything systematically. One day, in a very out-of-the-way place, he fell into a cataleptic state, and was supposed to be dead. According to the rapidity of American movement, instead of bringing the undertaker to him, they took him to the undertaker, who fitted him with a coffin and left him, laying the coffin lid loosely on the outside of it. In the middle of the night he awoke from his trance, pushed off the lid, and finding himself in a place alone surrounded by a quantity of coffins, he jumped up and pushed off the lid of the coffin nearest to him. He found nothing. He tried another: nothing. "Good God!" he cried, "I've been late all my life, and now I'm late for the resurrection!"

July 14 [1876]. —Luncheon at Mrs Lowe's. One day when Mrs Lowe was inveighing against the absurdity of the marriage service—of the bridegroom's statement, "With all my worldly goods I thee endow," even when he possessed nothing and it was just the other way, and when she was saying, "Now when I married

Mr Lowe, he had nothing whatever but his brains" —a deep voice from the end of the room growled out, "Well, my love, I certainly did not endow you with those."

"Why contend against your natural advantages?" said Mr Lowe one day to a deaf friend who was holding up an ear-trumpet to listen to a bore.

Holmhurst, Sept. 1 [1876]. —I had rather dreaded the *tête-à-tête* journey with the Duchess today, and truly it was a long one. At Ampthill she told me how she was going into London to meet Admiral Inglefield, who was going to help her to "pick a child out of the gutter." "That child," she said, "will some day be Earl Powlett. Lord Powlett took a wager that he would run away with the lady love of one of his brother officers, and he did run away with her; but she made it a condition that he should marry her before a Registrar, which he believed was illegal, but it was not, and they were really married. Her only child, a boy, was brought up in the gutter. His name is Hinton, and he is present-able, which his wife is not, for she is a figurante at the opera; but she gets more than the other danseuses, because she has the courage to stand unsupported on a tight-rope, which the others have not. Powlett offered his son £400 if he would go away from England and never come back again, but he refused, so he would only give him £100. He lives by acting at small theatres, but sometimes he does not live, but starves. He had four children, but one is dead. It is the eldest I mean to take away and place with a clergyman and his wife, that he may learn something of being a gentleman. I shall undertake him for three years, then I shall see what he is likely to be fit for. If I live so long, I can settle it; if not, I must leave means for it. Facts are stranger than fiction."

Lord Hinton afterwards used to play a barrel-organ in the

streets of London, with an inscription over it in large letters, "I am the only Viscount Hinton." He would play it for hours opposite the windows of Lord Powlett in Berkeley Square.

Sarsden House, Chipping Norton, Oct. 4—I came here on Monday. On Tuesday afternoon I drove to Heythorp. In the evening Lord Denbigh told us: —

Dr Playfair, physician at Florence, went to the garden of a villa to see some friends of his. Sitting on a seat in the garden, he saw two ladies he knew; between them was a third lady dressed in grey, of a very peculiar appearance. Walking round the seat, Dr Playfair found it very difficult to see her features. In a farther part of the garden he met another man he knew. He stayed behind the seat and asked his friend to walk round and see if he could make out who the odd-looking lady was. When he came back, he said, "Of course I could not make her out, because when I came in front of her, her face was turned towards you." Dr Playfair then walked up to the ladies, and as he did so, the central figure disappeared. The others expressed surprise that Dr Playfair, having seen them, had not joined them sooner. He asked who the lady was who had been sitting between them. They assured him that there had never been any such person.

The next morning, Dr Playfair went early to see the old gardener of the villa, and asked him if there was any tradition about the place. He said, "Yes, there is a story of a lady dressed in grey, who appears once in every twenty-five years, and the singular part of it is that she has no face." Dr Playfair asked when she had appeared last. "Well, I remember perfectly; it was twenty-five years ago, and the time is about coming round for her to appear again."

A delightful old Mrs Stewart has arrived from Scotland. I sat by her at dinner. She described an interview Mrs Grote had with Madame George Sand. She said to Madame Sand that it was a pity she did not employ her great powers for the leavening and mellowing of mankind, as Miss Austen had done. "*Madame,*" said Madame Sand; "*je ne suis pas philosophe, je ne suis pas moraliste, et je suis romancière.*"*

Nov. 21 [1876]. —We have been out to New Hailes, the old Dalrymple house, now inhabited by Lord Shand. The characteristic of the house is its library, which, however, is rather useless, as the bookcases are seventeen feet high, and there is no ladder to reach the upper shelves by.

Osterly, Dec. 16 [1876]. —I came here about tea-time to what Horace Walpole calls "the Palace of Palaces." It is a magnificent house. *Dec. 17* —Mr Spencer rails at everything supernatural, so we spoke of the story in his own family, and he told us the *facts* of the Lyttleton ghost, declaring that everything added to them about altering the clock, &c., was absolutely fictitious.

Thomas Lord Lyttleton was at Peel House, near Epsom, when a woman with whom he had lived seemed to appear to him. He spoke of it to some friends and said that the spirit had said he should die in three days, and that he believed he should certainly do so. Nevertheless, on the following day he went up to London, and made one of his most brilliant speeches, for he was a really great speaker—in the House of Lords. He was not well at the time. On the third evening, his servant, after the custom of that time, was in his room assisting him to undress. When the clock struck twelve, Lord Lyttleton counted the strokes, and when it came to the last, exclaimed, "I have cheated the ghost," and fell down dead: he must have had something the matter with his heart.

6 Bury Street, Feb.13 [1877]. —Last night I dined with the

---

* "I am not a philosopher, I am not a moralist and I am a novelist."

Haygarths. The Dowager Lady Spencer was there, who gave an amusing account of her Irish experiences, when her stepson was Lord Lieutenant. One day he was hunting, and had just leapt a hedge into a lane, when he was aware that a funeral was coming up. He thought it might hurt the feelings of the mourners if he passed them hunting, so he hid himself. But as the funeral came by the hounds appeared, and instantly, setting the coffin down in the road, mourners, pall-bearers and all started in hot pursuit, and Lord Spencer found himself left alone with the body.

Feb.14 [1877].—Luncheon at Miss Davenport Bromley's to meet Mr Portal. Mr Portal described his feeling of desolation when he first arrived in England—"not one soul he knew amongst all these millions;" that the next day a lady asked him to conduct her and her child to a pantomime. He consented, without understanding that a pantomime meant Drury Lane Theatre and his horror was intense when he "found himself, a clergyman of forty years' standing" in such a place. This however, was nothing to what he felt "when a troop of half-naked women rushed in and began to throw up their legs into the air;" he "could have sunk into the ground for shame . . . . Was not the mother of our Lord a woman? Was not my mother a woman? Is not my wife a woman? Are not my daughters women? And what are these?"

Mr Knowles, the ex-editor of the *Contemporary Review*, who was at luncheon, said that he had taken Alfred Tennyson to see a ballet with just the same effect. When the ballet-girls trooped in wearing "*une robe qui ne commence qu'à peine, et qui finit tout de suite*,"[*] Tennyson had rushed at once out of the box, walked up and down in an agony over the degradation of the nineteenth century, and nothing could induce him to go in again.

Feb. 28 [1877].—A charming visit to old Lord John Thynne,

---

[*] "A frock which hardly begins and which finishes at once."

then to Mrs Duncan Stewart, who was sitting almost on the ground, covered with an eiderdown. She told how, when her child was dying—she knew it must die—the clergyman came, and used to kneel by the table and pray that resignation might be given to the mother to bear the parting, and resignation to the child to die; and how she listened and prayed too; and yet, at the end, she could not feel it. She did not, and—though she knew it was impossible—she could not but break in with, "Yet, O Lord, yet *restore* her."

"Do you know," said Mrs Stewart, "that till I was thirty, I had never seen death—never seen it even in a poor person; then I saw it in my own child, and I may truly say that then death entered the world for me as truly as it did for Eve, and it never left me afterwards—*never*. If one of my children had an ache afterwards, I thought it was going to die; if I awoke in the night and looked at my husband in his sleep, I thought—'He will look like that when he is dead.'

"Do not think that I murmur, but life *is* very trying when one knows so little of the beyond. The clergyman's wife has just been, and she said, 'But you must believe; you must believe Scripture literally; you must believe all it says to the letter.' But I cannot believe it literally: one can only use the faith one has, I have not the faith which moves mountains. I have prayed that the mountains might move, with all the faith that was in me—*all*; but the mountains did not move. No, I cannot pray with the faith which is not granted me.

"I think that I believe all the promises of Scripture; yet when I think of Death, I hesitate to wish to leave the certainty here for what is—yes, must be—the uncertainty beyond. Yet lately, when I was so ill, when I continued to go down and down into the very depths, I felt I had got so far—so very far, it would be difficult to travel all that way again—'Oh let me go through the gates now.' And then the comforting thought came that perhaps after all it might *not* be the will of God that I should travel the *same* way again, and that when he leads me up to the gates for the last time, it might be His will to lead me by some other, by some quite different way."

XVI. VISITS AND TALES

THE NAYLOR LANDING, HOLMHURST.

JOURNAL. *Holmhurst, April 6 [1877].* — At Llanover, almost the
only other guest was Miss Geraldine Jewsbury, the intimate and
faithful friend of Mrs Carlyle. I found it difficult to trace in the
ancient spinster the gifted brilliancy I had heard described,
though of her strong will there was abundant evidence. During an
illness of Mrs Carlyle there was comic evidence of this. Miss
Jewsbury had unlimited faith in black currant jelly for a cold.
Now Mrs Carlyle's throat was very bad, and Miss Jewsbury took
some of her jelly to her. "But I will not take it; I will not take it,
Geraldine," said Mrs Carlyle, with her strong inflexion on the
"ine." So Miss Jewsbury sat by the head of the bed and kept her
black currant jelly well out of sight. But a moment came when
Mrs Carlyle fell fast asleep, and—if the truth must be told—
opened her mouth very wide. It was Miss Jewsbury's opportunity, and she filled a spoon full of jelly, and popped it into the open
mouth. "Good, God! Geraldine, what was that?" exclaimed Mrs
Carlyle, waking up.—"*That* was the black currant jelly."—"Good
God, Geraldine! I thought it was a leech gone the wrong way."

April 14— The other day I dined at Lord Charlemont's. Sir

Julius Benedict was at dinner, a most amusing person. He told us that—

One day an American bishop called in his carriage at Hunt & Roskell's. He asked to see some bracelets, mentioning that he was returning to America and wished to take a present to his wife. Nothing very expensive, he said; he could not afford that, but something about £70 or £80. Eventually he agreed to take a bracelet that cost £100. He said that he would pay for it with a £100 note which he had with him: it happened to be the only money he had at the moment, but he would wait while they sent it to the bank to ascertain that it was all right; he should really prefer doing this. They sent it to the bank and received answer that it was perfectly correct.

Having paid for his bracelet, the bishop took it, and was just about to step into his carriage, when a policeman tapped him on the shoulder and said, "Hallo, Jim! You're up to your old tricks again, are you? You'll just come along with me," and he brought him back into the shop. Hunt & Roskell said there was some mistake, that the gentleman was an American bishop, that he had just bought a £100 bracelet and paid for it with an excellent £100 note. "Just let me look at the note, will you?" said the policeman. He looked at it and said, "Yes, it's just as I thought; this note is one of a particularly clever batch of forgeries, which are very difficult to detect, and the man is no more of a bishop than you are. We will go off to the police station at once. I will take the note and go on with the prisoner in the carriage, and you must send your men in a cab to meet us and bear witness." So the police took the bishop and the bracelet and the note, but when Hunt & Roskell's men reached the police station, they had not yet arrived; and they have never been heard of since!

June 3 [1877].—I have dined several times with Miss Wright to meet the Charles Wilbrahams. Mr Wilbraham was amusing with some of his American experiences. He told of two young girls who were stopped going through a turnpike gate. "What are your charges?"—"Half a dollar for man and horse."—"Well, then, just stand on one side, will you, for we are two girls and a mare, so we've nothing to pay." He said he had asked an American at Florence what he thought of Venus de Medicis. "Wal, I guess I'm not so partiklar overpowered by stone gals," was the reply.

JOURNAL. *Walton Heath Oct. 6*—I have come here to Miss Davenport Bromley at a quaint cottage, partly built out of a church, in a corner of the vast Walton Heath, but full of artistic comfort and brightness within. Another pleasure has been finding Mrs Henry de Bunsen here. She told me—

"There was, and there is still, living in Cadogan Place, a lady of middle age, who is clever, charming, amiable, even handsome, but who has the misfortune of having—a wooden leg. Daily, for many years, she was accustomed to amble every morning on her wooden leg down Cadogan Place, and to take the air in the park. It was her principal enjoyment.

"One day she discovered that in these walks she was constantly followed by a gentleman. When she turned, he turned: where she went, he went: it was most disagreeable. She determined to put an end to it by staying at home, and for some days she did not go out at all. But she missed her walks in the park very much, and after a time she thought her follower must have forgotten all about her, and she went out as before. The same gentleman was waiting, he followed her, and at length suddenly came up to her in the park and presented her with a letter. He said that, as a stranger, he must apologise for speaking to her, but that he must implore her to take the letter, and read it when she got home: it was of great importance. She took the letter, and when she got home she read it, and found that it contained a violent declaration of love and a proposal of marriage. She was perfectly furious. She desired her lawyer to enclose the letter to the writer, and say that she could not find words to describe her sense of his ungentlemanly conduct, especially cruel to one afflicted as she was with a wooden leg.

"Several years elapsed, and the lady was paying a visit to some friends in the country, when the conversation frequently turned upon a friend of the house who was described as one of the most charming, generous, and beneficent of mankind. So delightful was the description, that the lady was quite anxious to see the original, and was enchanted when she heard that he was likely to come to the house. But when he arrived, she recognised with consternation her admirer of the park. He did not, however, recur to their former meeting, and after a time, when she knew him well, she grew to esteem him exceedingly, and at last, when he renewed his proposal after an intimate acquaintance, she accepted him and married him.

"He took her to his country house, and for six weeks they were entirely, uncloudedly happy. Then there came a day upon which he announced that he was obliged to go up to London on business. His wife could not go with him because the house in Cadogan Place was dismantled for the summer. 'I should regret this more,' he said, 'but that where two lives are so completely, so entirely united as ours are, there ought to be the most absolute confidence on either side. Therefore, while I am away, I shall leave you my keys. Open my desk, read all my letters and journals, make yourself mistress of my whole life. Above all,' he said, 'there is one cupboard in my dressing-room which contains certain memorials of my past peculiarly sacred to me, which I should like you to make yourself acquainted with.' The wife heard with concern of her husband's intended absence, but she was considerably buoyed up under the idea of the three days in which they were to be separated by the thought of the very interesting time she would have. She saw her husband off from the door, and as soon as she heard the wheels of his carriage die away in the distance, she clattered away as fast as she could upon her wooden leg to the dressing-room, and in a minute she was down on all fours before the cupboard he had described.

"She unlocked the cupboard. It contained two shelves. On each shelf was a long narrow parcel sewn up in canvas. She felt a tremor of horror as she looked at them, she did not know why. She lifted down the first parcel, and it had a label on the outside. She trembled so she could scarcely read it. It was inscribed—'In memory of my dear wife Elizabeth Anne, who died on the 24th of August 1864.' With quivering fingers she sought for a pair of scissors and ripped open the canvas, and it contained—a wooden leg!

"With indescribable horror she lifted down the other parcel, of the same form and size. It also bore a label—'In memory of my dearest wife Wilhelmine, who died the 6th of March 1869,' and she opened it and it contained—another wooden leg!

"Instantly she rose from her knees. 'It is evident,' she said, 'that I am married to a Blue Beard—a monster who collects wooden legs. This is not the time for sentiment, this is the time for action,' and she swept her jewels and some miniatures that she had into a handbag and she clattered away on her own wooden leg by the back shrubberies to the highroad—and there she saw the butcher's cart passing, and she hailed it, and was driven by the butcher to the nearest station, where she just caught the next train to London, intending to make good her escape that night to France and to leave no trace behind her.

"But she had not consulted Bradshaw, and she found she had some hours to wait in London before the tidal train started. Then she could not resist employing them in going to reproach the people at whose house she had met her husband, and she told them what she had found. To her amazement they were not the least surprised. 'Yes,' they said, 'yes, we thought he ought to have told you: we do not wonder you were astonished. Yes, indeed, we knew dear Elizabeth Anne very well; she was indeed a most delightful person, the most perfect of women and of wives, and when she was taken away, the whole light seemed blotted out of Arthur's life, the change was so very terrible. We thought he would never rally his spirits again, but then after two years, he met dearest Wilhelmine, to whom he was first attracted by her having the same affliction which was characteristic of her predecessor. And Wilhelmine was perhaps even a more charming person than Elizabeth Anne, and made her husband's life uncloudedly happy. But she too was, alas! early snatched away, and then it was as if the whole world was cut from under Arthur's feet, until at last he met you, with the same peculiarity which was endeared to him by two lost and loved ones, and we believe that with you he has been even more entirely, more uncloudedly happy than he was either with Wilhelmine or Elizabeth Anne.'

"And the wife was so charmed by what she heard, that it gave quite a new aspect to affairs. She went home by the next train. She was there when her husband returned; and ever since they have lived perfectly happily between his house in the country and hers in Cadogan Place."

Mrs De Bunsen said that a cousin of hers was repeating this story when dining at the Balfours'. Suddenly he saw that his host and hostess were both telegraphing frantic signals to him, and by a great effort he turned it off. The lady of the wooden leg and her husband were both amongst the guests.

Milford Cottage, Oct. 8—I came here with Miss Bromley on Saturday to visit Mrs Greville and her most engaging mother, Mrs Thellusson.

This afternoon I have been with Mrs Greville to Mr Tennyson at Haselmere. It is a wild, high, brown heath, with ragged edges of birch, and an almost limitless view of blue Sussex distances. Jammed into a hollow is the house, a Gothic house, built by Mr Knowles, the editor of the *Nineteenth Century*—'that young bricklayer fellow that Alfred is so fond of,' as Mr Carlyle calls him. Though the place is a bleak, wind-stricken height, where the flowers in the garden can never sit still, the house is pleasant inside and well and simply furnished, but is without any library whatever. Tennyson is older looking than I expected, so that his *unkempt* appearance signifies less. He has an abrupt, bearish manner, and seems thoroughly hard and *un*poetical: one would think of him as a man in whom the direst prose of life was absolutely ingrained. Mrs Greville kissed his hand as he came in, which he received without any protest. He asked if I would like to go out, and we walked round the gardens.

By way of breaking the silence I said, "How fine your arbūtus is."—"Well, I would say arbŭtus," he answered, "otherwise you are as bad as the gardeners, who say clemātis." When we returned to the house, Hallam Tennyson brought in his mother very tenderly and put her on a sofa. She is a very sweet-looking woman, with "the glittering blue eyes" which fascinated Carlyle, and a lady-abbess look from her head-dress—a kind of veil. Tennyson then insisted that I should tell him some stories. I did not like it, but found it was no use to resist; I should have to do it in the end. He asked for "a village tragedy," so I told him the story of Caroline Crowhurst: he said he should write it in a play or a poem. He was an atrociously bad audience, and constantly interrupted with questions.

On the whole, the wayward poet leaves a favourable impression. He could scarcely be less egotistic with all the flattery he has, and I am glad to have seen him so quietly. For the poet's bearish manners the Tennyson family are to blame, in making him think himself a demigod. One day, on arriving at Mrs Greville's, he said at once, "Give me a pipe; I want to smoke." She at once went off by herself down the village to the shop, and returning with two pipes, offered them to him with all becoming subservience. He never looked at her or thanked her, but, as he took them, growled out, "Where are the matches? I suppose now you've forgotten the matches!"—"Oh dear! I never thought of those."

Babworth, Oct. 14—This house overflows with loveliness in the way of amateur art, and the drawings of its mistress, Mrs Bridgeman Simpson, are most beautiful.

Oct. 15—Mrs Simpson's very charming Polish sister-in-law, Mrs Drummond Baring, recounted yesterday evening a curious story out of the reminiscences of her childhood, of which her husband from knowledge confirmed every fact. Her father, Count Potocka, lived in Martinique. His wife had been married before, and her beautiful daughter, Minetta, idolised by her second husband, had made a happy marriage with the Marquis de San Luz, and resided at Port Royal about five miles from her parents. The father was a great naturalist, and had the greatest interest in introducing and naturalising all kinds of plants in the West Indies. Amongst other plants, he was most anxious to introduce strawberries. Everyone said he would fail, and the neighbouring gardeners especially said so much about it that it was a positive annoyance to them when his plants all seemed to succeed, and he had a large bed of strawberries in flower. His stepdaughter, Minetta, came to see them, and he always said to her that, when the strawberries were ripe, she should have the first fruit.

A ball was given at Port Royal by the Governor, and there her parents saw Minetta, beautiful and radiant as ever; but she left the ball early, for her child was not well. As she went away, she said to her stepfather, "Remember my strawberries."

Her parents returned home in the early morning, and a day and a night succeeded. Towards dawn on the second morning, when night was just breaking into the first grey daylight, the mother felt an irresistible restlessness, and getting up and going to the window, she looked out. A figure in white was moving to and fro amongst the strawberries, carefully examining each plant and looking under the leaves. She awoke her husband, who said at once, "It is one of the gardeners, who are so jealous that they have come to destroy my plants;" and jumping up, he put on his gola—a sort of dressing-gown wrapper worn in Martinique—

and, taking his gun, rushed out. On first going out, he saw the figure in white moving before him, but as he came up to the strawberry beds it seemed to have disappeared. He was surprised, and turning round towards the house, saw his wife making agonised signs to him to come back. Such was her livid aspect, that he threw down his gun upon the ground and ran in to her. He found her in a dead faint upon the floor. When she recovered, she said that she had watched him from the window as he went out, and that, as he reached the strawberry beds, the figure seemed to turn round, and she saw—like a person seen through a veil and through the glass of a window, and, though perfectly distinct, transparent—her daughter Minetta. Soon after describing this, she was seized with violent convulsions. Her husband was greatly alarmed about her, and was just sending off for the doctor, who lived at some distance, when a rider on a little Porto Rico pony came clattering into the court. They thought it was the doctor, but it was not; it was a messenger from Port Royal to say that Minetta was dead. She had been seized with a chill on returning from the ball, and it had turned to fatal diphtheria. In her last hours, when her throat was so swelled and hot, she had constantly said, "Oh, my throat is so hot! Oh, if I had only some of those strawberries!"

April 3 [1878].—On Monday, March 25, as I was breakfasting at the Athenaeum, I glanced into the paper and the first thing which met my eyes was the news of the total loss of the *Eurydice*, with dear good Marcus Hare and more than three hundred men. It was a terrible shock, and seemed to carry away a whole mass of one's life in recollections from childhood . . . . It is many days ago now, and the dreadful fact has seemed ever since to be hammering itself into one's brain with ceaselessly increasing horror. How small now seem the failings in Marcus's unselfish and loving character, how many the virtues. It is difficult also to realise that there is now scarcely anyone left who really cares for the old traditions of the Hare family, the old portraits, the old memorials, which were always so much to him, and which I hoped, through him, would be handed down to another generation.

April 14—I have little to tell of London beyond the ordinary experiences, except perhaps having been shocked by the slanderous malignity of so-called "religious people," as I have been charmed by the chivalrous disinterestedness of many who do not aspire to that denomination. Of the many dinner parties I have attended, I cannot recollect anything except that someone —I cannot remember who—spoke of Disraeli as "that old Jew gentleman who is sitting on the top of chaos."

JOURNAL. *London, April 29 [1879].*—I have heard again the curious story of Sir T. Watson from Mrs T., to whom he told it himself, so will write it down.

Sir Thomas Watson, better known as Dr Watson, was a well-known physician. During the last years of his life he was in failing health, and only saw patients at his own house, but till then he went about in England wherever he was sent for. One day he was summoned to attend an urgent case at Oxenholme in Cumberland. There was only one carriage in the train which went through to Oxenholme, and in a compartment of that carriage he took his seat. He tipped the guard, and said he should be glad to be alone if he could.

The train at Euston was already in motion, when a young lady came running down the platform, with a porter laden with her handbags and cloaks. The man just contrived to open the carriage door, push the young lady in, throw in her things after her, and the train was off. The young lady, a very pretty, pleasing young lady, took the seat opposite Dr Watson. Being a polite, gallant old gentleman, very soon Dr Watson began to make himself agreeable: "What beautiful effects of cloud there were. How picturesque Harrow church steeple looked through the morning haze," &c. &c., and the young lady responded pleasantly. At last, as their acquaintance advanced, Dr Watson said, "And are you travelling far?"—"Oh yes," said the young lady, "very far, I am going to Oxenholme in Cumberland."—"How singular," said Dr Watson, "for that is just where I am going myself. I wonder if you happen to know Lady D. who lives near Oxenholme."—"Yes," said the young lady, "I know Lady D. very well."—"And Mrs P. and her daughters?" said Dr W.—"Oh yes, I know them too."—"And Mr Y.?"—There was a moment's pause, and then the young lady very naïvely and ingenuously said, "Yes, I do know Mr Y. very well; and perhaps I had better tell you something. I am going to be *married* to him tomorrow. My own parents are in India, and I am going to be married from his father's house. Since I have been engaged to him, I have made the acquaintance of many of his friends and neighbours, and that is how I know so many people near Oxenholme, though I have never been there before."

Dr Watson was charmed with the simple candour of the young lady. They went on talking, and they became quite friends. The train arrived at Rugby, and they both got out and had their bun in the refreshment room. They were in the carriage again, and the train was already moving, when, in great excitement, the young lady called out: "Oh stop, stop the train, don't you see how he's urging me to get out. There! That young man in the brown ulster, that's the young man I'm going to be married to." Of course it was impossible to get out, and the young lady was greatly distressed, and though Dr Watson assured her most positively that there was no one standing where she described, she would not and could not believe him.

Then Dr Watson said, "Now, my dear young lady, you're very young and I'm very old. I am a doctor. I am very well known, and from what you have been seeing I am quite sure, as a physician, that you are not at all well. Now, I have my medicine chest with me, and you had better let me give you a little dose." And he did give her a little dose.

The train arrived at Stafford, and exactly the same thing occurred. "There, there! don't you see him! *That* young man with the light beard, in the brown ulster, don't you see how he's urging me to get out?" And again Dr. Watson assured her there was no one there, and said, "I think you had better let me give you another little dose;" and he gave her another little dose.

But Dr Watson naturally felt that he could not go on giving her a dose at every station all the way to Oxenholme, so he decided within himself that if the same thing happened at Crewe, the young lady's state indicated one of two things: either that there was some intentional vision from Providence, with which he ought not to interfere; or that the young lady was certainly not in a state of health or brain which should allow her to be married the next day. So he determined to act accordingly.

And at Crewe just the same thing happened. "There, there! Don't you see him! He's urging me more than ever to get out," cried the young lady. "Very well," said Dr Watson, "we will get out and go after him," and with the young lady, he pursued the imaginary figure, and of course did not find him. But Dr Watson had often been at the Crewe station before, and he went to the hotel, which opens on the platform, and said to the matron, "Here is this young lady, who is not at all well, and should have a very quiet room; unfortunately I am not able to remain now to look after her, but I will leave her in your care, and tomorrow I shall be returning this way and will come to see how she is." And he slipped a five-pound note into the woman's hand to guarantee expenses.

Dr Watson returned to the railway carriage. There was another young lady there, sitting in the place which the first young lady had occupied—a passenger who had arrived by one of the many lines which converge at Crewe. With the new young lady he did not make acquaintance; he moved his things to the other side of the carriage and devoted himself to his book.

Three stations farther on came the shock of a frightful accident. There was a collision. The train was telescoped, and many of the passengers were terribly hurt. The heavy case of instruments, which was in the rack above the place where Dr Watson had first been sitting, was thrown violently to the other side of the carriage, hit the young lady upon the forehead and killed her on the spot.

It was long before the line could be sufficiently cleared for the train to pass which was sent to pick up the surviving passengers. Many hours later, in the middle of the night, Dr Watson arrived at Oxenholme. There, waiting on the platform, stood the young man with the light beard, in the brown ulster, exactly as he had been described. He had heard that the only young lady in the through-carriage from London had been killed, and was only waiting for the worst to be confirmed. And Dr Watson was the person who went up to him and said: "Unfortunately it is too true that a young lady has been killed, but it is not your young lady. Your young lady is safe in the station hotel at Crewe."

34 Jermyn Street, London, May 13 [1879].—This morning I went with Mrs Duncan Stewart and a very large party to Whistler's studio—a huge place in Chelsea. We were invited to see his pictures, but there was only one there—"The Loves of the Lobsters." It was supposed to represent Niagara, but looked as if the artist had upset the inkstand and left Providence to work out its own results. In the midst of the black chaos were two lobsters curvetting opposite each other and looking as if they were done with red sealing-wax. "I wonder you did not paint the lobsters making love before they were boiled," aptly observed a lady visitor. "Oh, I never thought of that," said Whistler! It was a joke, I suppose. The little man, with his plume of white hair ("the Whistler tuft," he calls it) waving on his forehead, frisked about the room looking most strange and uncanny, and rather diverted himself over our disappointment in coming so far and finding nothing to see. People admire like sheep his pictures in the Grosvenor Gallery, following each other's lead because it is the fashion.

May 17 [1879].—At luncheon at Lady Florentia Hughes's I met George Russell, who told me a story which Lord and Lady Portsmouth had just brought back from Devonshire.

On the railway which runs from Exeter to Barnstaple is a small station called Lapford. A farmer who lives in a farmhouse near that station awoke his wife one night, saying that he had had a very vivid dream which had troubled him—that a very valuable cow of his had fallen into a pit and could not get out again. The wife laughed, and he went to sleep and dreamt the same thing. Then he wanted to go and look after the cow. But the wife urged the piercing cold of the winter night, and he went to sleep instead, and dreamt the same thing a third time. Then he insisted upon getting up, and resisting his wife's entreaties, he went out to look after the cow. It was with a sense of bathos that he found the cow quite well and grazing quietly, and he was thinking how his wife would laugh at him when he got home, and wondering what he should say to her, when he was aware of a light in the next field. Crawling very quietly to the hedge, he saw, through the leafless branches of the hawthorns, a man with a lanthorn and a spade, apparently digging a pit. As he was watching, he stumbled into the ditch and the branches crackled. The man, hearing a noise, started, then threw down the spade and ran off with the lanthorn.

The farmer then made his way round into the next field and came up to the place where the man had been digging. It was a long narrow pit like an open grave. At first he could make nothing of it, then by the side of the pit he found a large open knife. He took that and the spade, and began to set out homewards, but, with an indescribable shrinking from the more desolate feeling of the fields, he went round by the lane. He had not gone far before he heard footsteps coming towards him. It was two o'clock in the morning, and his nerves being quite unstrung, he shrank from meeting whoever it was, and climbed up into the hedge to conceal himself. To his astonishment, he saw pass below him in the moonlit road one of the maids of his own farmhouse. He allowed her to pass, and then sprang out and seized her. She was most dreadfully frightened. He demanded to know what she was there for. She tried to make some excuse. "Oh," he said, "there can be no possible excuse; I insist upon knowing the truth." She then said, "You know I was engaged to be married, and that I had a dreadful quarrel with the man I was engaged to, and it was broken off. Well, yesterday he let me know that if I would meet him in the middle of the night, he had got something to show me that would make up for all the past."—"Would you like to know what he had to show you? It was your grave he had to show you," said the farmer, and he led her to the edge of the pit and showed it to her.

The farmer's dream had saved the woman's life.

June 15—A quiet luncheon with Lady Reay. Afterwards to Mrs. Duncan Stewart, who told me: —"A great friend of mine was living lately in Brittany, and, while there, made acquaintance with a lady and her daughter who were staying in the same place —the mother a commonplace woman, the daughter a pleasant interesting girl.

"A short time after, the mother and daughter came to England, and my friend, who was in very delicate health at the time, invited them to visit her. The mother was prevented coming at first, but sent her daughter and said that she would follow.

"One day my friend was sitting in her boudoir, of which the door was ajar, very little open. The girl had gone to her own room, which was immediately above the boudoir, saying that she had letters to write.

"Suddenly my friend was aware that *something* was coming in at the door, not pushing it wider open, but gliding through the opening which already existed, and to her horror, she saw, perfectly naked, propelling herself serpent-like on her belly, with her hair rising like a crest over her head, and her eyes, without any speculation in them, staring wide open, the figure of a young girl, whom she recognized as her guest.

"With snake-like motion the girl glided in and out of the furniture, under the chairs, sofas, &c., but touching nothing, and with her eyes constantly fixed upon my friend, with an expression which was rather that of fear than anything else. At length she glided out of the room as she came in.

"As soon as my friend could recover herself a little, she pursued the girl to her room and quietly opened the door. To her horror, all the articles of crockery in the room, jug, basin, &c, were dispersed about the floor at regular intervals and in a regular pattern, and through them all, in and out, without touching them, the girl was gliding, snake-like, with her head erect, and her vacant eyes staring.

"My friend fled to her room and began to think what she should do; but such was her horror that she thinks she fainted; at any rate the power of action seemed to fail her. When she could move, she thought it her duty to go up to the girl's room again, and perhaps was almost more horrified than before to find the room in perfect order and the girl seated dressed at the table, writing. She sent for the girl's mother, who was terribly distressed. She allowed that her daughter had had these utterly inexplicable attacks before, but long ago, and she had hoped that she was cured of them.

Mrs Stewart told this story to Mr Fergusson the great naturalist, who only said, "I am not the least surprised: there is nothing extraordinary in it. There have been many other instances of the serpent element coming out in people."

Glamis Castle, Aug. 13 [1879].—I arrived at Glamis at 9 p.m. and found an immense party in the house. Miss Erica Robertson said: —

"Bishop Wilberforce was going, in a visitation tour, to stay at a very humble clergyman's house. The maid was instructed that, if he spoke to her, she was never to answer him without saying, 'My Lord.' When the Bishop had written his letters, he asked who would take them to the post. 'The Lord, my boy,' said the terrified maid."

Osterley Park, Nov. 13—I came here yesterday, most kindly welcomed by the good old Duchess of Cleveland, who is delightful. *Nov. 14*—In the afternoon we went to Ham House—a most curious visit. No half-inhabited château of a ruined family in Normandy was ever half so dilapidated as this home of the enormously rich Tollemaches. All the members of the family whom I knew were absent, but I sent in my card to Mr Algernon Tollemache, who received us. As the door at the head of the entrance-stair opened, its handle went through a priceless Sir Joshua [Reynolds] of Louisa, Countess of Dysart; it always does go through it. We were taken through a half-ruined hall and a bedroom to an inner room in which Mr Algernon Tollemache (unable to move from illness) was sitting. It presented the most unusual contrasts imaginable—a velvet bed in a recess backed by the most exquisite embroidery on Chinese silk; an uncarpeted floor of rough boards; a glorious Lely portrait of the Duchess of Lauderdale; a deal board by way of washing-stand, with a coarse white jug and basin upon it; a splendid mirror framed in massive silver on a hideous rough deal scullery table without a cover; and all of Mr Tollemache's most extraordinarily huge boots and shoes ranged round the room by way of ornament. . . .

We were sent over the house. All was of the same character —a glorious staircase with splendid carving in deep relief; the dismal chapel with the prayer-book of Charles I, in a most wonderful cover of metallic embroidery; marvellous old rooms with delicate silk hangings of exquisitely beautiful tints, though mouldering in rags; old Persian carpets of priceless designs worn to shreds; priceless Japanese screens perishing; beautiful pictures dropping to pieces for want of varnish; magnificent silver tables; black chandeliers which look like ebony and are solid silver; a library full of Caxtons, the finest collection in the world except two; a china closet with piles of old Chelsea, undusted and untouched for years; a lovely little room full of miniatures, of which the most beautiful of all was brought down for us to examine closer. "Do you see that mark?" said Mr Tollemache. "Thirty years ago a spot appeared there upon the miniature, so I opened the case and wetted my finger and rubbed it: I did not know paint came off (!). Wasn't it fortunate I did not wipe my wet hand down over the whole picture: it would *all* have come off!"

And the inhabitants of this palace, which looks like that of the Sleeping Beauty in the Wood, have wealth which is inexhaustible, though they have scarcely any servants, no carriage, only bread and cheese for luncheon, and never repair or restore anything.

All the family have had their peculiarities. The late Lord Huntingtower was at one time separated from his wife, and when he was persuaded that he ought in common justice to allow her to return to Ham, he assented, but he draped the gates and portico with black cloth for her reception, and he put a band of black cloth round the left leg of every animal on the estate, the cows in the field, the horses in the stable, even the dogs and cats. *His* grandfather, Lord Huntingtower, was more extraordinary still. When he bought a very nice estate with a house near Buckminster, he bought all the contents of the house at the same time. There was a very good collection of pictures, but "What do I want with pictures? All that rubbish shall be burnt," he said—"But, my lord, they are very *good* pictures."—"Well, bring them all down here and make a very great fire, and I will see them burnt." And he did.

There is a ghost at Ham. The old butler there had a little girl, and the Ladies Tollemache kindly asked her to come on a visit: she was then six years old. In the small hours of the morning, when dawn was making things clear, the child, waking up, saw a

THE SAVOY CHURCHYARD

little old woman scratching with her fingers against the wall close to the fireplace. She was not at all frightened at first, but sat up to look at her. The noise she made in doing this caused the old woman to look round, and she came to the foot of the bed, and grasping the rail with her hands, stared at the child long and fixedly. So horrible was her stare, that the child was terrified, and screamed and hid her face under the clothes. People who were in the passage ran in, and the child told what she had seen. The wall was examined where she had seen the figure scratching, and concealed in it were found papers which proved that in that room Elizabeth, Countess of Dysart, had murdered her husband to marry the Duke of Lauderdale.

Holmhurst, Nov. 24 [1879].—I have heard a very eerie story from Lady Waterford:—There is a place in Scotland called Longmacfergus. Mr and Mrs Spottiswoode lived there, who were the father and mother of Lady John Scott, and they vouched for the story. The villagers of Longmacfergus are in the habit of going to do their marketing at the little town of Dunse, and though their nearest way home would be by crossing the burn at a point called "the Foul Ford," they always choose another and longer way by preference, for the Foul Ford is always looked upon as haunted. There was a farmer who lived in Longmacfergus, and who was highly respected, and very well-to-do. One night his wife was expecting him back from the market at Dunse, and he did not appear. Late and long she waited and he did not come, but at last, after midnight, when she was very seriously alarmed, he knocked violently at the door and she let him in. She was horrified to see his wild and agonised expression, and the awful change which had taken place in his whole aspect since they parted. He told her that he had come home by the Foul Ford, and that he must rue the day and the way, for he must die before morning. He begged her to send for the minister, for he must see him at once. She was terrified at his state, and implored him rather to send for the doctor, but he said, "No, the minister—the minister was the only person who could do him any good."

However, being a wise woman, she sent for both minister and doctor. When the doctor came, he said he could do nothing for the man, the case was past his cure, but the minister spent several hours with the farmer. Before morning he died, and what he said that night to the minister never was told till many years after.

Naturally the circumstances of the farmer's death made the inhabitants of Longmacfergus regard the Foul Ford with greater terror than before, and for a few years no one attempted to use it. At last, however, there came a day when the son of the dead farmer was persuaded to linger longer than usual drinking at Dunse, and after being twitted by his comrades for cowardice in not returning the shortest way, he determined to risk it, and set out with a brave heart. That night *his* wife sat watching in vain for his return, and she watched in vain till morning, for he never came back. In the morning the neighbours went to search for him, and he was found lying dead on the bank above the Foul Ford, and—it is a foolish fact perhaps, but it has always been narrated as a fact incidental to the story, that—though there were no marks of violence upon his person, and though his coat was on, his waistcoat was off and lying by the side of his body upon the grass; his watch and his money were left intact in his pockets.

After his funeral the minister said to the assembled mourners and parishioners, that now that the second death had occurred of the son, he thought that he should be justified in revealing the substance of the strange confession which the father had made on the night he died. He said that he had crossed the wooden bridge of the Foul Ford, and was coming up the brae on the other side, when he met a procession of horsemen dressed in black, riding two and two upon black horses. As they came up, he saw amongst them, to his horror, everyone he had known amongst his neighbours of Longmacfergus, and who were already dead. But the man who rode last—the last man who had died—was leading a riderless horse. As he came up, he dismounted by the farmer's side, and said that the horse was for him. The farmer refused to mount, and all his former neighbours tried to force him on to the horse. They had a deadly struggle, in which at last the farmer seemed to get the better, for the horseman rode away, leading the riderless horse, but he said, "Never mind, you will want it before morning." And before morning he was dead.

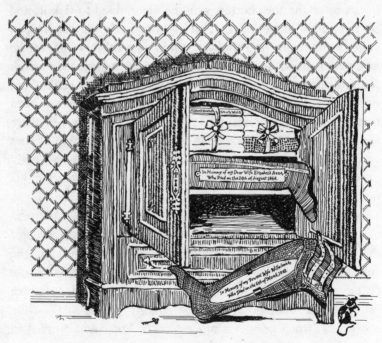

XVII. A Halt in Life

Augustus J. C. Hare, 1879.

In May, 1878, my publishers, Messrs Daldy and Isbister, had astounded the literary world by becoming bankrupt. They had been personally pleasant to deal with; I had never doubted their solvency; and I was on terms of friendly intercourse with Mr Isbister. In April 1878 he wrote to me saying that he knew I applied the interest of money derived from my books to charitable purposes, and that he would much rather bestow the large interest he was prepared to give for such purpose than any other, and he asked me to lend him £1500. About a week later, I lent it to him. Then, within a month, the firm declared itself bankrupt, owing me in all nearly £3000, and the £1500 and much more was apparently lost forever. I had always been given to understand that I never parted with the copyright. I believe that most publishers would have informed an ignorant author that the very unusual forms of agreement they prepared involved the copyright, but I was allowed to suppose that I retained it in my own hands. I first discovered my mistake after their bankruptcy, when, besides owing me nearly £3000, Messrs Daldy and Isbister demanded a bonus of £1500 (which I refused, offering £850 in vain) for giving me the permission to go on circulating my own books through another publisher.

As it was impossible to come to terms, my unfortunate books lapsed.

These circumstances made such a discouragement for any real work, that for two years I did nothing of a literary character beyond collecting the reminiscences contained in these volumes.

In November 1879 an event occurred which would at one time have affected me very deeply—the death of the Mary Stanley who for many years ruled my adopted family by the force of her strong will, and who, after my dearest mother was taken away from me, remorselessly used that power to expel me from the hearts and homes of those over whom she had any influence, in her fury at the publication of the "Memorials of a Quiet Life."*

I only wish, as regards her, I could have profited more by words of Mrs Kemble, which I read too late to apply them— "Do you not know that to misunderstand and be misunderstood is one of the inevitable conclusions, and I think one of the especial purposes, of our existence? The principal use of the affection of human beings for each other is to supply the want of perfect comprehension, which is impossible. All the faith and love which we possess are barely sufficient to bridge over the abyss of individualism which separates one human being from another; and they would not, or could not, exist, if we really understood each other."

June 15[1880].—Luncheon with Lady Dorothy Neville in her charming house in Charles Street, which has all the attractions of an old manor. She and Lord Houghton were very amusing

---

* A book written by Hare about the life of his mother which enraged some members of the family.

over Mr Wolff, who married her aunt, Lady Georgiana. Nothing could persuade him to cleanliness. Once they tried to insist upon his washing his hands, and took him to a jug, basin and clean towel for the purpose, but he would only dip the ends of his fingers in the jug and dry them on his pocket-handkerchief. If he went to stay anywhere, he would never take any luggage. He was, however, persuaded for three days to take three clean shirts, but he arrived with them all on, and peeled gradually.

Mr Wolff went to stay with George Anthony Denison, who was frightfully bored with him. He stayed a week. As he was in the carriage going off from the door, Mr Denison said to him, "Well, goodbye, my dear fellow; I'm sorry you're going." — "Are you sorry I'm going?" said a gruff voice from the carriage; "then I'll stay another week."

July 14 [1880].—Dinner at Lady Charlemont's. Lady Charlemont talked much of the Lord Chancellor Thurlow.

A clergyman desirous of a living went to the Bishop of London and asked him for an introduction to the Lord Chancellor Thurlow. The Bishop said, "I should be willing to give it, but an introduction from me would defeat the very end you have in view." However, the clergyman persisted in his request, and the introduction was given.

The Lord Chancellor received him with fury. "So that damned scoundrel the Bishop of London has given you an introduction; as it is he who has introduced you, you will certainly not get the living."—"Well, so the Bishop said, my lord," replied the clergyman.—"Did the Bishop say so?" thundered Lord Thurlow; "then he's a damned liar, and I'll prove him so: you *shall* have the living," and the man got it.

At Arundel the guests were astonished by the butler coming in one day abruptly and saying to the Duke, "May it please your Grace, Lord Thurlow has laid an egg." It was one of the owls which existed at Arundel till the time of the present owner. Lord Thurlow's daughter, going round their cages in the wall, had stopped opposite one of them, and, looking at the blinking bird, said, "Why, he's just like papa." The bird was ever after called Lord Thurlow.

July 17 [1880].—Sat by Matthew Arnold at breakfast. Speaking of the odd effect misspelled words often produced, he quoted a begging letter he had just received from a lady who said she had a decided claim upon charity, being the "sole support of an aged Ant."

Two days ago I went to Lady Airlie's, where a large party was collected to hear Mr Browning read. I never heard anyone, even a child of ten, read so atrociously. It was two of his own poems —"Good News to Ghent" and "Ivan Ivanowitch," the latter always most horrible and unsuitable for reading aloud, but in this case rendered unintelligible by the melodramatic vocal contortions of the reader.

Melchet, Hants, Oct. 23 [1880].—Lady Marian is here, always pleasant with her ripple of conversation and anecdote. She has been very amusing about her mother's parrot, which used to hop about on the lawn. One day it was carried off by an eagle. Old John Tooch, one of the dynasty of John Toochs who worked in the garden, was mowing the lawn, and as the parrot, in the eagle's grip, was sailing over his head, he heard a voice in the air call out, "We're ridin' noo, John Tooch, we're ridin' noo;" at which strange sound the eagle was so dreadfully frightened that he let the parrot fall, so that John Tooch took it home to its cage again.

Holmhurst, Nov. 13 [1880].—Mr and Mrs Paterson have been here for the day. He told me this story: —

A lady was awoke in the night with the disagreeable sense of not being alone in the room, and soon felt a thud upon her bed. There was no doubt that someone was moving to and fro in the room, and that hands were constantly moving over her bed. She was so dreadfully frightened that at last she fainted. When she came to herself, it was broad daylight, and she found that the butler had walked in his sleep and had laid the table for fourteen upon her bed.

JOURNAL. *Jan. 11 [1881].*—There is a large party here (at Tortworth) but one forgets all its other elements in dear Mrs Duncan Stewart. Today, at luncheon, Mrs Stewart talked much of Paris and of her intercourse with a French physician there. Dr—— spoke to her of the happy despatch, and unhesitatingly allowed that when he saw a patient condemned to hopeless suffering, he practiced it. "But of course you insist on the acquiescence both of the patients and of their families," said Mrs Stewart. "*Never,*" shouted Dr——. "I should be a mean sneak indeed if I waited for *that.*"

Mrs Stewart also talked of Trollope's novels, and said how Trollope had told her of the circumstances which led to the death of Mrs Proudie. He had gone up to write at the round table in the library at the Athenaeum, and spread his things all over it. It was early in the morning, and there is seldom any one there at that time. On this occasion, however, two country clergymen were sitting on either side of the fire reading one of his own books: after a time they began to talk about them. "It is a great pity Trollope does not get some fresh characters," said one. "Yes," said the other, "one gets so tired of meeting the same people again and again, especially of Mrs Proudie." Then Trollope got up, and planting himself on the rug between them with his back to the fire, said, "Gentlemen, I do not think it would be honest to listen to you talking about my books any more, without telling you that I am the victim; but I will add that I quite agree with what you have been saying, and that I will give you my word of honour that Mrs Proudie shall die in the very next book I write."

Jan. 12—Mrs Stewart has been talking of the cases in which a lie is justifiable. Of herself she said, "There was once a case in which I thought I ought to tell a lie, but I was not sure. I went to Dr and Mrs Bickersteth, and I asked them. They would only answer, 'We cannot advise you to tell a lie;' they would not advise it, but they did not forbid it. So when a husband came to question me about his wife, I equivocated. I said, 'She was certainly not seduced by that man.' He said to me very sternly and fiercely, 'That is no answer; is my wife innocent? I will believe you if you say she is.' And I said, 'She is.' I said it hesitatingly, for I knew it was false, and he knew it was false; he knew that I had lied to him, and he did not believe me in his heart; but he was glad to believe me outwardly, and he was grateful to me, and that husband and wife lived together till death. I believe that was one of the cases in which it is right to tell a lie. You will say that it might lead me to tell many others, but I don't think it had. Stopford Brooke once said that strict merciless truth was the most selfish thing he knew."

March 22 [1881].—The London world has been full of the "Reminiscences of Carlyle," published with furious haste by Froude a fortnight after his death. They have dwarfed their subject from a giant pigmy. His journal and letters speak well of no one except his own family, and assail with the utmost vituperation all who differ from him. For his wife there is a long wail of affection, which would be touching if the devotion had not begun after her death. "Never marry a genius," she said to Lady Ashburton; "I have done it, and suffered from it; but then, after my death I shall have an apotheosis"—and she has had it. Much of Carlyle's virulence arose from the state of his health: he used to say, "I can wish the devil nothing worse than that he may have to digest with my stomach to all eternity; there will be no need of fire and brimstone then."

March 28—Dined at Lady Lyveden's. Sat by Lady S., who was very pleasant. She talked of Tennyson, who had been to stay with her. He desired his sons to let her know that he should like to be asked to read some of his poems in the evening. Nevertheless, when she asked him, he made a piece of work about it, and said to the other guests, "I do it, but I only do it because Lady S. absolutely insists upon it." He read badly and with too much emotion: over "Maud" he sobbed passionately.

Afterwards, at Lady Ridley's party, Lord Houghton talked to me about Carlyle—of how his grimness, which was unrelieved in the "Reminiscences," was relieved in the man by much kindly humour. He said that he and Lady Houghton were almost the only people spoken well of in the book. Mr Spedding used to say that Carlyle always needed that kind of indulgence which most of us need in a fit of violent toothache.

Penrohs, Anglesea, Oct. 9 [1881].—We have been to see the ruins of a deserted manorhouse which belonged to Sir George Aubrey. It was abandoned on account of a family tragedy. Sir George's only son, a little boy, one day refused to eat his pudding. "You must," said the father. The child said he really could not, and implored with strange anguish to be excused, but the father insisted. Three hours after, the child died in frightful agonies. That day the cook, by mistake, had put arsenic into the pudding instead of sugar.

London, June 4 [1882].—In the last week I have spent three pleasant days with the Husseys at Scotney, a lovely place, where an old tower of Richard the Second's time and a ruined house by Inigo Jones stand in a wooded hollow, surrounded by a moat so clear that its reflections are even brighter than the reality . . . .

In the evening the conversation turned on witchcraft, and on Mr Maitland, author of "The Church in the Catacombs," who undertook to prove the absurdity of belief in witchcraft, but, on examination, found such incontrovertible evidence of its reality, that he abandoned the subject. Talk of strange relics led to mention of the heart of a French king, preserved at Nuneham in a silver casket. Dr Buckland, whilst looking at it, exclaimed, "I have eaten many strange things, but have never eaten the heart of a king before," and before any one could hinder him, he had gobbled it up, and the precious relic was lost for ever. Dr Buckland used to say that he had eaten his way straight through the whole animal creation, and that the worst thing was a mole—that was utterly horrible. (Dr Buckland afterwards told Lady Lyndhurst that there was one thing even worse than a mole, and that was a blue-bottle fly.)

July 5 [1882].—Dined with Miss Courtenay. We had all been reading and generally enchanted with Mrs Kemble's "Later Reminiscences," and Mr Reeve of the *Edinburgh Review* was delighted to have much to say of his personal remembrance of her, much that certainly was not favourable. She says little of the separation from her husband (Mr Butler) in her book, but Mr Reeve remembered her intensely overbearing manner to him.

Once when he was travelling with them in Belgium, Mr Butler, with great difficulty, procured a very beautiful bouquet for her for the evening. He gave it to her. "I have been all over the town, my dear, to get this bouquet for you," he said. She sniffed at it, said contemptuously, "There are no gardenias in this bouquet," and threw it into the back of the fire.

Mrs Kemble always disliked those who were afraid of her, but she hated those who were not.

JOURNAL. *Babworth Hall, Notts, Oct. 7 [1882].*—Yesterday we went by appointment to Welbeck, arriving by the darksome tunnel, more than two miles long, upon which the late Duke spent £60,000 and £60,000 more apiece upon banking up (and spoiling) his sheet of water with brick walls and building a gigantic riding school. The house itself stands well, considering the ugliness of the park, and is rather handsome; vast as it is, it has no staircase worth speaking of. The late Duke lived almost entirely in a small suite of rooms in the old part of the house. He inherited the peculiarity of his mother, who would see no one, and he always hid himself. If he gave permission to anyone to visit Welbeck, he always added, "But Mr So-and-so will be good enough not to *see* me" (if they chanced to meet). He drove out, but in a black coach like a hearse, drawn by four black horses, and with all the blinds down; and he walked out, but at night, with a woman, who was never to speak to him, and always to walk exactly forty yards in front, carrying a lanthorn. When he went to London, it was in a closed brougham, which was put on a railway truck, and which deposited him at his own house at Cavendish Square, his servants all being ordered out of the way: no one ever saw him go or arrive. When he needed a doctor, the doctor only came to the door, and asked questions through it of the valet, who was allowed to feel his pulse.

The Duke's mania for a hidden life made him build immense suites of rooms underground, only approachable by a common flight of steps leading to a long tunnel, down which the dinner is conveyed from the far-distant kitchen on a tramway.

All is vast, splendid, and utterly comfortless: one could imagine no more awful and ghastly fate than waking up one day and finding oneself Duke of Portland and master of Welbeck.

Alas! whilst I was enjoying this Babworth visit, the greatest sorrow which still remained possible for me was preparing, and a few days later it fell.

All the familiar figures of my childhood are swept away—all the uncles and aunts, brothers and sister; all the old neighbours;

THE VENETIAN WELL, HOLMHURST.

nearly all the old friends; the dear Mother; Marcus Hare; Arthur and Mary Stanley; and now my own dear Lea: all the old homes too are broken up, pulled down, or deserted; only I and the ruins of the castle seem left.

Holmhurst, Nov. 14—The winds are howling round and I sit alone in my home. The silence is sometimes awful, for I never hear the human voice now, for my only attendant, the faithful Anne, who waits upon me, is stone-deaf, so that all communication with her is in writing.

It may seem odd, but my dear Lea's removal really makes a greater blank in my life than even the Mother left behind. My mother had so long taken the child's place to be loved and taken care of: Lea, to her last hour, took as much care of me as in the first year of my life. I have the piteous feeling that there is none now to whom I *signify*: it can really 'matter' to no one whether I live or die. My friends are very kind, and would be sorry to lose me, but in this rapid world-current a few days would see them well out of their grief. And my dearest Lea, who cared—who would have cared while life lasted, rests now under a white marble cross like my mother's, inscribed—

MARY LEA GIDMAN,
June 2, 1800–Oct. 19, 1882
Through fifty-four years
Devoted, honoured, and beloved
In the Hare family.

June 19—Dined with Lady Airlie, only meeting Mrs Duncan Stewart and Lady De Clifford.

Lady Airlie said she had known Leigh Hunt very well when she was a child. He had taken her into the garden, and talked to her, and asked her what she thought heaven would be like, and then he said, "I will tell you what I think it will be like: I think it will be like a most beautiful arbour all hung with creepers and flowers, and that one will be able to sit in it all day, and read a most interesting novel."

Of her early acquaintance with Washington Irving, Mrs Stewart said "It was at Havre. My guardian was consul there. People used to say, 'Where is Harriet gone?' and he answered, 'Oh, she is down at the end of the terrace, busy making Washington Irving believe he is God Almighty, and he is busy believing it.'"

Mrs Stewart told of Miss Ruth Paget, one of many sisters, who went down at night to the kitchen to let out her little dog for a minute, and found her brother Marco, who was a midshipman in the Mediterranean, sitting on the kitchen table, swinging his legs, and pouring with wet. She said, "Good heavens, Marco, how did you come here?" He looked at her, and only said, "Do not tell any one you have seen me." She looked round for an instant to see if anyone was coming, and when she turned, he was gone.

Ghastly pale, she went upstairs. Her sisters said, "You look as if you had seen a ghost," and they tried to insist on her telling them what had happened to her. She put them off by complaining of headache and faintness; but she was terribly anxious.

Three months afterwards she heard her brother was coming home, then that he had arrived at Portsmouth, then he came. The first time she was alone with him she said, "I must tell you something," and she told him how he had appeared to her, and then she said, "I wrote it down at the time, and here is the paper, with the date and the hour."

He looked shocked at first, and then said, that at that very moment, being absent from his ship without leave, his boat had been upset, and he had been as nearly drowned as possible—in fact, when he was taken out of the water, life was supposed to

be extinct. His first fear on recovering was that his absence without leave would be detected by his accident and become his
ruin, and his first words were, "Do not tell any one you have seen
me."

June 21—At Madame de Quaire's I met Oscar Wilde and
Mrs Stewart. He talked in a way intended to be very startling, but
she startled him by saying quietly, "You poor dear foolish boy!
How can you talk such nonsense?" Mrs M. L. had recently met
this "type of an aesthetic age" at a country house, and described
his going out shooting in a black velvet dress with salmon-
coloured stockings, and falling down when the gun went off, yet
captivating all the ladies by his pleasant talk. One day he came
down looking very pale. "I am afraid you are ill, Mr Wilde," said
one of the party. "No, not ill, only tired," he answered. "The fact
is, I picked a primrose in the wood yesterday, and it was so ill, I
have been sitting up with it all night." Oscar Wilde's oddities
would attract notice anywhere, but of course they do so ten times
more in the *plein midi**of London society, where the smallest
faults of manner, most of all of assumption, are detected and
exposed at once.

July 2 [1883].—I have just heard again the ghost story so often
told by Mrs Thompson Hankey:

Two beautiful but penniless sisters were taken out in London
by an aunt. A young gentleman from the north, of very good family and fortune, fell in love with one of them, and proposed to her,
but she was with difficulty persuaded to accept him, and afterwards could never be induced to fix a date for their marriage. The
young man, who was very much in love, urged and urged, but,
on one excuse or another, he was always put off. Whilst things
were in this unsettled state, the young lady was invited to a ball.

* Broad daylight.

Her lover implored her not to go to it, and when she insisted, he made her promise not to dance any round dances, saying that if she did, he should believe she had ceased to care for him.

The young lady went to the ball, and, as usual all the young men gathered round her, trying to persuade her to dance. She refused any but square dances. At last, however, as a delightful valse was being played, and she was standing looking longingly on, she suddenly felt herself seized round the waist, and hurried into the dance. Not till she reached the end of the room, very angry, did she succeed in seeing with whom she had been forced to dance: it was with her own betrothed. Furious, she said she should never forgive him. But, as she spoke, he disappeared. She begged several young men to look for him, but he could not be found anywhere, and, to her astonishment, everyone denied altogether having seen him. On reaching home, she found a telegram telling her of his death, and when the hours were compared, he was found to have died at the very moment when he had seized her for the dance.

Whitburn, Dec. 28 [1884].—Lizzie Williamson says she wonders very much that, when our Saviour was on earth, no one thought of asking Him if people ill of hopeless and agonising complaints, idiots, cretins, &c., might not be put out of the way —"the Bible would have been so much more useful if it had only given us a little information on these points."

JOURNAL. *July 25 [1885].*—Mrs Rogerson, working in the east end of London met with a family of poor children—very hopelessly poor children—whom she knew, with a dog. She stopped and told them that, as they could not keep themselves, she wondered they could keep a dog. The eldest boy answered rather savagely, "Father bought it: Father gave sixpence for the dog, and right well he did too, for the rats wos so many, they wos, they used to eat our toes at night, and the dog keeps them off."

Campsea Ashe, Suffolk, Aug. 22—James Lowther, who is at home now, is certainly one of the pleasantest and best-informed young men of the day. He has just been very amusing about answers in Board Schools, telling, amongst others, of a child who was asked "If King Alfred had been alive now, what part would he have taken in politics?" and replied, "If King Alfred had been alive now, he would have been far too old to have taken part in politics at all!"

The last owner of Campsea Ashe, Mr Shepherd, was the grandson of a gardener. The Mr Shepherd who then owned Campsea adopted a nephew, a young Frere. The nephew invited his friends to Campsea, and after the fashion of the time, they sat up drinking. Very late, young Frere rang the bell and ordered another bottle of port. The butler, very cross, went up to his master's room and woke him up, saying that Mr Frere wanted some more port and that he must have the key of the cellar. Old Mr Shepherd, furious, gave the key, but next morning sent for a lawyer and disinherited his nephew, and, no one else being handy, and having a gardener he liked who bore his own name of Shepherd, he left him his fortune.

Burwarton, Shropshire, Oct. 23 [1885].—This is a beautiful place of Lord Boyne's, high in the Clee hills. The house is modern, but has good pictures, several representing members of the Medmenham brotherhood, and one a Lady Paisley, an ancestress, who declared that she did not wish to go to heaven if poor people went there.

The latter months of 1885 found me quietly at home, exceedingly busy over my work on France. As at all other times, except in fine summer weather, I was chiefly alone, save when on Sundays some of my young men friends—"the boys"—were generally at Holmhurst for two nights, for I have always felt how much, in similar circumstances, I should have cared myself to have a friend and a homelike little refuge to go to. But it must be allowed that, except in very rare cases, those I tried to be useful to in former days turned out very ill. Here are just a few instances: —

No. 1 was a gentleman once in a good position, who had fallen into extreme poverty. I gave up being in London, I gave up going abroad, I always went in an omnibus instead of a cab, always travelled second class instead of first, to have £50 a year to give to No. 1. But when I found that my poor gentleman always took a hansom even to cross Eaton Square, I drew in my purse-strings.

No. 2 seemed very different. Rudely nurtured, he minded no difficulties, and was willing to live hardly. He only cared for work, and his work was science. He threw his whole life into it, and seemed on the eve of great discoveries—in fact, he made them. But he had no one to help him to buy the patents that were necessary, and I spent £800 for this, and altogether many thousand pounds in his behalf. He was to have repaid this sum if he became successful in life, but he made a very large fortune, and "forgot to pay it." Then, having lost his fortune again, his originality and cleverness took another direction: he suddenly turned Buddhist, cared for nothing but the divine essence, and went off to India to join a brotherhood in which, after years of prayer and fasting, he might hope to obtain the distinction of "a little yellow garment." He wrote then that his religion itself would prevent his ever again forgetting that he owed me four thousand pounds with interest. Yet, after his return, he repudiated his debt altogether, and denied that he had even the slightest obligation to me. All I had spent was thrown away! No. 2 was an utter collapse.

No. 3 wanted to be married. He had led a wild life, and his marriage would "be the saving of him;" with his marriage a new page of his life would be turned over; but to enable the marriage to be, a loan of money was necessary. I sent the money, but the marriage never took place, and the loan was never returned. No. 3 vanished into chaos.

No. 4 was very engaging and I became very fond of him. He was perpetually at my home, where I always treated him as a younger brother, giving him money when I was away for whatever he wanted. When he wished to give a party to his friends in London, the food, the wine, the flowers, came from Holmhurst. He had to work hard in a public office, so every year I gave him money for the change of a Continental tour, and on one occasion, when he had no other companion, I took him myself, and showed him the whole of a foreign country. This went on for nine years. Then a circumstance occurred which made me feel that he, in his turn, might, not even for one day, but for one hour, be useful to me. Under these circumstances I asked a favour of him. "No," it was refused at once, "it might not be to his advantage: it might even possibly be rather inconvenient." No. 4 collapsed.

No. 5 was a very young and ingenuous boy. I met him first when he was at Oxford, when his family—country gentlefolk—were trying to compel him to take Orders. He confided to me his misery about it, and his utter unfitness. I backed him up in resisting. From that time I saw a great deal of him. He was very affectionate to me, and I grew very fond of him. His family, irritated at his opposition to taking Orders, refused to go on spending money upon his education. I continued it, or thought I did, by letter, sending him daily questions to answer by post, and receiving *précis* of History from him and correcting them. He was also very frequently at Holmhurst for a long time together, and had more of a real home there than with his own parents. Once, without my knowledge or that of his family, he went to London, and got into terribly bad companionship and disgracefully bad habits. He was plundered of all he possessed, and had to pawn his watch to get away. To prevent the discovery of this, which would have hopelessly estranged him from his family, I redeemed his valuables for a considerable sum. He then seemed penitent, promised amendment, and took refuge at Holmhurst again. About a year after I found him on the eve of wilfully making an acquaintance which was sure to cause his ruin. I pointed out to him the misery he was bringing upon himself, and he promised to give it up. Then I found that all the while he was promising to do nothing of the kind, he had been constantly writing to the person in question, with whom he had no previous acquaintance, making assignations for meetings, &c. From that time he got into one miserable scrape after another. He sank and sank. Whenever he has made a promise, he has always broken his word; nothing he says can be believed; his every act must be mistrusted . . . . Now, he has taken Holy Orders! This is the end of No. 5.

No. 6 was very dear to me. I had known him intimately from his earliest childhood. Exceedingly unprepossessing in appearance, he gave the most brilliant promise of a distingushed career. To me he showed the most unbounded affection and confidence, but he never told the truth. This led to a series of miserable deceptions which caused his expulsion from school and brought about his failure everywhere. Dreaded, mistrusted, he became alienated from his family, almost from his fellow-men. No opportunity of extravagant folly occurred but was greedily seized upon, to be followed by fresh falsehood. His whole life has been a sorrow to those who know him, and who think mournfully of its beautiful "might have been."

I met No. 7 when he was eighteen. Of very lowly origin but gentle instincts, he had been turned adrift at seventeen upon London to earn his own living, and he seemed at first to be earning it bravely and honestly. He was clever and was anxious to improve himself, and he spent all his evenings in reading, and succeeded in teaching himself French. By his own unaided efforts he had really given himself an education. At first I used only to lend him books and do what I could to help his reading. Then I frequently invited him to Holmhurst, and paid for his coming there. He had a bad illness in London, when I went constantly to him in his miserable garret, and supplied all his little comforts. About a year after I first knew him, he yielded to a great temptation in misappropriating a large sum of money belonging to the firm he was serving, and spending it in a very disgraceful manner. It seemed as if he really did this under a diabolic influence, and as if he really believed that he should be able to replace the money before the theft was discovered. But the time drew very near when his accounts would be examined, and there was no chance—there never had been—that they would be found correct. Then the full agony of his position came upon him, and he confessed the whole to me and implored me to save him. The day before the examination of accounts I replaced the stolen money, and the defalcation was never discovered.

From this time he seemed to go on well, and I became much attached to him. Five times a year I paid his expenses to Holmhurst, to give him country air, treating him like my own son when he was with me. Then came a time when, after several years, he fell into feeble health, and had to leave his situation. I was then not perfectly satisfied with the way in which he was going on, and did not think him as frank and candid as he had been, but I took him home with me for a month to recruit. At Holmhurst he had every kindness and indulgence, and was received not only as an equal, but almost as a child of the house. At the end of a month, he told me that he had heard of some very suitable employment in London, and hoped that I would not object to his going to town to see about it. I said, "Certainly not; but what is the employment?" To my surprise, he said that he could not tell me then, but I should know later. I was more surprised because, when he left, he was so unusually affectionate—"I am very glad you are so fond of me, but I cannot imagine why you should show it especially to-day, as you are coming back in a few hours." He never came back. It was many days before he wrote. Then I had a formal letter saying that, when he went up to London, he had been received into the Church of Rome at Brompton Oratory, and enclosing a list of his possessions left at Holmhurst, and directions for sending them. Since then he has sunk lower and lower. I have often heard of him, and always a worse account. He is utterly lost to me. That is the end of No. 7.

No. 8 was excessively good-looking, had pleasant manners, and was especially winning to ladies. I had known his family long ago, and his home, a very quiet rectory in a desolate fen district. When he was at Oxford, I found him, like No. 5, very unhappy at being expected to take Orders, for which he honestly felt himself unfitted, and I persuaded him to tell his father that it was impossible. Then, as he was penniless and had no prospects, it was necessary that a profession should be found for him, and I obtained a nomination for him for the Foreign Office from Lord Granville. He came to London to work for this, and he worked well. Feeling that it would be most undesirable for him to go on in London, especially to enter the Foreign Office, knowing no one in society, I took him out with me every day to parties, and introduced him everywhere, claiming all kindness for him as my intimate friend. His good looks and pleasing manners made him very welcome. But he fell in love with an Earl's daughter. Strange to say, his suit was not rejected, though a probation of two years was required, during which he must begin to make an income. With this view, he abandoned all thought of the Foreign Office and took to the Stock Exchange. A week before the end of the two years' probation, the lady, of her own accord, threw him over, but, as far as love went, her place was soon supplied. By this time, too, the young man had acquired *l'habitude de société*, had begun to despise his humble relations, to cut his old friends, and a shake of the Prince of Wales's hand finally turned his head. He scarcely speaks to me now when we meet. He openly says that, as he has gained all he can from me, he naturally prefers "those who can be more useful" to him.

No. 9, poor fellow, was long a great anxiety to me. He was of good family. He fell often—fell into the most frightful vice and shame. He repented bitterly, and then fell again worse than before. But in one of his best and truest times of repentance, God saw that he was positively unable to cope with temptation, and he died—died most mercifully, full of faith, hope, and gratitude. This was the end of No. 9. Thinking of him has often brought to my mind Rossetti's lines —

> Look in my face: my name is Might-have-been,
> I am also called No-more, Too-late, Farewell.

London, Dec. 6 [1886].—Luncheon with Miss Seymour to meet Madame de Quaire. She had met Lady Colin Campbell at dinner and sat opposite to her, but she did not know her. She could not help being attracted by the necklace she wore, it was so very extraordinary. After a time it seemed to be moving by itself. She fancied at first that this must be a delusion, but, putting up her glasses, she certainly saw the necklace writhing around Lady Colin's throat. Seeing her astonished look, Lady Colin said, "Oh, I see you are looking at my snake: I always wear a live snake round my throat in hot weather; it keeps one's neck so cool;" and it really was a live snake.

Dec. 9—Dined with M. B., who told me of Lady Vane being quite worn-out by the ghastly noises at their place in Cumberland: it was as if some one were always trying to climb up a disused chimney in the wall, and then falling violently down again. But lately, when Sir Henry Vane was away, she had the wall opened. Inside she found a wide and very lofty closet, narrowing into a funnel as it reached the roof, where it opened by a very small hole to the sky. In it were human bones, a broken water-bottle, and the cover of an old Bible, which bore a date. Lady Vane had the bones gathered up and put into a box, which was left in a corner of Sir Henry Vane's room till his return.

When Sir Henry Vane came home, he was exhausted by a long

journey and went at once to rest. Lady Vane did not intend to tell him of her discovery till the next day. But suddenly, late in the afternoon, she heard a tremendous noise in her husband's room. She rushed in, and found Sir Henry in a state of the greatest agitation. He said, "I have seen the most frightful apparition—a woman in that corner," pointing to where the box of bones had been deposited.

From old family archives they found that, some years before, exactly at the date upon the Bible cover, a woman had been walled up in the house. She had made desperate efforts to escape up the funnel of the disused chimney, and had always fallen down again. Sir Henry and Lady Vane themselves buried the bones in the churchyard, and the house has been at peace ever since.

XVIII. Adventure in France

Courmayeur.

On the 26th of February 1889, I left England again for my French book. During the latter part of this French tour I had an unpleasant adventure, which excited more attention than I ever anticipated at the time. On April 19 I had gone from Gap to visit Embrun, a curious little town in the Alpes Dauphinoises. I had not long left the station before I was aware that I was watched and followed wherever I went. However, at last I contrived to dodge my pursuer, and made, from behind a wall, the sketch of the cathedral which I wanted, and then had dinner at the hotel. When I was returning to the station, separated by a desolate plain from the town, I saw, by the faint waning light, the same figure following wherever I went. It was dark when the train by which I was to leave was to start. I had taken my place, and the train was already in motion, when it was stopped, and an official accompanied by a gendarme entered the carriage and demanded what I had been doing at Embrun. "Visiting the cathedral." "Why should I visit the cathedral?" and so on, through a long series of questions of the same kind. My passport was demanded, and, though not usually considered necessary for English travellers, I happened to have one. It was, however, refused as an identification, not being dated in the present year. Fortunately, I recollected having in my pocket-book an order from the Préfet de la Seine authorising me to draw in all the palaces in Paris and elsewhere in France, and this was considered sufficient. The train was allowed to move on just as a crowd was collecting.

At Briançon (where I spent the following day), I carefully abstained from drawing, as it was a fortified town. But on April 23 I left the station at Vizille to visit the old château of the famous Lesdiguiéres, two miles distant. I had seen the château, and began to occupy the quarter of an hour which remained before the omnibus started for the station by sketching it from the village street, when I was pounced upon by a gendarme. "Who has authorised you to sketch the château of Vizille?"—"No one."—"If you can draw this, you may also have drawn other places. You will go with me to the gendarmerie;" and I was marched through the long street of Vizille, followed by a crowd, and with the hand of the gendarme occasionally grasping me by the shoulder. At the gendarmerie a superior officer appeared, and, with the most extreme insolence of manner, demanded what I had been doing in France, &c. "What had I drawn?"—"Churches and mountains."—"Ah! Mountains! then it has been very easy for you to make a little mark in the drawing, known only to yourself, meaning here is a fortress, and there a fortress."—"But I am an Englishman."—"Oh, you are, are you? Then I am all the more glad that we have taken you, for we shall probably soon be at war with England, and then you will make your sketches useful to your Government; so you will consider yourself under arrest." The letter of the Préfet de la Seine was treated as worthless because it had no seal. The passport was rejected altogether with contempt.

After this, all further protestations and remonstrances were answered by an insolent shout of— *"Taisez vous donc, vous êtes en état d'arrestation."*[*]

Then the first gendarme was sent with me to the station, where my portmanteaux were opened and ransacked, the contents being tossed out upon the platform. Two suspicious articles were found. First, a slight sketch of the gorge at Sisteron (not the fort; the fort is on the other side of the rock), and, far worse, three volumes of the *Guide Joanne* for France. "What did I want with guide-books?"—"To study the country."—"Ah! that is just what I thought;" and all the officials of the station were called in to witness the discovery. The gendarme then declared that I must return with him and be locked up at Vizille, but a train coming up

MONTMAJOUR.

at that moment, I made a dash into it, and probably thinking a public scrimmage impolitic, the gendarme allowed the station-master to fasten my boxes and bring me a ticket. The gendarme

* "Shut up, you are under arrest."

then took his place opposite to me in a first-class carriage.

At 5 p.m. the train arrived at Grenoble. At the station the gendarme of Vizille summoned a gendarme of the town, and I was conducted as a prisoner by the two to the Hôtel Monnet. The gendarme of Vizille then left me in care of the other, shut up in a room of the hotel, where the gendarme of Grenoble sat silent opposite to me till 6:30. I thought that then the other gendarme would come back from the Préfecture with an order that I was to be freed from further annoyance. Not a bit of it! He came back with an order that all my possessions were to be carefully ransacked, and all the contents of my boxes were turned out upon the floor.

All suspected articles—all my sketches, manuscripts, letters, and all the volumes of the *Guide Joanne* were then put into my smallest portmanteau, which one of the gendarmes carried, and I was marched between the two to the old palace of the Dauphins, where the courts are. Here two clerks (or secretaries of the Préfecture) subjected me to a long examination—who I was, what was my employment, where I had been, &c. The English letters found in my blotting-book (ordinary family letters) were translated into French by a clerk who understood English. All my drawings (chiefly of church architecture) were examined in detail, and their objects inquired into. The terrible *Guides Joanne* were passed in review and, after an hour, I was told I was free, but without a single word of apology or regret.

On parting, the gendarme of Vizille was told in my presence that he had only done his duty in arresting me for having ventured to draw the Château of Lesdiguiéres; and he left, carrying off in his pocket (by accident no doubt) a sealed packet which he had taken from my dressing-case. I called the next day upon my examiners to ask them to obtain restitution of the packet, but they declined to take any trouble.

I wrote this story in the train, and posted it at one of the stations to the editor of the *Times*, who inserted it in the paper, so that when I reached home I found England ringing with it, and a question asked in the House about it. I also complained to the Foreign Office, and Lord Salisbury sent me afterwards the French answer to the inquiries made. They allowed the facts of the examination, but denied that I had ever been arrested, though the leading feature through the whole had been that whenever I attempted to speak I had been silenced by a shout of "*Taisez-vous donc; rappelez-vous donc que vous êtes en arrestation.*"* The sealed packet was never restored.

I returned home on May 3, and at the beginning of June was at Scotney Castle.

Mr Hussey told me that an old Mr and Mrs Close of Nottingham were very rich and great misers, and they both made wills leaving all they possessed each to the other. However, as they died within a few hours of each other, that made very little difference to anybody.

When the heirs-at-law arrived at Nottingham—young people full of spirits—they were greatly excited and brimming with curiosity. It was known that there were splendid diamonds, and that vast wealth of every kind existed, but at first nothing seemed to be forthcoming. Cupboards and drawers were ransacked in vain. Nothing particular was found.

At last, in a room at the top of the house a great trunk was discovered. "Here," they said, "it all is; we shall find all the treasures now." But when the trunk was opened, the upper part was found to be full of nothing but scraps of human hair, as if for

* "Shut up; remember that you are under arrest."

years the off-scourings of all the old hair brushes had been collected; then below that was a layer of very dirty old curl-papers; and the bottom of the box was full of still more dirty old corsets of ladies' dresses, and—the box was alive! When young Mrs Close had dived into the box, she exclaimed, "What disgusting old creatures our relations must have been! This horrible mess might infest the whole house; we must have it burnt at once." So she had some men up, and the trunk carried down into the courtyard of the house, and a huge bonfire made there, and the trunk upset into it.

As it was burning, she stood by, and heedlessly, with her stick, pulled one of the curl-papers towards her, and poked it open at her feet. It was a £50 note! In an agony, she scrimmaged at the fire, and raked out all she possibly could, but it was too late; most of the notes were burnt; she only saved about £800.

Naturally her husband was furious, and of course he was very unjust. "Any one but you would have examined the box carefully; there never was such an idiot of a woman," &c. And every time he saw the burnt heap in the courtyard, he burst forth afresh. So she sent for the dustman round the corner, and had all the ashes carefully cleared away.

Still nothing had been found of the diamonds. They had certainly existed; there were always the diamonds to fall back upon. But though they searched everywhere, nothing could be found of them. At last they asked the only old lady with whom Mrs Close had visited if she knew of any one who could help them. "Yes, certainly," she said; "there's old Betty Thompson at the almshouses, she was always in and out of the house as charwoman; she knew more of Mrs Close and her ways than any one else." So away they went to the almshouses, and asked Betty Thompson.

"Oh yes," she said, "she knew very well that there were diamonds, very fine diamonds indeed, but small good *they* ever did to old Mrs Close, for she always kept them sewn up and hidden away in her old stays."

The stays had all perished in the fire; the diamonds would not have burnt, but then the very ashes had been thrown away; there was no trace left of them. The bank-notes were all very old—the few that were saved—but they were quite good; but there was very little else left of the great inheritance.

LETTER. *Jermyn Street, June 19 [1887].*—Lady Dorothy Neville has been most funny about a burglary at Lady Orford's. While the family were away, a man came to the door, who said he was sent to measure the dining room chimney-piece, and asked the old woman who was taking care of the place to go up to the top of the house to get him a piece of tape for the purpose. When she came down, the man was gone, and so were two of the best pictures. "I could swear to the pictures anywhere," said the old woman afterwards, "for they were of members of the Orford family." "They were the Virgin Mary and St. Sebastian," added Lady Dorothy, "and I leave you to imagine how far *they* were ever likely to have been members of the Orford family!"

Chief-Justice Morris said he was sitting on the bench in Ireland, and after a case had been tried, he said to the jurymen, "Now to consider this matter, you will retire to your accustomed place," and two-thirds of them went into *the dock*.

Another time he said to a culprit, "I can produce five witnesses who saw you steal that cow."—"Yes," said the prisoner, "but I can produce five hundred who did not."

When I was at Hornby, I went up with the present Duchess of Leeds into a tower into which a former Duchess had carried a quantity of books, because, she said, "there were enough down-stairs." They had been taken up at haphazard, and some of them were of extraordinary value: there were wonderful editions of Aretino there, excessively improper, but nobody could read them. The tower had been open to the bats and owls, and when we took out the books, many of them were matted together in one solid mass: they bore the name of Hewit Osborne, the apprentice who jumped from London Bridge to save the life of his master's daughter, and, afterwards marrying her, founded the family; he was a great Italian scholar.

July 15 [1887].—I heard such a charming story of little Jane Smith the other day. Her nurse told her to say her prayers. She wouldn't; she said God wouldn't expect her to. "But He always expects it," said the nurse. "No, He doesn't," replied little Jane, "for I told Him the other day I couldn't say them, I was so sleepy, and He said, "Don't mention it, *Miss Smith*.""

July 20 [1887].—Tea with Mrs Ford—always interesting. Mr Browning described how he had been asked to dinner by two elderly ladies—sisters. He did not know them, but it was very kind of them to ask him, and he went. Going down to dinner, the lady who fell to his share suddenly said to him, "You are a poet, aren't you?"—"Well, people are sometimes kind enough to say that I am."—"Oh, don't mind my having mentioned it: you know *Lord Byron was a poet!*"

Browning is unlike Tennyson; he does not write from inspiration but by power of work. He says he sets himself a certain number of lines to write in a day, and he writes them. Sometimes he says, "Tomorrow morning I will write a sonnet;" and he writes it. Nevertheless he is always greater in aspiration than in achievement. Mr Carlyle could not bear his poems. "What did the fellow mean by leaving that car-load of stones at my door?" he said to Alfred Tennyson when Browning left one of his poems there.

Oct. 2 [1887].—Again at Highcliffe with Lady Waterford, whose conversation is as charming as ever. Here are some fragments from her lips:—"That is like the priest who, when he was remonstrated with for eating meat on Friday, said, 'All flesh is grass.'"

XIX. In Pleasure and Pain

THE AVE-VALE STEPS, HOLMHURST.

A FEW DAYS AFTER I reached home, two more volumes of mine were published, "Paris" and "Days near Paris." They had been the engrossing work of the last two years. My hourly thought had been for them, and I had taken all the pains I could with them. I knew their faults, and know them still; but all the same I am conscious, and I am sure it is not conceit, that no better general books on those subjects have ever been written. I suppose it is one of the penalties of a lonely life that it seemed that no one spoke of them; that day after day passed on and no one mentioned their existence. And then came a Review—a leading article indeed—in the *Athenaeum*, not of mere abuse of the books, though no words were strong enough for that, but of such bitter personal malignity against myself, as gave one the shuddering conviction that one must indeed have an enemy as virulent as he was unscrupulous. Most of the Reviews of my books have been unfavourable, but the books have always contrived to outlive them; and generally, when they have been found fault with, I have felt almost grateful for such lessons of humility.

It is curious, certainly, how one has only to turn to the pages of a book which collects Reviews of past authors, like "Alibone's Dictionary," to find plentiful consolation. I chanced to open it on Thackeray, and found the *Edinburgh Review*, after abusing "Esmond" in the most contemptuous tones, saying patronisingly, " . . . a parody three volumes long becomes tiresome." The same *Edinburgh Review* advised Byron to abandon poetry and apply his talents to some better use; and declared Coleridge's "Christabel" to be "a thing utterly destitute of value."

Even honest reviewers seldom read beyond the first chapter of a book; *that* they usually read, and occasionally criticise; but even then the tendency to save themselves trouble generally causes a great deal of copying.

In the middle of October [1887] I went North for a short time.

JOURNAL. *Ruby Castle, Oct. 27*—Mrs Forester, wife of the Duke of Cleveland's nephew, who is here, told me much that is curious.

A Mrs A. had had an intimate friendship at school with two other girls, and when they parted, they made each other a solemn vow that if either of the three were in any real trouble in after life, the others would do all they could to help her. Mrs A. was left a widow with several children, and almost in a state of destitution. In all her troubles, she had continued to confide in Lady B., one of the three friends. At one time especially, Lady B. was perplexed as to how she could help her, and spoke of it to her husband, who said, "Well, there is at least one thing I could do for her: there is that old place of ours in Dorsetshire, where nobody lives. It is all being kept up for nothing, so if Mrs A. likes to go and inhabit it, she is quite welcome; only, you know, she ought to be told that it is said to be haunted."

Lady B. made the proposal to Mrs A., who was enchanted, and she moved at once with her children to the house in Dorsetshire, where she seemed to find a refuge from her troubles and every comfort. She asked the servants whom she found in the house about the ghosts, and they said, "Oh yes, the great hall and the rooms beyond it are said to be haunted, but we never go there, and the ghosts never come to our part of the house, so we are never troubled by them in the least." For several years Mrs A. lived most happily in the old house, and nothing happened.

At last, on one of her children's birthdays, she invited some children from the neighbourhood to come and play with her own children, who begged that, after tea, they might all go and play hide-and-seek in the great disused hall. The children had finished their games, and Mrs A. was alone in the hall setting things to rights afterwards, about 8 p.m. in the evening, with an unlighted candle in her hand, when she heard someone call out loudly, "Bring me a light! Bring me a light!" Then, almost immediately, the door from the inner passage leading to the farther rooms opened, and a lady rushed in, beautifully dressed in white, but with all her dress in flames. She ran across the hall screaming "She's done it! She's done it!" and vanished through a door on the other side. Mrs A. instantly lighted her candle, and ran with it up the passage from which the lady emerged, but she found all the doors locked. The next night, at exactly the same hour, she came again to the hall, and exactly the same thing happened. She then wrote to Lady B. that she should be obliged to leave the place, unless Lord B. could explain the mystery.

Lord B. then said that an ancestress of his—a widowed Lady B.—had an only son, who fell in love with the charming daughter of a neighbouring clergyman. The young lady was lovely, fascinating, and very well educated, but the mother regarded it as a mésalliance and would not hear of it. The young man, who was a very dutiful son, consented to gratify his mother by waiting, and went abroad for two years. After that time, as their attachment was unbroken, and he was of age, he married the young lady.

It was with joyful surprise that the young married pair received a very kind letter from the mother, saying that as all was now settled, she should make a point of welcoming the bride as her daughter, and always living happily with her afterwards. They went home to the mother at the old house which Lord B. had lent to Mrs A., and were most kindly received. All seemed perfectly smooth. At last a day came on which the mother had invited an immense party to be introduced to and do honour to the bride. The evening arrived, and the young lady was already dressed, when her mother-in-law came into the room, kissed her affectionately, and then said to her son, "Now that she is indeed my daughter, I am going to fetch the family diamonds, that I may have the pleasure of decorating her with them myself." The diamonds spoken of were really the property of the son, but he had never liked to irritate his mother by claiming them, and rejoiced that his wife should accept them from her.

The mother then went to fetch the diamonds, the son lighting her. As they were coming back, they heard the voice of the young lady calling to her husband to bring her a light. "Oh, I will take it to her," cried the mother suddenly, and snatched the candle out of his hand. In another instant the girl rushed by with her white dress enveloped in flames, screaming "She's done it! She's done it!" The mother confessed that her hate and jealousy had been too much for her.

Now the house is pulled down, and a railway passes over its site.

JOURNAL. *Dec. 11 [1888].*—My old cousins, Mr and Mrs Thurlow, who had often invited me before to their house of Baynards, wrote that this week was my last chance of going, as Baynards was just sold, so I have been for one night. The house is partly modern, but the place was an ancient royal residence, and was part of the dower of Katherine Parr. A pretty statue of Edward VI was discovered there walled up, and Margaret Roper lived there afterwards, and long kept her husband's head in a box, which still exists at the foot of the staircase . . . .

Mrs Thurlow says that Cardinal Wiseman went to dine with some friends of hers. It was a Friday, but they had quite forgotten to provide a fast-day dinner. However, he was quite equal to the occasion, for he stretched out his hands in benediction over the table and said, "I pronounce all this to be fish," and forthwith enjoyed all the good things heartily.

LETTER. *Holmhurst, Aug. 15 [1889].*—You would be amused with my hearing the other day that one of the servants had said, "Our master's a gentleman as knows his place," which meant that I never find fault with an under-servant except through an upper, or cast even the faintest shadow upon an upper-servant if an under-servant is present. After all, it is only another form of Landor's observation—"The spider is a gentleman, for he takes his fly in secret."

LETTER. *St Michael's Mount, Sept. 7 [1889].*—A child at Whiteway, being asked where the eggs were laid, answered, "On an average."—"What do you mean? Who told you so?"—"Father;

he said the hens laid, on an average, twenty eggs a day."

LETTER. *Holmhurst, Nov. [1889].*—From Ingmire I went to Muncaster, which I thought even more beautiful and delightful than before. The Bishop of Carlisle had just been at Muncaster, who said that a boy in a Board-school examination, being asked one of the foolish Catechism questions of "Why is a boy baptized when by reason of his tender age &c.?" wrote, "Why indeed?"

Another child in a higher class, being asked to define faith, said it was "the power of believing absolutely what was utterly incredible."

In quoting so constantly from journal and letters, I do not think I have mentioned how much poverty had been pressing upon me in the last few years. Not only had Messrs Daldy and Virtue, representing my first publishers, ceased to pay even the interest of their large debt, or paid it most irregularly, but under my second set of publishers I had made nothing whatever during the seven years I had been with them. Their accounts showed that 28,000 of my books had been sold in the time, but the innumerable percentages, &c., had swallowed up the whole of the profits, leaving me nothing but the loss of money expended on woodcuts, &c.

While I was at Muncaster, however, Mrs Arthur Severn came to the castle, and told me how Mr Ruskin also had made nothing by his books in the hands of my then publishers, but that they had brought him in a good income since they were removed to the hands of Mr Allen of Orpington. To his hands, therefore, I soon after removed all my books. I had no complaint of unfairness to make against those I had lately employed: they only acted according to their agreements and their usual method, which I had long hoped against hope might eventually result to my advantage: and they behaved very handsomely about parting with the books, though it must have been both a loss and disappointment to them.

LETTER. *Nov. 10 [1890].*—C. writes to me for advice, but I feel more and more diffident about giving any. I found such a capital bit about this in an American novel called "Margaret Maliphant," the other day. The old servant Deborah says, "What you think's the right way most times turns out to be the wrong way; and when you make folks turn to the right when they was minded to turn to the left, it's most like the left would have been the best way for them to travel after all. I've done advisin' long ago; for it's a queer tract of country here below, and every one has to take their own chance in the long run."

LETTER. *Nov. 30 [1890].*—I had a pleasant visit at St Audries, Sir A. Acland Hood's beautiful place. Mr W. Neville, who was one of the guests at St Audries, had been to hear Dr Parker, of the Congregational Hall, preach. He began his sermon by saying, "My brethren, I have received a letter from a gentleman saying that he intends to be present today and to make a philosophical analysis of my discourse to you. I am sure you will all sympathise with me in the embarrassment and nervousness which I must experience on such an occasion, though certainly I may derive some little comfort from the fact that my correspondent spells 'philosophical' with an 'f.'"

LETTER. *Rome, April 26 [1892].* —It has been a great pleasure to see a good deal of "Mark Twain" (Mr Samuel Clemens) and his most charming wife. He is a wiry, thin old man, with abundant grey hair, full round the head, like an Italian *zazzara*. He speaks very slowly, dragging his words and his sentences laboriously, and is long in warming up and when he does, he walks about the room whilst he makes all his utterances, which have additional drollery from the slowness with which they are given. A rival to Mark Twain, or rather one who draws him out capitally, is an American Miss Page, a very handsome elderly woman like an ancient Juno. "My cousin was begged of by a woman one night," said Miss Page. "She was very violent, and she said, 'You must give me money, you *shall*, or I'll say you're Jack the Ripper.' He went close up to her, and in sepulchral accents whispered, 'I *am!*' and the woman ran off as hard as she could."

JOURNAL. *Jan. [1893].*—Mrs Kemble was certainly the living person I wished most to see, but I have let too many opportunities slip, and she has passed away without my knowing her. She must have been a great and generous woman, and those who knew her always loved though they feared her. Miss (Harriet) Hosmer has often told me how dearly she and her companions loved Mrs Kemble when she (Miss Hosmer) was at school in America near the place where she (Mrs Kemble) lived. She would come voluntarily and read to the schoolgirls half a play in the morning and would finish it in the evening. Once, when she was reading, snow came on, and when she was to go home it was quite deep; so all the schoolgirls turned out with spades and brooms and cleared it away before her.

But her severe manner terrified those who were given that way. "We had some private theatricals," Mrs Story told me, "and Mrs Kemble came to look on at the rehearsal, at which a girl was acting who was supposed to do it very well. Afterwards, when she came in, Mrs Kemble walked up to her and "*Are* you a fool?" was all she said.

Dr Silas Bertol, the Unitarian minister at Boston, took his girl to see Mrs Kemble. He was nervous, and said, "My daughter wished so much to have the honour of knowing—rather of hearing—rather of seeing Mrs Kemble, that I have ventured to bring her." Mrs Kemble bowed stiffly, and motioned them to sit down, but said nothing. The girl only sat and stared at her. Then the father tried again—"My daughter is very young—is very nervous—is very shy." Then Mrs Kemble looked at them both, and, in her most sephulchral accents, said, "Shy! I also am shy. And since your daughter has nothing to say to me, and since most assuredly I have nothing to say to her, I will wish you good morning."

When in Boston long ago, while she was reading in public, she ordered dresses, pink and blue satin, at the great shop, the Marshall & Snelgrove of the town, but gave no address. The shopmen were afraid to ask her. The manager felt he must run after her and ask where the things should be sent. Unfortunately, to attract her attention, he touched her. "Unhand me, ruffian," she shouted in her most ferocious tone. "And such was the man's terror," said my informant, "that, though he was quite young, his hair was turned white that night."

A lady was once alluding to the hope she entertained of retaining her figure. In her most tragical voice, Mrs Kemble said, dwelling on every syllable, "With a hereditary tendency to fat, nor exercise, nor diet, nor grief may avail."

JOURNAL. *Dec. 7 [1893].*—Another delightful sitting with Mr Eddis. He talked of his own early life as a student . . . .

"Turner often used to come in and look at us and our work. There was a student amongst us who had painted in a red background, and he painted it the crudest, brightest red he could manage. Turner came in and said, 'Come now, this will never do; give me your palette and brush,' and in a few minutes he had toned and mellowed it down with a hundred delicate gradations of tint. 'Well now, don't you think it's improved?' said Turner. 'No, I don't,' answered the man; 'I think it was much better before,' which annoyed Turner rather."

LETTER. *London, April [1894].*—I have had a pleasant time here and as usual have found that there is more to be learnt by enduring the ups and downs of social pleasures than by withdrawing from them . . . . A little Gould child said the other day, "Can God Almighty do everything, Mother?"—"Yes, my dear, God is omnipotent."—"I know one thing He couldn't do, Mother."—"Quite impossible, my dear."—"Yes, Mother; God couldn't make a stone so big that He couldn't carry it."—Deep unconscious theology.

Bishopthorpe, Oct. 16 [1894].—The dining room here is hung with Archbishops, a very fine set of portraits. Talking of the portraits led to Sir T. Lawrence, who was an endless time over his pictures. That was the case with his portrait of Lady Mexborough and her child. Lord Mexborough asked to have it home again and again, but it was no use. At last he said he *must* have the picture. "Well," said Sir Thomas, "I've been a long time, I allow; but I've got well forward with Lady Mexborough: it's the baby wants finishing. Now if Lady Mexborough would kindly bring the baby and give me another sitting, I really will finish."—"Well, Sir Thomas," said Lord Mexborough, "my wife will be happy to give you another sitting whenever you like, but *the baby's in the Guards*!"

Nov. 16 [1894].—At Letton, the pleasant house of the Gurdons in Suffolk, I have met a large party, including the Hamonds of Westacre, into whose courtyard an invisible horse and rider clatter whenever any death is about to occur in their family. Several curious stories were told: —

Some young men once determined to frighten the famous naturalist Cuvier. One of them got horns, hoofs and a tail, and appeared by Cuvier's bedside. "I am the devil," he said, "and I am come to eat you." Cuvier looked at him. "Carnivorous! Horns— hoofs—impossible! Good-night," and he turned over and went to sleep.

LETTER. *London, Feb. 2 [1895].*—I dined with my two friends, Lewis Gilbertson and Frank Cookson, who live so happily together in the charming little canonical house of the former in Amen Court. Gilbertson told me how Mr Spooner of Oxford, celebrated for his absence of mind, was one evening found wandering disconsolately about the streets of Greenwich. "I've been here hours," he said. "I had an important appointment to meet someone at The Dull Man, Greenwich, and I can't find it anywhere; and the odd thing is no one seems to have heard of it." "You idiot!" exclaimed his wife; "why, it was the Green Man, Dulwich, you had to go to."

LETTER. *Penrhyn Castle, Sept. 22 [1895].*—I heard an amusing story the other day. Mr Parke of Andover, a great American philosopher and thinker, at one time quite lost the power of sleep. He said he had long tried all remedies in vain, but at last found a remedy which never failed. It was to have a book read to him, the story of a woman's life. It always took effect at once, and soothed him into the sweetest slumbers. If he was nervous, his wife would take the book and begin—"Elizabeth Fry was born"—"But," said Mr Parke, "she has begun that book constantly for two years, and I have never found out where she was born yet, for with the first words I am in dreamland."

Miss R. told me how the Bishop of Winchester and the Dean of Windsor were walking together down the street of Windsor, when they saw a little boy struggling to reach a bell. "Why, you're not tall enough, my little man; let me ring the bell for you," said the Bishop. "Yes, if you please, sir," said the boy modestly. So the Bishop gave the bell a good pull. "Now then, sir, run like the devil," shrieked the boy, as he made off as hard as he could.

Little E. L. was very naughty indeed the other day, and not only scratched her governess, but spit at her. "How can you have been so naughty?" said her mother, "It can only have been the devil who made you do such a thing." "Well, perhaps it was the devil who told me to scratch her," replied little E., "but as for the spitting, it was entirely my own idea."

Hams, Birmingham, Nov. 30 [1895].—This is a large house of extreme comfort, and its owner, Lord Norton, who looks sixty, though he is eighty-two, is one of the most agreeable hosts in England. Walking on the terrace this morning, [there was] the view of the pretty windings of the Thames. The river was terribly polluted by Birmingham, and Lord Norton went to law about it. "Should the convenience of one man be considered before that of millions?" exclaimed the Birmingham advocate at the trial. "Yes," shouted the opposition,"for the grandeur of English law is that millions may not interfere with the comfort and well-being of a single individual." Now the pollution is partially diverted into a sewage farm five miles in extent.

Bishopthorpe, Oct. 23—Lord Falkland has been here. He had been lately at Skelton Castle. His hostess, Miss Wharton, took him to his room, down a long passage—a large room, panelled with dark oak and with a great four-post bed with heavy hangings. It was very gloomy and oppressive, Lord Falkland thought, but he said nothing, dressed, and went down to dinner.

When he came upstairs again, he found the aspect of the room even more oppressive, but he made up a great fire and went to bed. In the night he was awakened by a pattering on the floor as of high-heeled shoes and the rustling of a stiff silk dress. There was still a little fire burning, but he could see nothing. As he distinctly heard the footsteps turn, he thought, "Oh, I hope they may not come up to the bed." They *did*. But then they turned away, and he heard them go out at the door.

With difficulty he composed himself to sleep again, but was soon reawakened by the same sound, the rustling of silk and the footsteps. Then he was thoroughly miserable, got up, lighted candles, made up the fire, and passed a wretched night. In the morning he was glad to find an excuse for going away.

Afterwards he heard an explanation. An old Wharton, cruel and brutal, had a young wife. One day, coming tipsy into his wife's room, he found her nursing her baby. He was in a violent temper, and, seizing the baby from her arms, he dashed its head against the wall and killed it on the spot. When he saw it was dead, he softened at once. Even in her grief and horror Mrs Wharton could not bear to expose him, and together they buried the child under the hearthstone; but she pined away and very soon she died.

She used to be heard not only rustling, but weeping, wailing, sobbing, crying. At that time the Whartons were Roman Catholics, and when the family were almost driven from their home by its terrors, they got a priest to exorcise the castle and to bury the baby skeleton in consecrated ground. Since then, there have been no sobs and cries, only the rustling and pattering of feet.

LETTER. *Oct. 26 [1896].*—The first three volumes of the "Story of my Life" are come out, and I send them to you. Even the favourable reviews complain vehemently about their length; and yet, if they were not in a huge type and had not quite half a volume's space full of woodcuts, they might easily have been two very moderate volumes.* Then, say the reviewers, "the public would have welcomed the book." But after all, it was not written or printed for the public, only for a private inner circle . . .! Then it is funny how each review wants a different part left out—one the childhood, one the youth, one the experiences of later life: there would be nothing left but the little anecdotes about already well-known people, which they all wish to keep, and, in quoting these, they one and all copy each other; it saves trouble. The *Saturday* had what the world calls "a cruel review" of the book, but what was really an article of nothing but personal vituperation against its author.

One of the things people find fault with is that I have not shown sufficient adoration for Jowett, who was so exceedingly kind to me at Oxford. But I always felt that it was for Arthur Stanley's sake. Jowett only really cared for three kinds of undergraduate—a pauper, a profligate, or a peer: he was boundlessly good to the first, he tried to reclaim the second, and he adored the third.

* The American edition, omitting nothing and doing full justice to the woodcuts, is in 2 rather thin volumes. — A.H.

XX. Farewell

Augustus John Cuthbert Hare

Letter, *Jan. 9 [1897]*.—Some people are very angry at me for telling the truth in the "Story of my Life" about my young years. They think that the portrait of a dead person should never be like a Franz Hals, portraying every "projecting peculiarity," but all delicately wrought with the smooth enamelling touch of Carlo Dolce. They wonder I can "reconcile it to my conscience: to hold another estimate of the Maurices to that which had been hitherto popular."

For myself I believe that the rule of after-death praise is a false one to be regulated by. I cannot feel that a faithful record of words and actions ought to be altered by the mere glamour of death, which so often gives an apotheosis to those who little deserve it.

Most extraordinarily virulent certainly reviews can be! *Blackwood* (*i.e.* the Maurice spirit in *Blackwood*), in an article which breathes of white lips . . . writes:—

"What is Mr Augustus Hare? He is neither anybody nor nobody —neither male nor female— Neither imbecile nor wise . . . As we wade through this foam of superannuated wrath . . . this vicious and venomous personal onslaught . . . Mr Hare's paragraphs plump like drops of concentrated venom over the dinted page . . . . Such a tenacity of ill-feeling, such a cold rage of vituperation, is seldom to be met with."

JOURNAL AND LETTER. *Castle Hale, Painswick, June 17 [1897].* — H. says that Count Herbert Bismarck went lately to a great function in Russia. While he wished to be incognito, he still did not see why he could not have the advantages of his cognito. "Stand back; you must keep the line," said an official as he was pushing through. "You do not know who I am; I am Count Herbert Bismarck."—"Really? Well, that quite *explains*, but it does not *excuse* your conduct," rejoined the officer.

LETTER. *March [1897].* —I think the reviews of the first three volumes of my "Story" must be coming to an end now. I have had them all sent to me and very amusing they have been, mostly recalling the dictum of Disraeli, that "critics are those who have failed in art and literature." Many criticisms have been kind. But the *Pall Mall Gazette* dwells upon the volumes' "bedside sentiment and goody-goody twaddle" and is "filled with genuine pity for a man who can attach importance to a life so trivial." The *Athenaeum* describes me as a mere "literary valet." *The New York Tribune* finds the book "the continuous wail of a very garrulous person."

LETTER. *Holmhurst, Nov. 16 [1897].* —Just now I have been laboring through the two long thick volumes which are called "Memoirs of Tennyson," though, when you close them, you have less idea of what the man was like than when you began—of the rude, rugged old egoist, who was yet almost sublimely picturesque; of the aged sage, who in dress, language, manners was always posing for the adoration of strangers, and furious if he did not get it, or—if he did. The book is most provoking, for it would by no means have destroyed the hero to have truthfully described the man.

LETTER AND JOURNAL. *Belvoir Castle, Nov. 18 [1899].*—I was two days at the familiar Campsea Ashe . . . . Mr Astor was there and was very funny about a man who was always late for everything, and who one day, when he was expecting a party to stay with him, rushed home after all his guests had arrived. On the stairs he met a man, with whom, to make up for lost time, he shook hands most warmly, saying, "Oh, my dear fellow, I'm so glad to see you; do make yourself quite at home and enjoy yourself." It was a burglar, very much surprised at his cordial reception, for he was carrying off all the valuables.

Helston, May 10 [1900].—Yesterday I breakfasted in the coffee-room with an old gentleman who was exceedingly angry with me because I did not think Sterne's "Sentimental Journey" should be one of the twelve novels to be saved if all the rest in the world were swept away—"only the most dense ignorance of literature" could make me confess such a thing!

Farewell.

I must close this book. Printers are calling for its last pages. It is like seeing an old friend go forth into a new world, and wondering if those who inhabit it will understand him and treat him well. Perhaps no one will read it except the intimate circle —a large one certainly—who have loved Hurstmonceaux, Stoke, and little Holmhurst at different times. But I can never regret having written it, and it has been so great an enjoyment to me, that perhaps others may like it; for I have concealed nothing, and Coleridge says, "I could inform the dullest author how he might write an interesting book. Let him relate the events of his own life with honesty, not disguising the feelings that accompanied them."

Most people will say two volumes would have been enough, but the fact is I have written chiefly for myself and my relations, and not for the general public at all. They may read the book if they like, but it was not intended for them.

Except that I have seen more varieties of people than some do, I believe there has been nothing unusual in my life. All lives are made up of joys and sorrows with a little calm, neutral ground connecting them; though, from physical reasons perhaps, I think I have enjoyed the pleasures and suffered in the troubles more than most. But from the calm backwater of my present life at Holmhurst, as I overlook the past, the pleasures seem to predominate and I could cordially answer to any one who asked me "Is life worth living?"—"Yes, to the very dregs."

Really I have been alone here for thirty years, twelve in which my dearest Lea was still presiding over the lower regions of the house, and eighteen in absolute solitude. It is the winter evenings, after the early twilight has set in, which are the longest. Then there are often no voices but those of the past. . . .

People say, "It is all your own fault that you are solitary; you ought to have married long ago." But they know nothing about it; for as long as my mother lived, and for some time after, I had nothing whatever to marry upon, and after that I had very little, and I have been constantly reminded that people of the class in which I have always lived do not like to marry paupers. Besides, the fact is, that except in one impossible case perhaps, very long ago, I have never loved anyone well enough to put myself in a noose for them: "It is a noose, you know." —George Eliot. What I have to regret is that I have no very near relations who have in the least my own interests and sympathies, though they are all very kind to me. I have far more in common with many of my younger friends, "the boys," who cease to be boys after a few years, and many whom, I am sure, turn to Holmhurst as the haven of their lives. But one feels that there would be this difference between any very congenial near relations and even the kindest friends: the latter are very glad to see one, but would be very sorry to see more of one; whilst the former, if they existed, would take it as a matter of course.

The greatest of all the blessings I have to be grateful for is that though since my serious illness six years ago, I have never been entirely without pain, I have, notwithstanding this, good health and a feeling of youth—just the same feeling I had forty years ago. I suppose there will be many who will be surprised to see in these pages how old I am; I am unspeakably surprised at it myself. I have to be perpetually reminding myself of my years, that I am so much nearer the close than the outset of life. I feel so young still, that I can hardly help making plans for quite the far-distant future, schemes of work and of travel, and I hope sometimes of usefulness, which of course can never be realised. I have very good spirits, and I feel that I should be inexcusable if I were not happy when I remember the contrast of my present life to my oppressed boyhood, or to the terrible trial of the time when every thought was occupied by such tangled perplexities as those of the Roman Catholic conspiracy.

My local affections are centred in Holmhurst now. Rome, which I was formerly even fonder of, is so utterly changed, it has lost its enchaining power, and, with the places, the familiar faces there have all passed away. I go there every third year, but not for pleasure, only because it is necessary for "Walks in Rome," the one of my books which pays best.

It is astonishing how little good can be derived from all the religious teaching which is the form and order of the day, from the endless monotony of services, from the wearisome sermons, not one of which remains with me from the thousands upon thousands I have been condemned to listen to, some few of them excellent, but most of them a farrago of stilted nonsense. I suppose that there are some types of mind which are benefited by them: I cannot believe that they were good for me. "Oh, stop, do stop; you have talked enough," my whole heart has generally cried out when I have listened to a preacher—generally a man whom one would never dream of listening to in ordinary conversation for a quarter of an hour. It is a terrible penalty to pay for one's religion to have weekly to hear it worried and tangled by these incapable and often arrogant beings. Whittier echoes my own thoughts when he says, "I regard Christianity as a life rather than a creed; and in judging my fellow-men, I can use no other standard than that which our Lord and Master has given us, 'By their fruits ye shall know them.' The only orthodoxy that I am especially interested in is that of life and practice."

When I look at the dates of births and deaths in our family in the Family Bible, I see that I have already exceeded the age which has been usually allotted to the Hares. Can it be that, while I still feel so young, the evening of life is closing in? Perhaps it may not be so, perhaps long years may still be before me. I hope so; but the lesson should be the same, for "man can do no better than live in eternity's sunrise."—Blake.

Index